Allegories
Underdev

C000256613

_ent

Allegories of Underdevelopment

Aesthetics and Politics in Modern Brazilian Cinema

Ismail Xavier

University of Minnesota Press

Minneapolis / London

Grateful acknowledgment is made for permission to reprint from *Poesia de Mario Faustino*, ed. Benedito Nunes (Rio de Janeiro: Civilização Brasileira, 1966)

Published by the University of Minnesota Press
111 Third Avenue South, Suite 290, Minneapolis, MN 55401-2520
http://www.upress.umn.edu
Printed in the United States of America on acid-free paper
Second printing 1999

Library of Congress Cataloging-in-Publication Data

Xavier, Ismail.
 [Alegorias do subdesenvolvimento. English]
 Allegories of underdevelopment : aesthetics and politics in modern Brazilian cinema / Ismail Xavier.
  p. cm.
 Includes bibliographical references and index.
 ISBN 0-8166-2676-6 (hc : alk. paper). — ISBN 0-8166-2677-4 (pb : alk. paper)
 1. Motion pictures—Brazil—History. 2. Motion pictures—Political aspects—Brazil. I. Title.
 PN1993.5.B6X3813   1997
 791.43'75'0981—dc21   97-6967

The University of Minnesota is an
equal-opportunity educator and employer.

Contents

Acknowledgments

This text synthesizes a body of work that began with my doctoral dissertation, "Allegories of Underdevelopment: From the Aesthetics of Hunger to the Aesthetics of Garbage," completed in 1982 at New York University. Many of its themes were reworked later, leading to two books in Portuguese: *Sertão Mar: Glauber Rocha e estética da fome* (1983) and *Alegorias do subdesenvolvimento: Cinema Novo, Tropicalismo, Cinema Marginal* (1993), both published by Editora Brasiliense in São Paulo. The structure of the present book and most of the text come from the NYU dissertation and the expanded Brazilian version, *Alegorias do subdesenvolvimento* (Brasiliense), but the Introduction and chapter 10 incorporate materials published later in different forms. The Introduction was entirely rewritten for the American reader but incorporates parts of an article published in Italy: "Il cinema brasiliano moderno," in *Prima e Dopo la Rivoluzione—Brasile Anni'60: dal Cinema Novo al Cinema Marginal,* edited by Marco Giusti and Marco Melani (Turin: Lindau Editore, 1995). Parts of chapter 10 rework material already published as "Transcending Cinéma Vérité," in *The Social Documentary in Latin American,* edited by Julianne Burton (Pittsburgh: University of Pittsburgh Press, 1990); as "Eldorado as Hell," in *Mediating Two Worlds: Cinematic Encounters in the Americas,* edited by John King, Ana López, and Manuel Alvarado (London: BFI, 1993); and as "Vicios Privados, Catástrofes Públicas: A psicologia social de Arnaldo Jabor," in *Novos Estudos— CEBRAP* 39 (July 1994). Chapter 1, although derived from my NYU dissertation, also incorporates material from the article *"Black God, White Devil*: The Representation of History," my contribution to *Brazilian Cinema,* edited by Randal Johnson and Robert Stam (New York: Columbia University Press, 1995: third and expanded edition).

I would like to thank the following persons and institutions for various forms of help and support. The Fulbright Commission and the

Brazilian Coordenadoria de Aperfeiçoamento de Pessoal do Ensino Superior (CAPES) provided me with grants that made possible my stay in New York during different stages of my research, in 1982 and 1986. The Brazilian Conselho Nacional para o Desenvolvimento Científico e Tecnológico (CNPq) provided me with grants from 1989 on, which made possible more recent research on the topic of allegory and national culture in Brazil and other countries. At NYU, I would like to express my appreciation to Annette Michelson, for her generous support as my adviser in the preparation of the dissertation finished in 1982, and for her subsequent intellectual stimulus in the development of my work up to the present. My gratitude to Randal Johnson, William Simon, and Rodriguez Monegal, readers of my dissertation committee, and to Carole and Tony Pipolo, who helped in the final edition of that work. Special thanks are due to Robert Stam, who has followed all the stages of this work, since its inception, and who first suggested that I submit the text to the University of Minnesota Press; I also thank him for the evolving discussions on Brazilian cinema, for the shared work done and for the patient revision and concrete suggestions that made possible the completion of the manuscript submitted to the University of Minnesota Press. My gratitude goes to Ana López for her helpful comments on the manuscript and to Kathy Delfosse for her careful and respectful copyediting in the completion of the final version of the text.

At the University of São Paulo, I would like to thank my advisers during my graduate studies in São Paulo, Paulo Emilio Salles Gomes and Antonio Candido de Mello e Souza. My friends from literary studies, Iumna Maria Simon, Vinicius Dantas, and José Miguel Wisnik, were very supportive on reading the Portuguese version of most of the chapters of this book; I deeply thank them. Maria Regina Martins and Zeca Mauro collaborated in the production of frame enlargements, and Heloisa Xavier helped me in the translation of those parts of the text that were first published in Portuguese. My gratitude also goes to the Cinemateca Brasileira and to the Fundação Nacional de Arte (FUNARTE), institutions that authorized the copying of film frames from their collection.

I would like to thank my wife, Isaura, who has been supportive and patient far beyond what I deserve.

Introduction

The Force of the Historical Conjuncture

The aim of this book is to characterize, through the analysis of Brazilian films made between 1964 and 1970, the allegorical representation of national history and contemporary society developed by young filmmakers who deeply transformed film culture in Brazil.

The period in focus is the height of Brazilian auteur cinema, which tightened relations between culture and politics as never before in the country; a moment in which the most interesting films—those of Cinema Novo and the so-called Marginal Cinema (1969-73)—were raising social issues and creating alternatives to the aesthetics of mainstream cinema.

Glauber Rocha, in the mid-1960s, summarized Cinema Novo's ideas in the expression "aesthetics of hunger," by which he meant the production of extremely low-budget politicized films taking an aggressive stance toward the dominant cinematic codes.[1] The overall demands of the modern European *cinéma d'auteur*—the denial of technical constraints, production values, and narrative codes—acquired, in Brazil, an anticolonialist thrust. Cinema Novo's search for a mode of production able to overcome economic underdevelopment led to the well-known axiom: To make a legitimate film, all one needs is "a camera in the hand and ideas in the head." Leaving behind industrial dreams and acknowledging its material disadvantages, the new cinema asserted its cultural value and ideological strength through its constant search for an original film style able to turn the scarcity of means into a channel for aesthetic experimentation. This implied the creation of an aggressive art cinema with national and political concerns.

Cinema Novo emerged around 1960. Its theory was explicated in Rocha's writings between 1963 and 1965, but its major ideas resulted from a debate that had begun in the 1950s around the notion of an

1

independent low-budget cinema inspired by Italian neorealism. This debate underwent parallel development in different countries outside Europe and the United States, and it had a central role in the rise of new cinemas in Latin America: Fernando Birri, the Argentinean film-maker, wrote about the question of a national cinema within underdevelopment in 1962; Jorge Sanjinés developed experiments in the Ukamau Group in Bolivia beginning in the mid-1960s; and a new Cuban cinema emerged in the postrevolutionary decade.[2] As social struggles developed and guerrilla warfare increased in Latin America, other oppositional cinema projects emerged on the continent, sometimes with more concrete links to political activism. In 1968, Fernando Solanas and Octavio Getino wrote the manifesto "Towards a Third Cinema," in which they criticized the art cinema premises accepted by some politically engaged filmmakers, arguing for a more radical and, in their own view, more politically consistent guerrilla cinema.[3] Third Cinema emerged in 1968 as a concept opposed to what Solanas and Getino called Second Cinema (nouvelle vague and other art cinemas) and comprised the combination of a subversive film style with a redefinition of spectatorship. Refusing the "concession to market values" detected in Second Cinema, which for them remained "bourgeois," they proposed a more systematic connection between the battle for a new audiovisual language and the effort to create new modes of address tailored for special audiences. Third Cinema implied a more specific dialogue with selected spectators inserted in circuits created by political mobilization in unions and underground meetings, involving the ideological organization of oppressed people.

During the 1980s, the notion of Third Cinema gained other meanings and was taken as a category appropriate to a variety of leftist anticolonialist film practices not only in Latin America but also in other countries, First World included.[4] I am not engaged here in the recovery of the original meaning of Third Cinema. I use this reference only to make clear that, whatever the radical position assumed by the filmmakers in their style and political concerns, the Brazilian films I will be focusing on were made for regular theatrical exhibition. Some tried to be popular in a "box office" sense, struggling against the hegemony of Hollywood in the Brazilian market. In terms of the distinctions established by Solanas and Getino, those films would indeed be closer to Second Cinema; but in terms of the expanded notion of Third Cinema typical of present-day film criticism, Rocha's "aesthetics of hunger," together with Julio Garcia Espinosa's 1969 "imperfect cinema," form part of the canonical texts that built the idea of Third Cinema in the 1960s.[5] Espinosa's text aimed at ratifying the aesthetic and political values of a low-budget, "open cinema" against a particular incorporation of production values that he feared was gaining ground in his own country. With "imperfect cinema," as with the "aesthetics of hunger," the central question was the defense of those principles that made possible the alternative film practices embodied in the new cinemas of social criticism that emerged from the late 1950s on, whatever the particular political action implied in their opposition to a dominant cinema more engaged in spectacle and technical achievement.

Allegories of underdevelopment made in Brazil form part of a film practice marked by a strong belief in ideas and their role in historical changes. This belief was held with rare intensity, and the filmmakers' mood could quickly switch from hope to despair, following the ups and downs of the political struggle. A lively cultural process made that period particularly dense in aesthetic proposals, which obliges me to cover a wide variety of filmic styles in this book. This does not mean that one finds here a panorama of Brazilian film production or an overall account of Cinema Novo.[6] I deal only with a selection of films chosen as being among the most significant expressions of a national debate involving aesthetics and politics, a debate inscribed in the productive, often conflictual, interaction between the leftist engagement within history and that constellation of phenomena formed by youth culture, cinephilia, and the will to explore national reality.

The international political and cultural conjuncture of that period allowed a significant affirmation of national cinemas in what seemed to be a first step toward a new order, more pluralistic both in the production and consumption of films; this expectation of a new order, in terms of the market at least, was buried in the 1980s. In fact, that period was a very special moment in the history of South America itself, marked by the polarization of ideological-political conflicts and by the radicalization of behaviors that eventually defined the dramatic tone of those times. It was a decisive time of struggle among different alternatives of change—guerrilla warfare led by radical Marxist groups; Marxist or Christian socialist reformism, sometimes linked to populist strategies; bourgeois conceptions of modernization within a capitalist framework, whether social democrat or authoritarian-conservative— all willing to consolidate hegemony as the sign of a long-term historical trend. During this period of excessive polarization, almost nothing was left out of the dichotomy between revolution and reaction. The Left—aware of the contradictions between imperialist and national interests and split between populist alliances and armed struggle—was defeated and had to face the right-wing administration, often under the military, of a model of economic growth that excluded the majority: a classic case of conservative modernization.

Brazilian cinema, my focus here, gave a critical response to this particular process of modernization in the peripheral countries. In this sense, it assumed political commitment and lined up with the radical spirit of the 1960s. However, its sense of ideological urgency did not prevent it from reworking traditional themes of the Brazilian cultural debate. Although concerned with present struggles, Cinema Novo filmmakers were deeply engaged in inherited controversies about the historical formation of the country and about the question of national identity in a postcolonial nation-state. Those controversies had been developing in Brazil since the nineteenth century and had permeated literary production and social-historical thought, playing a central role in the process that built a tradition of high culture. As part of its political agenda, Cinema Novo self-consciously inscribed itself in that tradition and claimed to be the first film experience in Brazil able to participate as an equal in the dialogues among literature, theater, and music. Considering that inscription, one can see Cinema Novo filmmakers as young radical heirs of a lineage of cultural nationalism born in Brazilian postindependence romanticism and deeply reworked by Brazilian modernism during the 1920s. Partially inspired by the European historical avant-garde, Brazilian literary, musical, and pictorial modernism articulated national concerns within an overall process of transforming and updating art production in the country. This combination of aesthetic experimentation and engagement with the national question, typical of the Brazilian cultural debate in the 1920s, was resumed by the political cinema in the 1960s as part of its effort to cope with contemporary challenges. And Cinema Novo gave political meaning to the demands for authenticity typical of the European art cinema, combining those demands with the careful observation of reality, especially in relation to the poorer sectors of the Brazilian society: the emblems of underdevelopment. Since the national question was taken as a central mediation for understanding human experience, the idea of nation worked as a structuring space of dramas involving the interplay of social structures and individual actions. The representation of Brazilian society acquired a pedagogical dimension, but the modernist concerns of the *cinéma d'auteur* defined the style and the scope of the representation. Thus the pedagogical mission ended up concretely embodied in original and complex films. Given the multiple cultural and political tasks assumed by the filmmakers, their films had to present a totalizing view of the country (or had to present a critique that referred to that view), and their attempt to provide condensed representations of society resulted in a preference for allegory.

My view of allegories as referring to "underdevelopment" assumes the spirit of the time, that ideological-political atmosphere that favored the effort toward an encompassing vision, toward a "state of the nation" discourse. Each film was to account for many aspects of reality and, at the same time, was to express that disseminated feeling of imminent revolution, a revolution mainly understood as national liberation.

Political concerns, questions of identity, formal choices linked to original answers given to technical problems, the attempt to present an all-encompassing, allegorical view of the country's history—dealing with this particular set of issues, this book encounters in the present conjuncture a specific context molded by recent debates on identity, politics and allegory, especially the debate about "national allegory" between Fredric Jameson and Aijaz Ahmad in *Social Text*.[7] Jameson, in his "Third World Literature in the Era of Multinational Capitalism," presented a totalizing view of the Third World experience that works as a kind of allegorical construction, perhaps too abstract to satisfy his readers who live in peripheral countries. Even though his remarks on Third World literature do manage to raise the question of the collective meaning of narratives and challenge his intended readers in the United States, they imply a schematic view of what are indeed more complex social formations and cultural processes. Ahmad has already pointed out a set of problems created, in that particular text, by Jameson's hypothesis about the close correspondences between modes of literary production and stages of economic development. My book brings into view aspects of the national allegories not accounted for in Jameson's essay and points out the almost simultaneous presence of a number of allegorical modes that he would link to different "stages of development," including the so-called postmodernity of the First World. I go from religious (and national) allegories to a critique of nationalism, from national teleology to an antiteleological understanding of the ways of society, dealing with a variety of strategies all found in this short period of Brazilian cinema, as they might also be found in many European cinemas or in U.S. cinema.

This book has at its core the issue of the representation of history and its crisis, notably national history, a topic of interest to both narratologists and historians. Today this issue motivates a theoretical production that involves authors such as Hayden White, Alex Callinicos, Homi K. Bhabha, Timothy Brennan, and Doris Sommer.[8] Their works are related to aspects of my analysis since I deal with audiovisual interpretations of a special moment of Brazilian political life, engaged recapitulations of national history that involve some notions currently on the agenda such as figurative imagination, allegory, invention of traditions, and deconstructive strategies.

The common point between my analysis of the 1960s and 1970s and the current debate defines my commitment to issues related to identity politics and its outcomes: revisions of history, critiques of the persistance of colonialist assumptions, attacks on ethnocentrism. However, this book is a revised and much expanded version of my doctoral dissertation, "Allegories of Underdevelopment," which was completed in 1982. Therefore it is a work that, although updated, ultimately emerges from the theoretical debate developed in Brazil in the 1970s and early 1980s on the value and the power of allegorical representations as a "source of knowledge" and as the embodiment of a critical view of history.

Within that Brazilian debate, the central theme was the issue of national identity in a peripheral country entangled in a heteronomous movement of modernization. The theoretical drama arose from the lack of synchronization between that modernization, already well advanced, and the egalitarian hopes of revolutionary projects, understood as a sui generis articulation of class conflict and national liberation, within a broader horizon of opposition between capitalism and socialism. Such projects were expressed in the Cinema Novo in the 1960s, among other cultural projects in Brazil, up to the moment when *tropicalismo*—a specific version of the decade's concerns—emerged to restructure the field. My work with the notion of allegory partly results from the controversy around this cultural movement, whose zenith occurred in 1968. A decisive essay in this controversy was the text written by Roberto Schwarz in 1969, "Culture and Politics in Brazil: 1964-1969," which brought the question of allegory to the foreground; it influenced the essays written in Brazil between 1969 and 1980 and is still echoing today.[9] I say "partly results" because, for Brazilian film critics, the question of allegory had already been on the agenda since the beginning of the 1960s, forced by the central presence of Glauber Rocha, whose cinema has always been an imaginary figuration of history, simultaneously working the issues of myth, revolution, and utopia. When the controversy around *tropicalismo* emerged, in popular music (Caetano Veloso and Gilberto Gil), in theater (José Celso Martinez Correa), and in cinema (Rogério Sganzerla), the debate on allegory merely took on new density and its fundamental terms became clearer. This happened, as we shall see, because *tropicalismo* saw the national question as central, criticizing both the tradition of leftist nationalist populism and the provincial values of a moralist and patriarchal Brazil, values supported by the military regime to co-opt the lower middle class and to keep the army united. Both on the Left and on the Right, *tropicalismo* introduced the shock of constructions and collages inspired by the Anglo-American pop art from the 1950s and 1960s. In the new context, such collages acquired new, different meanings because they melded signs coming from both modern and historic Brazil. This contamination was shocking for some leftist sectors, who considered the areas of the country untouched by development as a kind of reservoir of national authenticity, a reservoir that was threatened by extinction. Choosing parody as its central strategy, *tropicalismo* assumed the ambiguities of its shock effect and novelty in the universe of kitsch and commodities, triggering a harsh debate on its political-ideological content: Was it a market affirmation? irony? national appraisal? a total denial of tradition? The discontinuities and the enigmatic tone of its representations were analyzed by intellectuals as a modern version of allegorical schemes. Here they followed Walter Benjamin's texts—which introduced to the criticism of this century a new matrix for thinking about the relations between the modern and the baroque worlds or the problematic relations between allegory and temporality. Benjamin's matrix inspired a new reflection on the vicissitudes of the 1964 Brazilian coup d'état and its representation. The frustration experienced then could be linked to the constellation of historical moments in which promising movements lost momentum and broke up, bringing to the surface the setbacks and the discontinuous face of history when observed from the point of view of the losers' aborted projects. *Tropicalist* collage showed an inventory of the losers' history, foregrounding the crisis of the subject in the contemporary world and, especially, the death of two historical subjects: that of the proletariat amid mass culture and that of the nation amid globalization.

Centered on the notion of allegory, the cultural debate in Brazil in the 1970s in a peculiar way connected the problems related to national identity (where allegory represents a residue of the sacred) with the problems of the crisis of the subject within a capitalist world (where allegory occurs as a reflection on commodity fetishism, on simulation, and on linguistic opacity). On the other hand, the censorship imposed by the authoritarian regime reinforced allegory as a pragmatic way to encrypt messages. Therefore it is not surprising that the series of films I deal with show a broad range of structures and allegorical strategies, precisely because they are overdetermined by these different inspirations.

The allegories studied here involve the careful consideration of a specific historical juncture, in a case study where it would be illegitimate to reduce the variety of representations into a sole master narrative, a supposed paradigm of any national allegory. I interpret Brazilian *cinéma d'auteur* from the 1960s as a pluralistic effort to rethink and clarify a country in transition, a country embedded in a crisis that at the time was difficult to evaluate and whose resolution launched Brazil on a historical path that gradually took it away from the nationalist ideology of the Left. Thus I avoid mechanically projecting current coordinates on a material that had another origin and met other demands. My conceptual framework responds to a material specifically anchored in its own time, a cinema in which the issues of class, race, and gender were subordinate to the national question, a time when totalizations were fashionable and the notion of underdevelopment was the nucleus of national thinking.

Today the reference to the reversal of the social, political, and aesthetic expectations occurring between the 1960s and the present is commonplace. In the 1960s there were great expectations in all Latin America, when the movement in world history seemed to elect the so-called Third World as the epicenter of change. Analyzing the Brazilian culture of that decade entails the discussion of the forms that artists gradually found to deal with the discrepancies between national expectations and reality. It is a privileged point of view because, at that moment, such discrepancies became clear and triggered the answers that produced an authentic revolution in the cultural sphere. The experience of the country was completely reevaluated, with increasing irony, because of conditions that were becoming more and more adverse. Both in culture and in politics, there was a bitter diagnosis of society: Underdevelopment became a central and tragic notion, bringing a connotation of failure that separated the experience observed from a more complete experience in "another place."

In Brazil, as Antonio Candido explains, quoting Mário Silva de Mello, we may identify two successive forms of perception of economic backwardness: There is the "soft" consciousness of underdevelopment, correlated to the idea of a "new nation with a great future," that was present up to the 1930s and that was linked to ornamental nationalism; and there is the catastrophic consciousness of underdevelopment, correlated with the idea of a poor country needing practical changes in the economic structure to overcome misery, that was present after World War II and that has been more obvious from the 1950s on.[10]

This distinction finds its translation in cinema, and not by accident: The 1950s and 1960s testify to the passage from the futuristic industrial dreams to a more aggressive posture of both Cinema Novo and Marginal Cinema, clear manifestations of the catastrophic awareness of underdevelopment. On the one hand, both movements were aware, in their own ways, of misery and of violence and domination. On the other, they were the first to give a more effective response to the "colonial condition" of the cinema itself: lack of resources and an unfavorable position in a domestic market ruled by Hollywood. In their struggle, a central problem was the dialogue with the audience, an issue that they tried to solve within a specific dialectics of seduction and aggression toward urban middle-class spectators.

For a generation oriented toward political cinema, the crucial dilemma was whether or not to adapt its language to market parameters. In the beginning of the 1960s, market efficiency, as a value, was questioned by Cinema Novo, and the idea of the *cinéma d'auteur* acquired an anti-industrial formulation. This resulted partly because the director, as an "industrial professional," was seen as a mere craftsman working for capital and partly because in Brazil the attempts at industrial cinema had led to huge bankruptcies, as happened with the Companhia Cinematográfica Vera Cruz, which collapsed in the mid-1950s.

As a question of principle and taking into consideration recent historical experience, the proposal of a political cinema turned art and commerce into enemies. Toward the end of the 1960s the question of the market was revised and the Cinema Novo group was more engaged in the idea of framing a national cinema with less immediate revolutionary consequences and more concerned with its own continuity.[11] In the turn from the 1960s to the 1970s, this more "institutional" position was one of the key issues in the controversy involving Cinema Novo and the Marginal Cinema filmmakers, who argued for continuity of the aesthetics of violence and of a radical *cinéma d'auteur* and against compromises with the commodity world.

During the late 1960s and early 1970s, the cinema debate between Cinema Novo and its more radical opponents was carried out under political and economic conditions that were difficult but that were far from the suffocating conditions that affected Brazilian cinematic culture from 1985 on. The ideas could carry more weight, the projects more élan, the filmmaker more confidence—and, often, more illusions—regarding his power. It was a period when the debate favored the creation of alternative forms, allowing for a series of experiences reconciling Brazilian cinema and modern aesthetics, despite technical and economic underdevelopment and a conservative political regime.

Linked to the consciousness of the crisis—in the country, in the language able to state it—the use of allegory was consolidated in the 1960s. This use cannot be reduced to a programmed and hidden exposure of the authoritarian regime. It comprises a vast range of motivations, varying with the aesthetic posture of the filmmaker, his way of conceiving space and time, and his modes of address to the spectator. My analysis tends to foreground the constructive processes and takes the discussion of the form of the works as a path toward the political, since the allegories are not only disguised discourse but also have an expressive dimension: They condense the filmmakers' response both to the vicissitudes of a social project and to the crisis of the cinema itself. In their confrontation with the Brazilian conjuncture, the films analyzed express the passage from the promise of happiness to the contemplation of hell that marked their historical moment, a passage that could not foster the production of a harmonious art; rather, it could only inspire an art that, internalizing history, recognized flaws and failures. As Benjamin would suggest, an art that assumes the crisis of its own time refuses to confirm mythically given totalities and bends to a criticism of both historical continuities claimed by the winners and of the "aesthetic of happiness," typical of consumerism.

The National Question

Today, nationalism is no longer in vogue as a driving notion for analysis or even for political action in Brazil; a strong contrast to its importance in the 1950s and 1960s.[12] At that time an anticolonialist thought articulated economics, politics, and culture to explain the key problems of the Third World countries. Frantz Fanon, Aimé Césaire, and Jean-Paul Sartre were among the central figures of this mode of thought. The relation between developed and underdeveloped countries was understood in terms of domination, of a colonial heritage assumed and renewed on a new economic and technical basis. It was difficult to think about development without simultaneously thinking about the political problem of "national liberation" and revolution. Nationalist cultural projects in countries like Brazil took the dialectics of affirmation of the self through the "negation of the other" as an essential aspect of their struggle. The body of work produced by the ISEB (Instituto Superior de Estudos Brasileiros), especially Roland Corbisier's book *Formação e Problema da Cultura Brasileira* (1958), followed this Fanonian pattern, also present in Rocha's manifesto "For an Aesthetics of Hunger."[13]

The terms of the economic debate, with clear reflections for culture, assume quite a different color today. A particular idea of modernization, understood as a submissive insertion into the international hegemonic order, is now predominant. A model of integration has replaced that of conflict. Previously the nationalist ideology worked the internal–external opposition in a simplified form and saw hindrances to development only in external interests; now we find the equally reductive reversals typical of neoliberalism. Neoliberals condemn domestic culture, mainly in the form of the state, and praise an international market equated with modernity and efficiency, as if politics, military interests, class hegemonies, and corruption did not play any role in the new world order. This game of sharp contrasts does not account for a complex network of interests and forces that only confirms the ambiguity of the national question and, at the same time, its survival in the world today. A mix of what Benedict Anderson called "imagined communities" and practical reality that involves a variety

12   Introduction

of opposed interests, the nation is this mutable historical form with different versions depending on the context.[14] The nation is a privileged field of mythologies, akin to religion—positive when inspiring the resistance of the oppressed, sordid when embracing an ideology of expansionist powers—and it remains, after all, a challenge to those who think about modern society, returning to the cultural debate when it seems to be a solved problem.

The political activism that takes the "national" as a positive value has already surfaced in many times and in many places; its imbrications with the cultural are clear enough, at least from the second half of the eighteenth century in Europe, whether in revolutionary France, where we see the political version of the national as popular sovereignty, or in the Germany of Johann Herder, whose cultural nationalism distrusts the universal ideas of the Enlightenment and limits the problem to culture, emphasizing the idea of the particular character of each people. Nationalism as an affirmation of a resistance to external dominance is, in its turn, typical of societies formed under colonial rules. In these societies, economic dependence—although in a different way from what happened in conservative Germany of the eighteenth century—also favored the nationalist focus on cultural identity and the questioning of universal values. In Brazil since the late nineteenth century, the discussion of the national has been linked to the search for reasons for the country's poor economic performance. This search brought to the agenda the role of different ethnic groups—European, African, Native. The question of the "national character" initially arose based on the French positivist-evolutionary theories on race, primarily the prejudice that the mixture of races was an inhibiting factor for achieving social development. Later there were variations within this paradigm in a history not worth rehearsing here, but as a reference I should recall the reversal performed by the leaders of modernism in the 1920s: Against this positivist ethnocentrism, they praised miscegenation and underlined positive, specifically national features derived from the Native and the African traditions.

When Glauber Rocha made Black God, White Devil (Deus e o Diabo na Terra do Sol, 1963–64), his concern with the forms of popular religion made him confront the tradition set by Euclides da Cunha's book Os Sertões, published in 1902.[15] Da Cunha was a premodernist, and his work was a key impulse to changes in conceptions of race and culture in Brazil, changes that culminated in the modernist Oswald de

Andrade's ode to carnival and the African heritage of the country. As a journalist, da Cunha was able to follow closely some of the events of the Canudos War in 1897, when four army expeditions fought the peasants in the backlands, followers of the millenarian leader Antônio Conselheiro. His book, although influenced by French positivism, eventually prodded the discussion on national character into new directions, driven by the shock caused by seeing the barbarism of the army in massacring the impoverished representatives of "impure races" in the name of reason and the republic. In 1963 Rocha went back to that experience to praise the peasants' revolt in new terms and, by showing the Canudos War and other struggles led by the social bandits, revealed the presence in Brazilian history of a tradition of rebellion, against the official version of the pacific nature of the people. In *Black God, White Devil*, Rocha wanted to mobilize his audience for political struggle, and the tone of the film was one of hope. After the 1964 coup d'état, the defeat of the leftist political project gave Cinema Novo other reasons to focus even more on the discussion of the "national character": One should understand the reluctance of the people to assume the task of the revolution. The emphasis given at that time of crisis to the discussion of mentalities turned Cinema Novo into a unique instance of the combination of two styles of reflection about Latin America usually taken as antagonistic: One, represented by Eduardo Galeano, emphasizes the framing of a continental identity based on a "practical reality," aiming at overcoming its destiny as a "locus of exploitation" by different European and, later, North American colonial enterprises. The other, represented by Octavio Paz, is more interested in the study of the "national character" in terms of a culturalism inflected by psychoanalysis and by a historical relativism that refuses both the evolutionist positivism of the nineteenth century and Marxism, definitely embedded in the symbolic field. That is, it is normal to see in the Brazilian films a schematization of the conflicts that links the material dimension of class conflicts and national interests to a symbolic dimension through which one tries to include, among other determinations of the political game, the decisive presence of mentalities framed in long-term processes. In the 1970s, this feature led to films oriented toward a new anthropology taken as an answer to the intellectual's disenchantment. The facts had denied the hypothesis that the working classes had a natural inclination toward contesting the bourgeois order in Brazil. Some popular practices—like carnival, soccer,

Afro-Brazilian religions—considered "alienated" in the 1960s, came to be seen as positive components of national identity.

In any case, Cinema Novo's ambiguous relation with religion and popular feasts was already there in the 1960s. Above everything, there was a zeal for cultural traditions derived from the lack of confidence in the modernization process in progress. Some could consider this zeal as a trace of conservative romanticism in the cinema. It is well known that romanticism can idealize the past taken as essence, as national mythical origin, as an experience of the lost union between human beings and nature. However, the cultural nationalism that I focus on here tried to avoid romantic organicism and also tried to distinguish its critical view of the myth of progress from another form of mythical reduction that would seek a return to a "state of nature." It was this mythical reduction that worried Walter Benjamin in his criticism of the organicism of the devotees of the "symbol" as a crystallization of an aesthetic ideal heedless of time and history. As he reinstated the value of allegory, the German philosopher praised it as a figure of speech in which one can recognize the action of history in the entanglement and fragmentation of meanings; in which distance in time and space is clearly related to the displacement of signification, implying losses never recovered. These data posed allegory as a privileged strategy for consciousness of language, a place for disjunctions as a desirable antidote to illusionary organic cohesions and regressive mythologies that were sometimes of a racial type and that could lead eventually to fascism.

Contrary to organicism, Brazilian modernist tradition had assumed, since the 1920s, a parodic stance, satirizing myths and ironically laughing at the reifications of the national character. That is, modernism and the cinematic production around 1968 "carnivalize," in Bakhtinian terms, the question of national character, without normative intentions. An excellent example of this posture is *Macunaíma* (1969), an adaptation of Mário de Andrade's book *Macunaíma o herói sem nenhum caráter*, first published in 1928, the same year in which Oswald de Andrade made anthropophagy a cultural metaphor. Through this metaphor, "digestion" was proposed as the central operation by which the oppressed should assimilate and subvert the oppressor's culture, instead of clinging to an essentialist idea of "national roots" to oppose the process of technical and economic modernization.[16] Oswald de Andrade was not concerned with praising the unchangeable essence of the national "primitivism," but, rather, with proposing a model of national experience based on the critical assimilation of all inflows. National features should be thought of as something dynamic, changeable, inserted in history. In tune with dissonances and gaps of the allegorical, he conceived of culture as an intersection, a flow of changes, mistakes, and rereadings, in a nonorganic growth. In 1968 a similar sense of irony allowed for a corrosive attack on the mythical regressions of the military regime's hallowing of tradition and nationality. If that was a moment of crisis and transition, then allegory had a chance to show itself as the language of crisis par excellence—and this actually occurred in modern Brazilian cinema. If the bourgeois view of progress organized world history as a teleological process to which the fate of all peoples is subordinated, then the democratic response to this ethnocentric content of capital expansion balanced on the razor's edge. The defense of a culture and of a lifestyle always has to consider the meaning of a tradition in the present, without turning it into a fetish, assessing the possibilities of a symbolic practice able to mediate past and current demands. For an art that faces such dilemmas, the image of the world becomes complex, and the tendency is, once again, to allegorize, that is, to condense an endless number of questions and experiences into a few individual characters whose life courses, nevertheless, represent a national fate, the destiny of an ethnic group or of a class.

In the Brazilian cinema of the 1960s and early 1970s, we find a search for a general diagnosis of the nation based on the representation of long-term historical journeys, much as we see happening in other contexts in which the filmmaker calls on allegory to speak about his or her country. Humberto Solas, in *Lucía* (1968), articulates three moments of Cuban history to discuss the role of women in society, always correlating the historical time and the style of representation, always using the female character as a strategic figure to condense the national destiny. Rainer Werner Fassbinder does the same in *The Marriage of Maria Braun* (1978), taking a feminine protagonist as an allegory of the nation in order to condense Germany's historical course from World War II to 1954. National allegories referring to a comprehensive historical process were present in the movies, from the works of D. W. Griffith to such industrial genres as the western. Cinema in the most varied countries is well supplied with emblematic characters and the condensed representation of history. Allegories, like the idea of nation, are polymorphous and require specification.

In my analysis, I acknowledge a plurality clearly shown both in allegory as form and style and in allegory as the site of enunciation. Such a plurality suggests that the whole issue of allegory in the Third World has more facets than Fredric Jameson's schematization indicated, although he was no doubt right to note a stronger tendency toward overt national allegory in certain specific historical junctures, forced by a desire for totalization on the part of the politically engaged writer or filmmaker. This clearly occurs in some of the films examined here, notably in Rocha's cinema. The effort of totalization, always problematic, is the preferred field for the figure of language and thought here studied.

The Path of the Allegories

My discussion of modern Brazilian cinema, from Cinema Novo to Marginal Cinema, takes allegory as a central category that allows me to point out identities and differences among films. In allegory, the narrative texture places the spectator in an analytical posture while he or she is facing a coded message that is referred to an "other scene" and not directly given on the diegetic level. The spectator's willingness to decode finds anchorage when this "other scene" is signalized as being the national context as a whole. This happens in most of the films discussed here, but not in all of them. The greater the pedagogic impulse of the allegory, the more unmistakable is this signalization toward the national, as seen in *Black God, White Devil* or in *Macunaíma*. In other cases, the accumulation of data creates the risk of fragmentation, making it more difficult to grasp the national as totality; in these cases the tension between the clear meaning and the absurd challenges the interpreter. There are cases in which the juxtaposition of data and the fragmentation of the discourse do not allow for any anchorage, and the film seems to go against the traditional vocation of allegory—to march from fragments toward totality. One faces a discourse that questions the totalizing movement and radicalizes the enigmatic nature of the universe to which the allegory refers.

The first step of my comparative study has been to select a diachronic series of texts in order to provide a clear perception of the transformations occurring from film to film along the axis provided by that dialectics of fragmentation and totalization. This dialectics sets up a play of oppositions involving specific ideas of the nation as a whole, or, rather, deconstructive attacks on the totalizations implied in the various forms of nationalism. As a result, at each stage of my analysis I find a particular configuration within the dialectics, from clear national allegories to experimental works that foreground the question of language and spectatorship.

Aware of structural differences among the films analyzed, I take the question of teleology as a central axis along which to establish the stages of my path. Teleology condenses the question of the fragment and of the whole, and it does so in a way that is appropriate for my project, as it immediately places the question of time both in the structure of the works and in the world they are trying to picture. My universe is that of narrative, a ground where teleology, as a specific time organizer, seems to come as a natural fact, to the extent that the succession of events becomes meaningful after a settling point that defines any previous moment as a stage to achieve the telos—an organic crowning of a whole process. Always present in the classic narrative, the teleological scheme is in crisis in the 1960s, when narratives were apparently "disordered" and awkwardly "inconclusive." The films I analyze are inserted in the decade of the modern cinema par excellence. Each allegory analyzed here has its specific form of articulating the two temporalities: that of the narrated historical experience and that of the filmic discourse in its internal structure. Depending on the choice made, they also search for different strategies in the interplay between text and audience. I try to correlate such structural variations— narrative teleology or its denial—with the different diagnoses of the human experience in time: historical teleology or its denial.

In the early 1960s, the order of time was seen as being shaped by revolution. The allegory can show a discontinuous image and sound texture but considers history as teleology, assumes time as a movement with reason and meaning, and supposes a march toward the telos. My trajectory starts with *Black God, White Devil*, a film made before the coup d'état. A special example of the adjustment between formal inventions and national allegory, Rocha's work here suggests past experience as a set of promises to be fulfilled by present struggle. Revolutionary violence would be on the national agenda. As a historical subject, the nation has a project; Rocha's hope finds support in an allegorical structure with Christian overtones. A new version of "figural realism" guides the representation of history.[17] After the coup d'état, the tone of Cinema Novo's reflection on history changes, and the search for a totalizing view of the nation produces, in *Land in Anguish* (*Terra em transe*, 1967), a dramatic representation of the crisis of the teleology assumed by *Black God, White Devil*; the allegory now forcefully reworks the figures of disenchantment typical of the baroque drama as depicted by Walter Benjamin. Sganzerla's *Red Light Bandit* (*O bandido da luz vermelha*, 1968) offers an ironic version of this disenchantment embedded in the collage that exposes the crisis of the individual subject and of the nation in the universe of commodities and the electronic mass media. Sganzerla's film attacks Cinema Novo and initiates a more radical plunge into discontinuity and fragmentation. Although the idea of a "peripheral condition" of the nation remains as a guideline, the national project begins to lose its force and will not have the same role in Marginal Cinema films like *The Angel Is Born* (*O anjo nasceu*, 1969) and *Killed the Family and Went to the Movies* (*Matou a família e foi ao cinema*, 1969), both made by Júlio Bressane in 1969, and *Bang Bang*, made by Andrea Tonacci in 1970. From 1969 on, the allegories of underdevelopment become expressions either of the crisis of historical teleology or of its more radical denial. In Marginal Cinema, perplexity and sarcasm foster structures of aggression that, denying any horizon of salvation, affirm an antiteleology as the organizing principle of experience. The new aesthetics provoke bewilderment and force a revision of the concepts of nation and subject.

Taking the question of teleology as an organizing principle, this book is composed of four sections of textual analyses, a penultimate section with an overview of further developments in the 1970s, and my concluding statements. Each of the four analytical sections corresponds to a new step within the gradual displacement in the response given by the filmmakers to the development of the Brazilian political process in the 1960s.[18]

In Part I, I analyze *Black God, White Devil*, the major formulation of an historical teleology of the Nation. In Part II, I analyze two films that mark the crisis of this teleology: *Land in Anguish*, the dramatic recapitulation of the fall of populism in 1964, and *Red Light Bandit*, a film that characterizes the passage from the "aesthetics of hunger" to the "aesthetics of garbage," a significant shift in the central metaphor of underdevelopment. In Parts III and IV, I examine the bifurcation that occurred after 1968, when the rupture with the teleology of revolution split into two basic attitudes. One of them shows the rise of an antiteleology on the level of the organization of content, in which teleology is erased as a societal feature focused on by the film but remains as a formal feature of representation. So we have the allegories that keep the pedagogic background and look for a narrative closure and a conclusive statement regarding national identity and its relations to the conservative modernization. Part III deals with Joaquim Pedro de Andrade's *Macunaíma* and Glauber Rocha's *Antônio das Mortes* (1969). In both films, typically Cinema Novo authors try to incorporate communicative patterns adapted to the market. Part IV deals with the opposite attitude—that which carries the signs of Marginal Cinema's rupture and shows an antiteleology pervading the style of representation itself, as expected in modern allegory with its refusal of synthesis. In these we notice a questioning of the narrative process itself; antiteleology is internalized, becoming the formal principle in *The Angel Is Born*, *Killed the Family and Went to the Movies*, and *Bang Bang*. Here deconstruction takes a political turn, completing the transformation of the allegorical discourse in Brazilian cinema from 1964 to 1970. We begin with allegory derived from religious faith and made "national" in Rocha's film; and, through a path of increasing irony, we finish with allegory as derived from a contemporary version of philosophical skepticism.

Based on these criteria, I try to take into account the change that occurs in the very meaning of the allegorical, in terms of the dialectics between fragmentation (which questions meaning) and totalization (which affirms it). This dialectics, as I have stated, is resolved differently in each film and allows for revelatory confrontations. Throughout history, allegory has been a protean device, as Angus Fletcher reminds us.[19] It has received new meanings according to the expressive forms and debates of different eras. Taking that into consideration, I chose to accept here a suggestion that emerged from close observation of the films: Through them, it is possible to describe the passage of one sense of allegory to another. It is possible to identify a more traditional allegory, sometimes inspired by the didactic fable, sometimes by the Christian paradigm—first the evangelical-figural (Erich Auerbach) then the baroque (Benjamin)—and it is possible to identify a modern allegory more related to concepts generated in the poststructuralist context (Jacques Derrida, Paul de Man) or in the revised Marxist views (Terry Eagleton, Fredric Jameson).[20] The presence of such different traditions is made clearer in the films as the dialogue among the filmmakers increases.

In narrative terms, the films under consideration present a great variety of plot structures, from romancelike heroic quests, sometimes subverted by parodic strategies, to enigmatic juxtapositions of violent episodes enacted as banal pieces of everyday naturalism. On the level of visual composition, we can have a modern allegorical style associated with discontinuity, collages, fragmentation, or other effects created by "visible" editing. Nevertheless, allegory can also be built from traditional schemes as the emblem, the caricature, or the collection of objects creating a "cosmic order" within which the characters find their places.

Once the variations are recognized, there is a common feature that deserves to be pointed out: the strong presence in the films of an interaction between mise-en-scène and explicit comment, a constant mark that underlines the formalizing gesture of the narration when the agencies of filmic discourse display their schemas. My demarcation in the use of the notion of allegory is exactly applied to this feature of sheer and self-conscious schematization, common to all films. In this regard, I follow Fletcher's formal characterization of allegory while dealing with its metamorphoses in time. He underlines the discontinuity and pictorial juxtaposition that form part of the matrix of modernity, but he also enhances this broader dimension of the schematization always present in narrative allegories. In this work I explore the tendency of allegory, in all its modalities, to offer clear configurations for the essential pieces of its game. There is a graphic isolation of the elements put into relation, and this does not always mean that there is a "clear message" because the proper disjunction of the terms, as in the collage, may be a stratagem to enhance ambiguity and enigma. On the level of the mise-en-scène, we can see characters whose masks are carefully built in order to function almost as a diagram, a constellation of typical traits that insert them into a clear oppositional system. At an extreme, such human agents are composed in such a way as to display their condition as "personifications" of forces within a hierarchical world (this is the case in Glauber Rocha's filmic agents); their actions, even when apparently linear or mysteriously simple, may acquire a ritual tone, as if of a journey consisting of obsessive search (perhaps for a sacred token, as in *Macunaíma*, or a messianic salvation, as in *Black God, White Devil*). Sometimes this journey is juxtaposed to parallel actions that rigorously mirror it, creating a game of repetitions evoking an enigmatic order (as in *Killed the Family and Went to the Movies*); in other cases there is a magic cause inserting the agents into a progression or convulsion in the world, not always univocal in its meaning (as in *Land in Anguish* and, parodically, in *Red Light Bandit*). The spaces for these actions and causes are structured as closed microcosms with revealing names (as with Eldorado in Rocha's *Land in Anguish* and Boca do Lixo in Sganzerla's *Red Light Bandit*), or they repeat a distinctive feature that signals an intentional schematization (for example, the open spaces in *The Angel Is Born* and *Bang Bang*).

Separation, clear display of elements; therefore a spatialization of forces, concepts, and flow of time—these strong allegorical traces encourage a characterization, film by film, of the mode by which the narrative portrays social experience, either in relation to the idea of a national-historical space or in relation to the question of the crisis of representation. The critical awareness of language and cinema mark the filmmakers studied here, with all the political meaning that the rupture with dominant modes of representation acquired in the period.

The Allegories and Their Context in the 1960s

Brazilian cinema began in the nineteenth century. However, after a ten-year period of growth in production alongside imported films, this cinema faced its first crisis. In the early 1910s international trade reached a level of development that allowed large U.S. and French companies to better control film exhibition in several countries. Placed in a peripheral zone, Brazil watched its market be organized to fulfill the interests of these foreign, mostly U.S., groups, especially after World War I. In the 1920s, the production of feature films was rare in Brazil, and the films produced had little access to the theaters; cinematic activity, apart from documentaries and short films, was confined to the so-called regional cycles. With few connections among them, none of these cycles lasted long, but silent cinema in Brazil did generate the works of filmmakers like Humberto Mauro, from Minas Gerais, the maker of *Ganga Bruta* (1933) and considered by the Cinema Novo leaders to be their major forerunner, and Mario Peixoto, from Rio de Janeiro, who made the outstanding avant-garde film *Limite* (1931).

The advent of sound, in the 1930s, was less favorable than was expected for Brazilian production. At the time, Brazilians thought that language would create a barrier to the foreign film and considered it a promising time for domestic film. The genre of the musical comedy emerged; it introduced the forerunners of the so-called *chanchada* that managed to achieve some communication with the audience, and it presented Carmen Miranda.[21] But on the whole Brazilian cinema did not take off. It was only after World War II that, still through the *chanchada*, a continuous relationship with a significant part of the audience was made possible. Domestic production grew, and cinema won a place within the market alongside radio broadcasting, sharing, although to a lesser degree, the position of mediator of an active popular imagery rejected by the bourgeoisie and by most intellectuals. Around 1950, seeing the *chanchada* as demonstrating the feasibility of a Brazilian cinema and, at the same time, as a film style to be refused, São Paulo industrialists invested in movie studios and built a mini-Hollywood to produce "international-quality films." This was the last dream of an industry built on the U.S. model to occur in Brazilian cinema: Companhia Vera Cruz, established by rich industrialists in 1949, went bankrupt after producing around twenty feature films and drawing some attention worldwide with *O Cangaceiro* (1953), directed by Lima Barreto and honored in Cannes.[22] Vera Cruz's collapse made clear the obstacles to planting an alternative culture to the *chanchada* within the Brazilian context, and leftist filmmakers, who had already criticized the Hollywoodian terms of the São Paulo project, saw their case for low-budget films gain momentum. From 1954 on Nelson Pereira dos Santos and others were able to make films within the principles of a cinema outside of the studios and closer to neorealism.

The 1950s, then, were a moment of continuity of the *chanchada*, of an early funeral for the Brazilian "classic industrial cinema," and of a growing affirmation of a popular national project fed by the Left. When, at the end of the 1950s, Cinema Novo emerged, the *chanchada* was declining, partly because of the expansion of TV, a new medium that absorbed the performers and the traditions once created by radio and cinema. The fall of the *chanchada* left Cinema Novo with a strong hegemony in the cinematic sphere: This was a factor that contributed to the euphoria with which (considering the political ambiance in the country) the new generation developed the project of a nationalist, leftist, and noncommercial audiovisual culture in Brazil. Such a proj-

ect, alert to the hindrances arising from the U.S. domination of distribution and because of the subversive aspects of the proposed cinema,
paid little attention to the media issue as a whole. Cinema Novo carried out its task of discovering the country and exposing Brazilian
social reality to their fellow countrymen, but its sphere—even in the
early 1960s—was much narrower than that of the radio-TV-press system. Out of this system, by the nature of its project, Cinema Novo was
touched by the expansion of the very thing it refused: kitsch and the
conservative culture of the hegemonic media. From 1964 on, with the
triumph of conservative modernization, the long-term tendency was
the consolidation of this culture administered by large corporations
rather than of the culture born in universities or leftist groups. The
capitalist growth of the country enacted, however crudely, the organization of a complex mass culture. Within this context, Brazilian TV,
supported by the military regime, reached a new stage in the late
1960s, when censorship and economic pressures created for Cinema
Novo even worse conditions.

Not by chance, during the second half of the 1960s a change occurred in the consciousness of artists and critics regarding the question
of the cultural industry in Brazil. The cultural and information market
had grown in importance and had become privileged areas of interest.
In daily life the young conquered space not only in the political and
leftist cultural sphere but also in the sphere of consumerism and advertising. On the aesthetic level the major expression of that confrontation of sensibilities with the changes in the cultural process was
the controversy that led to *tropicalismo*. The debate around this movement expresses a clear awareness regarding the more complex nature
of power in modern society and the crisis of the political art sustained
by the nationalist ideas of the 1950s and early 1960s. In the arts and in
the social sciences, the post-1964 period is one of strong political and
aesthetic criticism of pre-1964 populism. A self-analysis of the intellectual was developed, and it was Rocha, in *Land in Anguish*, who on
the aesthetic level best formulated the reflection on the failure of the
revolutionary project. In his own audacious style, he, in this film, enhances the grotesque dimension of the political moment. His infernal
image of the country's elite opens space for the ironic inventory of the
mythical regressions of the conservative Right that will be performed
by *tropicalismo* in 1968. And Rocha's image of the people is the exasperated answer to the classical question: What really determined the

failure in the struggle for changes? What in the cultural formation of the majority engendered apathy toward the coup?

Since 1964 Cinema Novo had been searching for answers, and when Rocha directed *Land in Anguish*, he placed his work among a very particular set of films that chose to directly approach the question of the intellectual facing the coup and the revolution: *The Challenge* (*O desafio*, Paulo Cesar Saraceni, 1965), *The Brave Warrior* (*O bravo guerreiro*, Gustavo Dahl, 1968), and *Hunger for Love* (*Fome de amor*, Pereira dos Santos, 1968). All these films were engaged in discussing the political illusions of the intellectuals, and Cinema Novo recognized the real country that had previously been invisible. *Land in Anguish* brought to the agenda "uncomfortable issues," especially those marked by stereotypes already sedimented in the idea of the "tropics" as a "specific cultural complex." In the reflection about power, the film did not exclude a symbolic appropriation of what in Brazilian tradition was an argument polished by the conservative thought in order to underline the peculiarity of the country. What would this inclusion mean in a leftist film framed against the military coup? My analysis discusses the way Rocha conceives the role of these representations related to the national character and to the "inferiority" of the tropical men.

My examination of the films that answered Rocha's seminal inquiry implies the analysis of other forms of appropriation of such representations of "inferiority." Since 1968 we have seen the renewal of a type of collage that brings a good-humored critique of the stereotypes of conservative iconography and celebratory official discourses. Such collages usually unfold into ironic quotations of the more scholarly tradition and of the kitschy products of local industrialized culture. Reading *Red Light Bandit*, I try to evaluate the view offered by the collage in 1968, when the primacy of a pedagogic political art collapsed and there was a search for a new aesthetics to cope with a more complex society, more mediated in its power structure, different from what had previously been expected. The artists left aside the illusion of communicating with the people and recognized their audience as consisting of the middle and upper layers of the population, particularly college students. Then cinema either foregrounded aggression—as in Bressane and Tonacci's work—or tried out new market strategies. In many cases, this implied the mobilization of national genres dismissed by early Cinema Novo: the revival of the *chanchada* as a legitimate cultural reference, performed not only in the *tropicalist Red Light Bandit* but also in Cinema Novo's *Macunaíma*.

One of the dimensions of the revision performed by the new stance toward urban culture in Brazil was a process of transcending the dualistic view of the country, the view that opposed rural authenticity (folklore) to urban "corruption" (the sphere of international commodities). The revision allowed for the incorporation of elements of mass culture and redirected the discussion of national identity toward a good-humored parody of the official nationalism. But this good humor did not last long and turned into a bitter irony when the country plunged into that combination of economic growth and political repression called the "Brazilian miracle." To express this irony, the filmmakers found multiple forms and fostered a convergence of inspirations, from Bertolt Brecht to Antonin Artaud, from Jean-Luc Godard to Jean-Marie Straub, a convergence of inspirations typical of various Brazilian arts in the 1960s. The modernization administered by the military regime, although repressive, received an active response from the artists who developed aesthetic experimentation to confront a country, a language, and an audience made strange.

In 1968 *tropicalismo* brought several traditions to the center of the market culture, asserting a very special poetics that reworked the anthropophagic strategies proposed by Oswald de Andrade and making intertextuality its major program. Today, when quotation is routine in the cultural industry, it is difficult to retrieve the context in which an intertextual program meant rupture. However, polemics at the time were harsh because *tropicalist* music, for example, offended a nationalism concerned with the supposed purity of Brazilian traditional sound; on the other hand, for some time, *tropicalist* performances managed to keep a subversive content, shocking their audiences with increasingly aggressive strategies. The repressive Institutional Act Number 5 (the AI-5) broke the flow of this rich experiment. While it lasted, this unique process (which also involved television) was the laboratory of a new articulation between culture and politics, an ultimate experience of loss of innocence while confronting the cultural industry in conservative modern Brazil.

In its game of deliberate mixings of high and low, national and foreign, avant-garde and kitsch, Brazilian cinema in the late 1960s exposed the mechanisms of cultural production. By using quotations it revealed another feature of modernity, equally programmatic and varied in its meanings: reflexivity, exposure of the materials, overt display of the work of representation itself.[23] In film reflexivity tends to acquire a particular dimension thanks to the intimate relationship between cinematic technique and illusionistic fascination. Godard's films, an emblem of the 1960s, illustrate the impact given by this exposure of materials in cinema and by a more open intertextual practice as well. This practice, at that time, privileged discontinuity and other modernist strategies of a conceptual cinema or parodic displacements of a political cinema concerned with its performance in the market. The incorporation of objects and icons of consumer society sometimes, as in Godard, gave a pop dimension to intertextuality. What is significant in this connection is the fact that, in Europe and in Brazil as well, this pop gesture by the artist usually acquired a clear political meaning linked to the critique of mass culture.[24]

Confronted with the mechanisms of mass culture, on the one hand, and the kind of rupture performed by the historical avant-gardes up to World War II, on the other, some experiments of the 1960s political art require a specific framework to be properly read. Their critique addressed the universe of cultural industry but left aside the utopian creation of a world saved from the media. In the new interaction with kitsch, the critical artist produced a vexing juxtaposition of previously separated spheres of culture. This juxtaposition articulated a project with a very peculiar pathos, proper to those who, at the time, were engaged in the alteration of the relationship between experience and language, between art and daily life. There is an uneasiness in the good-humored collection of Godardian quotations, a romantic trace that becomes clearer when observed after cinema's later developments. This uneasiness, also present in Sganzerla's *Red Light Bandit*, is evident in Bressane's aggressive films made in 1969. This idea of pathos, of the drama lived by a generation in its daily confrontation with the media, refers here to that deep experience, crucial to the artist's expression, usually not acknowledged in recent recollections. More involved with the postmodern, these recollections project an air of the 1980s while observing the films of the 1960s.

In Brazil 1968 ended with the imposition of the AI-5, a political landmark that established a very clear relationship between the aggressive tone of the experimental cinema produced after 1969 and the definite tightening of the regime. In Marginal Cinema there are elements that reflect this relationship: desperation and references to repression and torture. But the variety of structures that one may find—a Tonacci film is quite different from a Luiz Rosemberg film or João Silvério Trevisan film—results from the positioning of particular films in different cinematic traditions. On the whole the films show different combinations of expressionist protest and constructive tendencies that translate the relationship of the artists to the Brazilian crisis, giving expression to a range of marginalized subcultures within a patriarchal context.

In the late 1960s there were signs of a "behavioral revolution" that reflected a culture of authenticity reworked by youth in their critique of common sense and bourgeois codes (patriarchal hypocrisy), a culture of authenticity that did not exclude leftist political engagement on the part of students. Under repression, this revolution was not merely an escape from the political, as many wanted, but a style of opposition to the established order that joined daily trangressions to artistic production. Just as had occurred in the period of the U.S. underground still influenced by the beat generation (1950s), in Brazil in 1969–70 this subculture came to articulate a moment of radical iconoclasm.[25]

The period I focus on constitutes a "frontier situation" in which confrontation increases: It is the key moment of the political, cultural, and even military struggle that resulted in the consolidation of the institutional picture sponsoring Brazilian modernization. In the 1960s and 1970s, the Brazilian process had very clear political demarcation points, a fact that favors interpreting the question of culture in the light of an analysis of the military regime. No doubt, much of what is expressed as disappointment and nihilism was a consequence of domestic political changes, including the consolidation of a system of telecommunications that promoted national integration under a conservative tutelage. However, one should note the changes taking place in culture from a broader perspective than the one given by the internal political evolution. The demolition of the imagery of the avant-garde and the atomization of cultural life within the sphere controlled by the electronic industry has an international dimension: They are part of a global process into which Brazil is integrated, a process that generates new forms of urban life and dissolves representation, creating what might be called a new regime of subjectivity.[26]

In Brazil political art, with its double movement of affirmation of utopias and loss of innocence in the face of an incipient consumer society, embodied quite well the dialectical tension of a kind of modernism that accepted the technical aspect of modern culture but criticized the content of its representations. On the one hand, this political art mobilized the dynamism of the modern trying to radicalize its corrosive power regarding the patriarchal side of the national tradition. On the other hand, it brought a reading of this tradition that, although irreverent, marked a continuity of references and underlined what was relevant to the "national question" in that sphere of the cultural process in which internationalization was clearer.

Considering the path of the conjunctions and disjunctions between avant-garde and nationalist concerns, what we see in the 1960s is a particular crossing of trends catalyzed by the politics of the decade. This crossing of trends can be now observed as the final stage of Brazilian modernism because it is a moment of crisis for two teleologies: that of the national revolutionary ideals and that of the avant-garde project.

In a kind of threshold of the "postmodern condition" in Brazil, the cultural process in the 1960s produced a zone of creativity in which, in its advances and retreats, the modern *cinéma d'auteur* still found a vigorous collective manifestation to express its oppositional stance toward conservative modernization.

Part I

The Teleology of History

1

Black God, White Devil: Allegory and Prophecy

Sertão and Sea: The Central Metaphor

At the beginning of the last sequence of *Black God, White Devil*, the main characters in the film, the peasant couple Manuel and Rosa, are about to witness a last great duel. Antônio das Mortes (Anthony of the Dead), the "*cangaceiro* killer,"[1] after a long chase, has the small group of outlaws in his sights. The chance to kill Corisco—the last *cangaceiro*—has finally come. Two shots showing Antônio das Mortes in his search provide the transition to this moment of confrontation while the ballad singer—the principal mediator in the storytelling process—comments on Antônio's will and perseverance in the accomplishment of his task. The encounter is first depicted in a long take beginning with the image of the small group—Corisco, Dadá (his wife), Manuel, and Rosa—in their flight through the *sertão*; they are tiny figures immersed in an "ocean" of dry land.[2] The camera then pans, and a zoom out expands our field of vision to include Antônio. He stands in the right-hand corner of the screen, close to the camera, with his back to us, observing the small group without being noticed. As a privileged observer, he sees without being seen.

Silence, tension, delay. Antônio points his gun in a slow easy gesture reminding us of many ambushes in the actual history of the *sertão*, in which crimes engendered by revenge or police repression succeeded given the advantage of surprise. In *Black God, White Devil* the chaser does not shoot. Briefly everything in the diegetic world is kept still. The ambush, the real pattern of the chaser's activity, has no place in this fiction. Antônio is not the image of the police officer, and his gesture does not follow a realistic representation. Antônio is an agent within the context of a legend—he waits, like everything else in the film. He waits, for the command of the storyteller. The order comes from the singer's voice on the sound track. Antônio begins to act ac-

31

32   *Black God, White Devil*

cording to a pattern of heroic gesture in perfect accord with the song, which explicitly organizes the representation of the episode. We hear the guitar and the singer's voice while Antônio raises his arm to call Corisco, synchronizing his gestures with the first verse of the song: "Surrender, Corisco." Released from the "arbitrary" stillness that interrupted the realistic mise-en-scène, the action develops with increasing rapidity. We are given short fragments of the scene in a succession of jump cuts. Camera and actors move in a way that translates the action described by the verses. The editing conforms to the rhythm and tone of the song in its reference to discontinuous fragments. When Antônio and Corisco are face-to-face, the *cangaceiro* refuses to surrender for a last time, and he jumps very quickly in all directions performing the magic gesture from which originates his legendary name (Figures 1.1–1.4; page 53). Despite Corisco's "closed body" magic, and speed, Antônio is stronger and manages to kill him.[3] In a theatrical gesture, he cuts off Corisco's head as the song invites everybody to celebrate the historical event.

The heroic tone given to the confrontation and the very style of Corisco's death—he dies with his body and outstretched arms forming a cross while he shouts, "Stronger are the powers of the people"— make clear that image and sound work together to express a particular view of things: Representation identifies the space of image and action with the space of guitar and verse. In this last episode of the narrative, the mediation of *cordel* literature controls all the elements of the mise-en-scène.[4] The telegraphic and awkwardly discontinuous style violates the codes of industrial cinema. Here the handheld camera and the series of jump cuts provide a cinematic strategy that fits the filmmaker's attempt to approach the oral tradition embedded in the "civilization of leather," as the region of the *sertão* is called.[5]

With Corisco dead, Antônio keeps his promise and lets Manuel and Rosa live. Maintaining the parallel evolution of song and image, the basic refrain—"The *sertão* will become sea and the sea *sertão*"—is heard, to be repeated many times while Manuel and Rosa are seen in their headlong *corrida* ("run") through the *sertão*.[6] Such a *corrida*— the first straight-line vector within a trajectory marked by constant circling of glances, movements, and even thought—reinforces the projection toward the glimpsed future and the certainty of the radical transformation suggested by the refrain. The same formula—"The *sertão* will become sea and the sea *sertão*"—was heard before in the film, coming from Sebastião (the *beato*, "saint") and from Corisco, in both cases used to express their ultimate dream of a happy life in the future. It was such a dream and such a formula that allowed them to conceive of their own practice as the accomplishment of a transcendental mission.

As the chorus repeats the refrain, the singer draws the moral of his story: "My story now is told, a story of truth and imagination, I hope you have learned the lesson: This world is wrong, ill-divided; and Earth [land] belongs to man, not to God or devil." Therefore while the chorus, repeating the central metaphor of transformation, reaffirms the formula that expressed the mystic certainty of *beato* and *cangaceiro*, the singer posits a secular, nonreligious conception of change that places history in the hands of human beings themselves, thus confirming many other allusions heard throughout the film. At the end of *Black God, White Devil*, the narration assumes the formula of its "alienated" characters; at the same time, through the singer's message, it completes its demystification of the metaphysics in both God and devil.[7] Facing such a paradox, we wait for some sign that could indicate which element prevails: the humanist secular notion of history or the metaphysical idea of fate. This sign does not come.

Manuel's *corrida* does not imply any "model for action" typical of political films with pedagogical concerns. It does not define a specific perspective; it merely evokes the possibility of perspectives. Though projective, it is simply availability for new engagements not yet defined. Nothing gives a clear direction to Manuel's path. The immediate aspect of this *corrida* is that of a blind flight across the *sertão*. Yet he keeps running in a straight line, and the song lends his *corrida* a note of hope that is reinforced by the subsequent movement of the narrative that does not end with Manuel's *corrida* or the verses of the folksong. The most explicit intervention of the narrator comes to offer a final reversal by reaffirming revolutionary certainty in the figurative language of images: The surf invades the screen, the *sertão* becomes sea, and the film visually realizes the metaphor of transformation used by both Sebastião and Corisco (Figures 1.5–1.7; page 53). The ritual sounds and voices of the Heitor Villa-Lobos choral music replace the popular ballad and punctuate the magic metamorphosis, *sertão* to sea. The presence of the sea connotes domination and fulfillment, and the music reinforces this feeling. Such a final stroke renders actual the telos that guides the main characters throughout the film, a telos that remains out of their reach.

This final celebration strengthens the formula of hope. There is, however, a discontinuity between the presence of the sea and Manuel's flight, confirming the hiatus between his particular experience and the future that is to come. The visual representation of the telos is not a projection of his thought or his particular hope—Manuel is far from the sea. This closing image, with its suggestion of ultimate fulfillment, results only from the intervention of an exterior narrative agency. Yet the sea on the screen remains closely connected with Manuel's straight-line *corrida* across the *sertão*. How can we relate Manuel's availability and this certainty affirmed at the end?

My hypothesis is that this hiatus between the metaphorical sea and Manuel's experience is fundamental to the economy of the film. The end undoubtedly points to the inevitable revolution, making the entire film the expression of a concrete hope. However, it is also made clear that effective attainment of the telos is neither in Manuel's and Rosa's adventure nor in Sebastião's or Corisco's practices—religious messianism and social banditry. How can we specify the connection between the projects of salvation experienced by the characters and the final proposal of the narration? My analysis of the basic episodes of Manuel's quest for justice intends to determine, if possible, where the final certainty finds its support. My reading focuses on the complex play of relations between the fictional world and the work of narration that constitutes that world. The film's style pleads for allegorical interpretation, whereas its internal organization defies the interpreter searching for a unifying "key." This resistance to interpretation is by no means incidental. I intend to demonstrate that it is structural.

The Weaving of the Narrative: Breaks and Discontinuities

The fable of *Black God, White Devil* is organized around a peasant couple, Manuel and Rosa. The film speaks of their social condition, their hopes and representations, and their links to two forms of contestation: messianic cults and *cangaço* (the activities of *cangaceiros*). We can identify, and the narration clearly distinguishes, three stages in their development. In the first stage, the cowherd Manuel lives with his wife Rosa and his mother on a backwoods plantation. He takes care of the local landowner's cattle in exchange for a small portion of the herd. Rosa, meanwhile, cultivates the crops necessary for their survival. In this stage, the first break occurs when Manuel, cheated out of his due allotment of cattle, kills the landowner (Colonel Morais), whose henchmen then pursue Manuel and murder his mother. Hounded by the powerful and seeing his mother's death as a sign from heaven, Manuel joins the followers of Sebastião, the miracle-working saint. In the second stage, Manuel, ignoring Rosa's objections, places his destiny in Sebastião's hands. To prove his devotion, he performs the necessary purification rites. Meanwhile Sebastião's cult begins to concern both the local landowners and the Catholic church. Together they call on Antônio das Mortes to suppress the movement. The break in this stage occurs when Antônio das Mortes agrees to exterminate the devotees (the *beatos*). At the same moment that Antônio massacres the *beatos*, Rosa slays Sebastião, ending his domination of Manuel. In the final stage, the blind singer Júlio leads Manuel and Rosa, the lone survivors of the massacre, to Corisco, the survivor of another massacre, that of the *cangaceiros'* major leader, Lampião, and his band. Manuel transfers his loyalty to Corisco, whom he sees as an agent of fate who will help him revenge Sebastião. He and Corisco discuss the role of violence in the struggle to master destiny. Their discussion revolves around the relative grandeur of Sebastião versus Lampião, and it comes to absorb all the protagonists: Manuel, Rosa, Corisco, and Dadá. The final break occurs when Antônio das Mortes fulfills his commission of eliminating Corisco. With both Sebastião and Corisco slain, the *sertão* opens up to the headlong flight of Manuel and Rosa.

The summary of the fable and the identification of three clearly separate stages gives the impression that the didactic aspect of the narrative implies a very simple conception of human and social temporality. The fable sets forth a linear disposition of events, which suggests a natural evolution within a notion of time as pure extension, as mere setting for the actions of men. This simplicity is deceptive. A consideration of the style of representation and the analysis of the three fundamental breaks will illuminate the film's temporal structure. In search of what is determinant in the legend of *Black God, White Devil,* I consider first the basic movement of expansion and contraction that characterizes its molding of time.

The three phases outlined here are not of equal duration in the narrative. The first is relatively short, suggesting a kind of prologue. In this phase, however, the film already develops its central procedure: the condensed representation of social existence. This procedure distinguishes *Black God, White Devil* from films like *Barren Lives* (1963), whose scenic conventions derive from the neorealist tradition. In opposition to a style that tends to privilege the intrinsic duration of episodes slowly exposing the characters' milieu, the prologue of Rocha's film already condenses situations, making ordinary activities emblematic of a whole mode of existence. The film's credits—superimposed over shots of arid *sertão*—announce the narrative style. The crescendo of Villa-Lobos's *Song of the Sertão* coincides with images (two close shots of the decomposing skull of an ox) symbolizing the drought afflicting the region. Contrasting in scale with the preceding long shots, these images are still in our mind when we first see Manuel. These brief shots, then, concentrate a dramatic charge of information about the drought and the precarious conditions of *sertão* life. The drama erupts and dissolves rapidly. The synthetic style and the shock image, condensing a broad range of significations, here anticipate the film's constant modulation of contrasts and energetic leaps.

This modulation becomes clearer during Manuel's conversation with Colonel Morais. Between the shots of the decomposing ox and this dialogue referring back to the dead animals, four scenes summarize the outlines of Manuel's life: his encounter with Sebastião; his attempt to convey the shock caused by this encounter to Rosa; he and Rosa producing manioc, their basic food; and their nocturnal conversation about the future, Manuel's hope contrasting with Rosa's skepticism. By the time Manuel goes to the town fair and crosses the corral to meet the colonel, these four scenes have already prepared us to grasp the significance of the dialogue in Manuel's life. The representation of this first break fully demonstrates the style of narration already announced in the prologue. Rather than evoking tension through a conventional play of shot–counter shot, Rocha exploits composition within the frame and the slow movement of the actors. The tension is primarily created by the dilation of the scene over time, especially in those moments preceding the conflict's resolution. Manuel's violence responds to the colonel's violence; it discharges the accumulated tension, finding resonance in the montage as long takes give way to a rapid succession of short-duration jump cut shots. The narration abbreviates the struggle between Manuel and the colonel, the chase, and the exchange of gunshots leading to the death of Manuel's mother. At the same time, coincident with this discontinuous visual montage, silence gives way to a saturated sound track that superimposes the sounds generated by the action on the music of Villa-Lobos. The aurally saturated scenes of the cavalcade and the gunfight in front of Manuel's house is followed by a long take in which Manuel, after closing the eyes of his murdered mother, slowly rises while looking back at the house. Complete silence, broken only by the singer's hushed lament, echoes the pensive immobility of the character. Within this sequence, then, dilated time, relative immobility, and silence "frame" a more contracted time of multiple actions and crucial decisions.

The second fundamental break follows a similar pattern. It is preceded by the long and exasperating sequence in which Manuel performs penance by carrying a boulder up an interminable slope. At the altar, Sebastião quietly tells Manuel to bring his wife and a child to the sacrifice. The film opposes the interior of the chapel, a space of ceremonial silence, to the exterior, a space of hysteria and agitation, evoked by the gyrating handheld camera and the strident cries of the *beatos* amplified by the blowing wind. This opposition follows the same dialectic of rarefaction–excess that governs the narrative as a whole. In the chapel, the ritual evolves in a silence marked by fixed glances and stylized gestures. The itinerary of the camera's glance, meanwhile, gradually transforms the central instrument of the rite (the dagger) into the center of the composition (Figures 1.8–1.11; pages 53–54). This hieratic disposition is broken only with Rosa's slaying of Sebastião and the fall of icons and candles from the altar, whose clatter signals the eruption of gunfire and the cries originating from the scene of the massacre. Extremely brief shots render the agitation and fall of the devout under the relentless fire of an Antônio das Mortes multiplied in a montage effect that makes his figure jump discontinuously while he shoots without interruption. The massacre over, the film reverts to slow camera movements over the victims, as a shot of a pensive Antônio installs a new phase of reflection.

This dialectic of scarcity and saturation is present in the breaks that carry us from one stage of the story to the next, and it also marks the temporality of *Black God, White Devil* as a whole. There are two significant examples of this: (1) the scene in which Rosa's mounting exasperation with Manuel's idolization of Sebastião results in a scream that "cues" Antônio's exuberant entrance into the film, in which the slow-paced sequence in Monte Santo involving Manuel, Sebastião, and Rosa is broken by the abrupt introduction of Antônio das Mortes, who is seen already in action; (2) the only love scene in the whole film, in which the slow perambulation and exchange of glances between Rosa and Corisco define a ceremonial approach that is broken by the sudden leap to a discontinuous series of handheld camera movements that figure a sexual intercourse celebrated by Villa-Lobos's "Bachianas."

This contrast between a lack and an overabundance of action functions decisively within the narrative economy and constitutes a rich source of meaning.

The Distended Time of Thought: Brecht and Eisenstein in the Pedagogy of the Sertão

On a semantic level, this narrative organization may be seen as a metaphor for the psychology of the characters, here taken as typical representatives of the peasant class. The exasperating passivity, the verbal awkwardness, the atmosphere of hesitant rumination, all alternating with sudden explosions of violence, thus find resonances within the narrative style. This metaphor could be extended to the environmental conditions of the *sertão*—where drought alternates with deluge—with its rude challenges to human survival. Undoubtedly, these metaphors form part of the film's structure and inform specific editing strategies and camera movements. Often the camera closely follows the actors' movements, fostering our identification with the quality of their experience. The mediation, however, does not always work precisely in this way. The singer, for example, takes us beyond the immediate experience of the characters and places the whole story within a broader perspective. There is a specific modulation of distance and identification created by the interaction of image and sound, pointing to fundamental changes in perspective within the relationship between the narration and the diegesis. To account for these changes, we need to place those metaphors within a broader frame of reference. In these terms, the plausible homologies between character and milieu are less important than the conception of temporality—historical in its decisive dimension—inherent in this modulation. The narrative, in its very texture, molds time so as to privilege disequilibrium and transformation. What seems to be immobility is in fact the accumulation of energy; moments of apparent stasis mask and express latent forces. The slow passages are not neutral moments of pure extension; rather, they engender the strong moments and the qualitative leaps. The internal movement of the narrative, in its swift changes and irreverent lack of measure, asserts the discontinuous but necessary presence of human and social transformation.

Given these contentions, the final leap from *sertão* to sea—the figurative representation of revolution—is totally coherent with the internal principle of the film. It epitomizes a basic discursive procedure of a film permeated by the irrepressible movement of humankind, a film in which history is a presupposition. If time accumulates energy and each single moment can reveal the gap (or the crisis) through which the revolutionary forces find their way, Manuel's *corrida* virtually demands the sea as its logical conclusion. Where violence and injustice form part of the human condition, insurrection is always potentially present. What *Black God, White Devil* proposes is that even when the oppressed seem to have acquiesced in alienation, they still carry within them the seeds of revolt.

Functionally this modulation opens breaches for the diverse interventions of the narrative voices, creating space for explicit commentary on the actions represented in the film and making possible the autonomous development of sound and image tracks (that is, a vertical montage). What guides the movement of the images, apart from the unifying stage of Monte Santo, is the contrasting articulation of Sebastião's messianic discourse and Rosa's disbelief. We accompany the play of questions and answers on the sound track; while a sentence or dialogue develops continuously, the image track displays a series of disconnected shots evoking the *beatos*' life in Monte Santo. The film's central purpose is to delineate the progression of an argument rather than to provide a continuous representation of individual scenes.

The same antinaturalist criteria operate in the *cangaceiro* episodes. The actors' performances acquire a clearly theatrical tone, and the editing structure alternates between long takes and abruptly discontinuous short pieces. At times, we follow Corisco's speeches presented directly to the audience through long takes. The tension of the argument is expressed through the duration of the shots and through the searching and "tactile" eye of a handheld camera positioned close to the actors' bodies. Sometimes the flux of time is interrupted to make room for Corisco's recollections. His tales are not conventional flashbacks; rather, they are framed as theatrical representations in which he plays two different roles: himself and Lampião (Figures 1.12–1.15; page 54).

Corisco's Brechtian theater functions as an interior monologue acted out. It breaks the continuity of action and is a veritable excursus designed to explain the decisive steps of the argument concerning the *cangaço*. The sequence in which Corisco, Manuel, Rosa, and Dadá discuss the legitimacy of violence versus the efficacy of prayer as a means to "change destiny" is a good example of this process. In his effort to preserve the myth of Lampião, Corisco, when threatened by opposing arguments, screams "It's a lie" directly to the camera, as if appealing for the audience's support (Figure 1.16; page 54). These words open the way for an excursus in which Corisco enacts Lampião's confession of fear and weakness. This confession completed, we immediately return to the space of the dialogue, with Corisco in exactly the same posture finally recognizing "It's true," thus closing the argument.

As this example illustrates, *Black God, White Devil* is dotted with ritual stagings of its own central ideological debate. The succession of phases weaves an overall movement of reflection, and everything in the film—the mise-en-scène, the montage, the singer-narrator, the dialogue, the discursive use of image and sound—foregrounds this movement. Although the film speaks of historical struggles, it is not concerned with reconstituting events as they actually occurred.[8] Rather than seeking legitimacy in the illusory transfer of the "real" life of another epoch to the fictional universe of the screen, *Black God, White Devil* attunes its style to the adverse economic conditions governing its production, expressing the basic principles of the "aesthetics of hunger." At the same time, this strategy forms part of the filmmaker's attempt to make his language akin to that of the *cordel* poet, a personage explicitly incorporated in the film's structure. It is no accident that the folksinger is a central narrative agency. Belonging to the same universe that constitutes the film's object of reflection, his role as mediating figure links *Black God, White Devil* with that tradition of popular culture celebrated by Cinema Novo.

This mediation, although not the sole carrier of the film's attitude toward historical data, partially explains the film's dismissal of rigorous fidelity to the official history of dates and documents in its discourse on Corisco, Lampião, and Antônio Conselheiro. The narrative transforms history into a referential matrix covered with layers of imaginary constructions. This precipitate of the popular imagination takes the form of exemplary tales whose purpose is not fidelity to fact but, rather, the transmission of a moral. The historical process turned into allegory is represented in a style reminiscent in its criteria of selection and its narrative poetics of the work of the traditional storyteller characterized by Walter Benjamin in his essay "The Storyteller."[9] Like the content of the imaginary world of the western, the material reworked by Rocha's film comes from popular ballads and stories, which transfigure the experience of social banditry within a context of land dispute in a social space controlled by landowners and cattle ranchers. Like the western, *Black God, White Devil* displays that rude landscape, the displacement in the wide-open spaces, the chase, and the heroic duels borrowed from the cavalier tradition. Unlike the classic western, however, Rocha's film does not convey the mythic past of the heroes who, defeating the emissaries of evil, led society from past barbarism to present civilization and legitimate order. The tradition embodied in the singer-narrator, with its metaphorical evocations of God and devil, is not the sole source of the discourse. The singer introduces the characters and makes his commentary, but it would be simplistic to see the narration as merely the expression of the singer's values. Popular poetry is but one of the multiple mediations that inform *Black God, White Devil*, for the movie exploits all the parameters of the film medium. The material of its representation (sound and image) is not homogeneous with the material of oral literature, and its conditions of production are not those of the *cordel* tradition. To state the obvious, *Black God, White Devil* is a film, with all that this fact implies. The mediation of *cordel* literature, resulting from an impulse of identification with popular art, interacts with the other processes involved in the film's construction, and this interaction generates the displacements that render the discourse ambiguous. The journey of Manuel and Rosa transfigures the accumulated experiences of the peasant community. These experiences, schematized and encapsulated within one linear trajectory, are mediated by narrative instances that constantly shift their position. In this sense, the film constitutes a decentered and ambivalent reflection on history itself, a reflection in which the memory of peasant revolts is both revealed and questioned from diverse points of view.

Sebastião and Corisco: Identity and Difference

How does the film depict its basic figures, Sebastião and Corisco?

In the accounts of both messianism and *cangaço*, the singer's narration, the work of the camera, and the musical commentaries are not always in accord. In the sequence of Manuel's first encounter with Sebastião, for example, the image of the sky coincides with the singer's first chord on the guitar. As the camera pans down to frame Sebastião, the singer begins his song. He presents the characters and anticipates the special nature of the encounter. The initial movement seems to define a unity of perspectives: Sound and image define the saint as blessed by God. As Manuel approaches on horseback, however, the voice of the singer is stilled and the visual composition interprets the encounter in a way that anticipates the subsequent unmasking of Sebastião. Manuel excitedly circles Sebastião and his followers, staring at the saint. The play of shot–counter shot, however, underlines Sebastião's indifference to Manuel. The subjective camera shows that the saint does not look at the peasant; Manuel becomes present to Sebastião only when he places himself directly before the saint's impassive eyes. This treatment helps characterize Manuel by discrediting in advance his account of the incident in the following scene. At the same time, the image does not support the singer's description of Sebastião. There is a divorce between the actor and the camera, and the distance that characterizes the play of glances only becomes more pronounced as the film progresses. In these encounters Sebastião remains an enigma as the camera more and more reflects the perspective of Rosa, the focus of skepticism. Sebastião, for his part, stimulates this skepticism by his air of aristocratic indifference and by a touch of sadism in his ministering of the ceremonies. His behavior results in an inglorious death, whose ordinary humanness contrasts with his former haughtiness and definitively unmasks him in our eyes. Only minutes before Rosa's attack, after all, had not this same man resolutely murdered a child?

This process of demystification, however, hardly exhausts the film's account of the social phenomenon of messianism. Manuel's surrender to Sebastião is constructed so as to celebrate a religious force capable of uniting the peasant masses. The camera anticipates Manuel and Rosa climbing the mountain to Sebastião's domain, thus providing a rare moment of apotheosis. Processions of banners and symbols outlined against the sky and blown by the wind find an echo in the symphonic music of Villa-Lobos. The solemn grandiosity of the scene comes, interestingly, not from the *cordel* singer's voice but, rather, from the music of a composer embedded in the erudite tradition. Even here, however, the figure of Sebastião is treated with great subtlety, since the camera emphasizes the pomp and circumstance surrounding him and the collective force of religious ecstasy. The following sequence points up the hysterically repressive side of this same religion, showing ritual humiliations and flagellations. The violent confrontation between the *beatos* and the larger society is rendered in a kind of strident shorthand, and the critique of messianism implicit in this passage is subsequently confirmed by the extended sequences on Monte Santo, the locus of retreat and contemplative longing. Metaphorically exploring the topography of the mountain—turned into a stage—the narration crystallizes the idea of proximity to Heaven and imminent ascension, of retreat to a kind of antechamber to Paradise. In this privileged space, detached from the impure earth, the possibility of direct intervention in the world ceases to be a goal. Messianic rebellion takes the peasants out of the process of production and distances them from the official church. It frees them from the domination of landlord and boss, but in its place it proposes only the passivity of prayer and the initiatory rituals that will define them as elect in the moment of cataclysm.

After the massacre, Manuel continues to be faithful to Sebastião. The saint's demystification takes place within the work of narration and without the character's knowledge. With the appearance of Corisco, however, the mise-en-scène changes significantly. An element from within the diegesis now becomes the focus of critical reflection. As master of ceremonies, Corisco addresses his words both to us as spectators and to Manuel within the fiction. From this point on, the extended passages of rarefied action involve the characters' discussion of their own experience, a discussion in which Corisco dominates. A new kind of dialogue appears with the insertion of the singer himself, or of his double, into the scene. At the same time, image and sound, by repeating similar insignia within apparently opposite conditions, suggest that Sebastião and Corisco are merely two sides of the same metaphysics; in the symmetry of their inversions lies a deeper unity.

The same voice (Othon Bastos) delivers the words of both Sebastião and Corisco.[10] And the same Villa-Lobos music consecrates Sebastião's triumph on Monte Santo and Manuel's initiation—by castrating the *fazendeiro* ("landowner")—into *cangaço* violence. The same metaphor marks the horizon of their practice: "The *sertão* will become sea and the sea *sertão*." Both speak in the name of good and evil. The unity that underlies their contradictions is expressed in symmetrical presentations: Corisco's presence in Manuel's path is also announced as a kind of advent ("as fate would have it") in versification similar to that of the beginning of the film.

At the same time, there are significant inversions: The vertical pan from sky to earth associated with Sebastião becomes a creeping horizontal pan over the *sertão* associated with Corisco. This inversion opposes Corisco's rootedness in the "lower" world of "that devil Lampião," to the "elevated" world of the saint. The *beatos*' straight-line progression toward Monte Santo, furthermore, is replaced by the back-and-forth movements of Corisco's violent rituals. In long shot he promises vengeance as his circular movements underline the clearly limited space of his action in the close-cropped *sertão*. The perspectival view of his stage, staked out by his immobile henchmen, projects on his figure the shadow of a closing and an absence of horizons that will only be reaffirmed and rendered explicit as the allegory progresses.

The *cangaceiro* phase of the film takes on the tone of a ritual of the living dead, of survivors without hope or prospect. More than once it is Corisco himself who enunciates this condition of living death. In his first appearance, as he introduces himself to the audience, Corisco refers metaphorically to his two heads (one killing, the other thinking). As a survivor of Lampião's army, he is a vestige of a historically condemned practice, which he carries to its foredoomed conclusion. Before we hear the sentence of death pronounced on the *cangaço* in the dialogue between Antônio das Mortes and the blind singer, Corisco himself suggests it, acting as the last embodiment of a condemned doctrine that is relived symbolically as a hymn of praise to violence as a form of justice. He speaks rather than effectively acts. As Corisco himself thematizes it, his violence involves no program beyond "turning things upside down" and vengeance. In his ceremonious speeches, he talks about himself at times as the agent of good and the figure of the just avenger (he is Saint Jorge, the people's saint, versus the dragon of wealth) and at times as the agent of evil in the figure of the condemned man who, when confronted with the greater indignity of death by starvation, chooses violence. His discourse is caught in self-defeating circularity, expressing the *cangaceiro*'s collapsing of means and ends as well as his alternation between revolt and accommodation with the enemy. The exuberant rhetoric with which Corisco demystifies Sebastião (Manuel's myth) implies the demystification of Lampião (his own myth). But we must acknowledge that, since his first intervention, it is Corisco himself who triggers the discussion leading to the recognition of Lampião's smallness. Moreover, his direct speech to the audience and his total lack of dissimulation contrast with Sebastião's enigmatic and self-sufficient attitude. Therefore, unlike Sebastião, he is accepted by Rosa. Unlike Sebastião, he interacts with the narrative agency embodied in the camera. Unlike Sebastião, he faces death with courage and has the right to fight Antônio das Mortes in a legendary duel reminiscent of the *cordel* tradition.

Antônio das Mortes: The "Daemonic Agent"

In its simultaneous praise and demystification of both Sebastião and Corisco, the narration discredits messianism and *cangaço* as practices likely to generate a more just human order. The underside of the metaphysics of good and evil is exposed in the equivocal expression of its rebellion. The film clearly favors the willed defeat and exemplary revolt of the *cangaceiro* to the alienation of the saint. Corisco's defense of violence seems to place him nearer the forces that command man's destiny. Unlike Sebastião, he establishes a dialogue of glances and gestures with the camera, a dialogue that allows him to participate in the discussion concerning his own social practice. The film suggests that there is a progression from the first chapter of Manuel's journey to the second. The *cangaço* is not just an experience coming after messianism; it is also an advanced stage within a specific teleology. The movement from stage to stage is not merely chronological; rather, it expresses a logical progression toward revolutionary consciousness. Antônio das Mortes is the "daemonic agent" of this progression, the figure of infallibility and enigma. Like Corisco, Antônio defends his own violence as a kind of euthanasia: The people must not die of hunger. He defines himself, furthermore, as the condemned agent of destiny within the same logic of "Kill and be killed." But while Corisco exposes his contradictions in a frenetic back-and-forth movement, Antônio is laconic, mysterious in his physical presence, and contradictory in his words.

When Antônio first appears in the film, the symphonic music celebrates him as a positive hero, but the folksinger presents him as the "*cangaceiro* killer," a condemned and proscribed figure. Antônio, by his own words, confirms such a role: "You need know nothing of me as an individual; I was condemned to this destiny and I have to fulfill it without thought or pity." His hesitation in accepting the task proposed by the priest and the colonel implies that he understands the conversation on some other level ("It is dangerous to meddle with the things of God"). When he accepts, with the words "Sebastião is finished," his tone of voice, suggesting both power and resignation, impresses solemnity on the moment. And in his conversation with blind Júlio, he posits once and for all the larger meaning of his acts, a meaning that his conscience intuits but that he never really explains: "One day there will be a great war in this *sertão*, a war without the blindness of God and devil; and in order to make way for this war, I killed Sebastião and I will kill Corisco. Then I will die, since we are all the same."

This dialogue between blind Júlio and Antônio interrupts the argument between Manuel and Corisco about the ends and means of justice. The song that introduces Antônio and Júlio's meeting in Canudos begins just after Corisco has repeated Sebastião's formula in a concluding statement. As a testament, Corisco says to Manuel: "When I die, go away with your wife and tell the people you see that Corisco was already more dead than alive. Lampião is dead, and Corisco died with him. For this very reason I needed to stand on my feet, fighting to the end, turning everything upside down. Till the *sertão* becomes sea and the sea *sertão*."

Comparing the two speeches, we can see that Antônio das Mortes goes further within the perspective opened up by Corisco. He declares the end of the *cangaço* to be necessary, and he foretells the advent of the great war. In his perspective, the willingness to fight "till the *sertão* becomes sea and the sea *sertão*" turns into an enigmatic consciousness of the preparatory mission of those who are not going to see the radical transformation because they are essentially immersed in the "blindness of God and devil." Antônio, in his posture of enigmatic sacrifice, reaffirms the certainty of the transformation through violence and brings us back to our initial interrogations, for his "great war" is nothing but the passage from *sertão* to sea that is postulated recurrently throughout the film. His infallible practice demonstrates an accord with the secret mechanisms of the world that bestows special authority on his words. And it is he who first enunciates the logic that regulates the progressive movement of Manuel's quest for justice. The final leap from *sertão* to sea sustains itself on this ascendant curve, which is only partially represented in the film. We see the enactment of prerevolution; revolution will necessarily come later.

Given this prophetic disposition, one can ask: Who (or what) in fact commands the progression of Manuel's journey? How can we relate Antônio's intervention to the ideas of destiny and history?

The Logic of the Prophecy

In the beginning of the film, by foretelling the outcome of the encounter between Manuel and Sebastião, the singer suggests the idea of destiny. The *beato* enters Manuel's life without Manuel having done anything to provoke the encounter. At the same time, Manuel's revolt is perfectly explicable in more earthly terms: the material conditions of his life, the social relations of his work, his visionary tendencies, Rosa's despair. To explain Manuel's violence, one needs only to assume a minimal notion of right and wrong and an elementary aspiration to justice. Angered by an obvious fraud and frustrated in a very specific hope (a hope for the possession of land), Manuel fails to understand the structural nature of his oppression and therefore invokes metaphysical entities to explain his adversity and to justify his revolt. He attributes the tragedy to a divine plan that requires his devotion to the saint, a choice that salves his guilty conscience and protects him from police pursuit. The providential presence of Sebastião offers to Manuel, at precisely the right moment, the option for which his consciousness is prepared. It is the singer, admittedly, who brings Sebastião to Manuel, but Manuel must also play his part for destiny to be fulfilled. It is this "coincidence" that triggers movement and makes concrete the first moment of rupture in the film.

In the second major break, the intervention of Antônio coincides with Rosa's act of violence. Her act too is explicable in terms of her own situation. She does not kill the saint in the service of some transcendent design but, rather, in her own name. Antônio's intervention, already ambiguous in itself, becomes doubly ambiguous by this precise coincidence with Rosa's violence. In the two decisive moments, external forces and human actions converge to create a turnabout that propels the characters into a new phase of life. Transformation arises from this correspondence, which marks a double determination: The narrative creates a situation in which the characters, unconscious of the stratagems mounted against them and moved by both personal and extrapersonal motives, act at the right time, participating actively in a process controlled by these same stratagems. In a peculiar translation of Hegel's "astuteness of reason," the film makes everything move toward a goal that remains unthinkable for the protagonists.

In reality, events do not proceed according to Manuel's expectations. In fact the narration works to discredit his interpretation, suggesting instead the existence of a preordained end. After the Monte Santo massacre, the projection of the singer, blind Júlio, into the story, visibly conducting Manuel and Rosa, makes palpable the presence of the agents of the grand plan behind the whole arrangement. In his first dialogue with Júlio at the crossroads, Antônio explains that he allowed Manuel and Rosa to survive so they could "tell their story." He makes Manuel and Rosa the bearers of his own legend, bastions of the oral tradition incorporated in the film. Thus, he hints at the very level at which the narration is engendered, for it is in the nature of the traditional narratives to organize themselves within a certain teleology. *Black God, White Devil* acknowledges this condition and comments on it even as it fulfills it.

The *cangaceiro* phase inaugurates a new system. Corisco arrives via the voice of the singer, and Manuel and Rosa come to Corisco via blind Júlio. Manuel, after the encounter, has his reasons for carrying out what has been predetermined: he joins the *cangaço* in order to avenge Sebastião. Prepared for violence, he sets out on a new trajectory of equivocations, in which his actions follow one design (that of a dimly glimpsed teleology) while his consciousness imagines another (based on the very metaphysics being discredited). Without knowing it, Manuel completes a circle; he descends from his messianic flight only to return to the down-to-earth practicality of Rosa. At this point, however, a subtle dislocation distances Manuel and Rosa from the central events of the fable. Although they remain present to the end of the film, their survival is determined by Antônio ("I didn't kill once, and won't kill again"). In the final sequence, the most relevant fact within the larger order is the duel between Corisco and Antônio; the song makes no reference to Manuel and Rosa. For the couple, survival marks a new opening and the reassertion of immediate natural bonds ("Let's have a son," Rosa proposes, and Manuel accepts). Their conscious future consists in liberation from both Sebastião and Corisco in favor of Rosa's life-oriented immediacy.

Although Manuel initially shows a capacity for revolt, by the end he shows only minimal initiative. Corisco gains strength, paradoxically, only insofar as he participates in the ritual representation of his own inevitable defeat. Antônio das Mortes, despite his infallibility, relinquishes all personal ambition, seeing himself as merely the doomed agent of a predetermined scheme. None of the agents in the film consciously makes his or her own history, taking control of destiny. The narration, for its part, moves from initial ambiguity toward explicit definition of a teleology. At first, this teleology is merely suggested by the singer and by the mise-en-scène, while the characters retain some initiative. With the dialogue between blind Júlio and Antônio, however, this teleological scheme, implicit in Corisco's style of representation, becomes explicit, defining the final term of the overall movement: "The great war, without the blindness of God and the devil." Antônio's own behavior, furthermore, favors this progression from implicit to explicit teleology. In his first intervention, his slaying of the *beatos* is explicable, on one level, by the earthly attraction of money, but his enigmatic attitude hints at more transcendent considerations. His duel with Corisco is not commercially motivated; killing *cangaceiros* is simply his destiny. In his final intervention, Antônio is only committed to the advent of the great war whose preparation is the only motive proposed for his action. The overall development of the film and Antônio's specific course suggest that progress is not determined by human beings. In this sense, the film moves toward a determination whose focus is outside of the characters and whose consciousness is capable, at best, only of vague intuitions of a more comprehensive order. And it is precisely Antônio who most clearly professes this radical agnosticism in his melancholy words.

There are, then, two major crisscrossing movements in the film: The questioning of a dualistic metaphysics in the name of the liberation of human beings as the subjects of history is superimposed on the gradual affirmation of a "larger order" that commands human destiny. These coexisting movements develop not along parallel paths but, rather, through a fundamental interdependence: The very agent who furthers liberation and humanistic values is also the demonic agent of a dim larger order. Antônio, collapsing in the same agent the usually contradictory features of alienation and lucidity, constitutes the nucleus of both movements, movements in which history advances along the correct path thanks to ambiguous and equivocal figures. Antônio's repressive violence is not a set of unfortunate incidents but a basic necessity, not a *despite* but a *through* by which history-destiny weaves itself. The story is composed as a propaedeutic recapitulation of a historical process (peasant's revolts) that the narration understands to be propaedeutic as well, as incorporating the movement toward the great war, an essential subterranean movement that the recapitulation, by its symbols, tries to make clear and palpable.

In this "making palpable," the *sertão* organizes itself as a cosmos. In its own internal movement, it must include all the essential forces that engender the future. Thus the invitation to action in the present must be based on the tradition of violence and rebellion celebrated by the legends. Therefore, in this "making palpable" the Marxist idea of historical necessity is transfigured into the idea of destiny, a version of necessity frequent in popular oral tradition.

The crucial point is that, in the form of destiny, the film paradoxically affirms the apparently opposite principle of human self-determination. The consummation of a telos is a given, but the particular form in which it is realized remains unspecified. Within the linear progression toward revolution, messianism and *cangaço* are moments by which human consciousness moves toward lucid acknowledgment of human beings themselves as the source, the means, and the end of transforming praxis. This ascension to consciousness does not find completion, however, within the perspective of the protagonists. There is a hiatus between their experience and the final term, the revolutionary telos around which the narration organizes its lesson. Manuel does not need to complete this trajectory because he does not liberate himself alone; he is not the center of his own trajectory. The horizon of history is not delineated by Manual or even by Rosa; the larger order requires that the certainty of the end be affirmed through incompletion. The essential element is hiatus. It is the lacuna that lends strength to prophecy. That is why we do not have all the links in the chain leading to revolution. We have only an overall design of history in which messianism and *cangaço* are included as the prefiguration of the telos that shall come to fulfill their promises and define their true meaning in the order of things. That is why, at the end of the film, in the final leap that constituted the point of departure of my analysis, hope could only be affirmed through the gap existing between Manuel's *corrida* and the sea. In Rocha's representation of the quest of the oppressed mind toward salvation, the arrangement of image, sound, and narrative reflects a typically figural (in Auerbach's sense) interpretation of historical facts. The allegory in this case corresponds to an impulse to redeem historical agents while acknowledging their limits and mistakes. There is a significant absence of any reference to the present. The representation is structured so as to read past events as evidences that support the prophetic vision of the future. The articulation past–future corresponds to that vertical relationship typical of the figural: past (prefiguration)–future (fulfillment).

The discontinuity between this narrative leap and Manuel's trajectory situates the certainty of transformation on the level of the universal ("man") and reaffirms the hiatus between Manuel's lived experience and his meaning as a figure within the allegorical design. His trajectory constitutes an oblique, transfigured representation of the certainty, just as Antônio's "repression" finally both liberates and represents this same certainty. Everything in *Black God, White Devil* denies the possibility of thinking in terms of lost trails, irrecoverable detours, or insurmountable gaps. The redemptive power of its teleology is radical. In its representation of the "machine of the world," the narration refers to the past or the future, leaping from genesis to apocalypse. Its figural view of history bridges the gap separating the realm of necessity from the realm of freedom. In its contradictory movement, the story evolves as the fulfillment of destiny at the same time that it grants humanity the condition of subject. Everything in the story only reaffirms this problematic condition, as it is expressed in the contradictory movement of the film.

The winds of history are ubiquitous. Their modulations are palpable in moments of violence, and there is no doubt about their final direction. But who or what impels them? *Black God, White Devil* gives no univocal response to this question; and it would be obtuse to ask for one, for what is fundamental in the film is not the precise determination of causality. The film's principle has been already defined: teleology and that specific ambivalence created by the interaction of voices and the crisscrossing movements through which man and destiny struggle for primacy. There is no definitive answer concerning the knowledge that sustains this certainty of revolution (the reaching of the telos) because the mediations in the film mark the coexistence of different systems of historical interpretation. The film assumes the didactic form of the moral lesson, but it decenters the focus of its pedagogic message. Its allegorical structure seems to simplify, but in fact it embraces in all its complexity the meditation on the meaning of the peasants' revolts and their specific forms of consciousness.

Crystallizing an aesthetic and ideological project that affirms popular forms of representation (as a focus of cultural resistance and as a logos where national identity is partially engendered) and striving for social transformation on the basis of a dialectical vision of history, the film neither idealizes nor downgrades popular culture. Rather than dismissing popular forms in the name of ideological correctness, Rocha uses them even as he questions the traditional character of their representations. Cinema Novo confronted this task—of reelaborating popular traditions as the springboard for a transformation-oriented critique of social reality—in diverse ways. *Black God, White Devil,* the major embodiment of the "aesthetics of hunger," is a key film because it incorporates within its very structure the contradictions of this project. It avoids any romantic endorsement of the popular as the source of all wisdom even as it discredits the enthnocentric reductionism that sees in popular culture nothing more than meaningless superstition and backward irrationality superseded by bourgeois progress and rationalism.

As a representation of the social bandit, Rocha's film develops a dialogue with the tradition of the western as a genre and especially with its Brazilian echo: the film O *Cangaceiro,* made by Lima Barreto in 1953 for the Companhia Vera Cruz. Criticizing the industrial exploitation of the popular hero, *Black God, White Devil* refuses both the image of the romantic outlaw—the Robin Hood model—and the stereotype of the "enemy of progress and civilization." Redeeming the violence of the rebel as a prefiguration of the future revolution—both are made of the same substance while existing in different historical conditions—Rocha's film replaces the teleology of progress within "law and order" with a teleology of history impelled by the spirit of rebellion. The fundamental fact is that the movement toward redemption interacts with a movement toward demystification, that is, the critique of alienation as embodied in the religious popular consciousness. The result, as demonstrated, is ambivalence, where the prophetic Christian view of history—embedded in the popular tradition—informs a film designed to perform a critique of religion. Conversely, the world of traditional allegory, projected into the texture of a modern discourse, loses its solid moral ground; and teleology, although emphatically asserted, suggests its problematic nature.

Figure 1.1

Figure 1.5

Figure 1.2

Figure 1.6

Figure 1.3

Figure 1.7

Figure 1.4

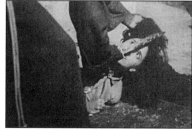

Figure 1.8

Figure 1.9

Figure 1.13

Figure 1.10

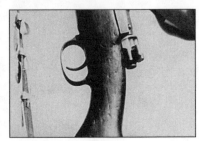

Figure 1.14

Figure 1.11

Figure 1.15

Figure 1.12

Figure 1.16

Part II

The Crisis
of Teleology

2

Land in Anguish:
Allegory and Agony

Vertical Montage: Structural Ambivalence

The dream is over. Revolution is no longer at hand. The conservative leader Porfirio Diaz has led a coup d'état, suppressed elections, and put an end to the political aspirations of the populist leader Vieira and his leftist supporters. Paulo Martins, poet, journalist, and political counselor, lies dying. Shot by the forces of repression after an isolated and romantic gesture of resistance, Paulo, before dying, recapitulates his political trajectory and the events that have led the country to the right-wing coup. The opening sequence of *Land in Anguish* offers a first representation of the hour of decision. The first images show the resignation of the populist provincial governor, Vieira, who refuses to follow Paulo's urging of armed resistance, preferring to avoid bloodshed. And we have heard Paulo's romantic cry, "I go to the very end, I'll take my chance," while Sara reminds him, in typically Brechtian terms, that Eldorado does not need heroes. Mortally wounded, the poet begins his recollection of the recent past—a flashback of ninety minutes—in an endless operatic agony. At the end of the film, with the circle of memories closed, we are led back to the hour of the coup and witness again Vieira's resignation, the tactical considerations of the Left, Sara's reasonable counsel, and Paulo's stubborn confrontation with repression. This reenactment adopts a tone similar to that of the beginning. However, instead of interrupting Paulo's delirious words and imagery just after he has been hit, in this second representation his immediate mental reaction to the shock of the bullet is foregrounded.

My analysis of *Land in Anguish* begins with the examination of this second representation, that is, of the critical moment when the film returns to the very beginning of Paulo's agony and reaches its climax in the presentation of a delirious imagery of frustrated desires and defeat.

The development of this closing sequence can be divided into four basic movements.

First Movement: The Alternation of Flashes

When Paulo is wounded at the wheel of his car, the film alternates images of his contortions with subjective flashes of a baroque ceremony revolving around Diaz (Figures 2.1–2.4; page 91). A long shot of this ceremony flashes by us four times, so rapidly that we are denied a clear view of the whole set; we barely recognize the images as representing Diaz's coronation. On the sound track, the noise of gunshots and the wail of a police siren create an irritating atmosphere while Paulo's voice-over begins an eloquent stream of consciousness speech: "Ah, this festival of medals can't go on; this happy apparatus of glories, this golden hope of the plateaus can't go on. . . . this march of banners with Christ and War in the same position can't go on."

Second Movement: Diaz's Coronation

We continue to hear Paulo's imprecation as Villa-Lobos's musical score, replacing the song of gunfire and sirens, underlines the spirit of his words:

> . . . the importance of faith, the *naiveté* of faith; this is a terrible time that we cannot bear any longer. . . . we are sons of darkness and Inquisition . . . and are infinitely, eternally sons of fear; we are always afraid of the blood pouring out of our brothers' bodies, we don't acknowledge our petty past of laziness and servitude to God and our Lords, of passive weakness typical of indolent people. . . . Ah, this can't be true, I cannot believe that all this is sheer truth. . . . How long can we stand it? How far beyond faith and hope, how far beyond our patience and love . . .

The flashes inserted within the first line of this speech are replaced by longer takes (Figures 2.5–2.9; pages 91–92). The image of the ceremony stabilizes, and the spectator now has time to examine Diaz's coronation. The awkward ceremony mixes modern and ancient costumes: Diaz wears a twentieth-century suit and a royal mantle; he seizes the royal scepter while, behind him, a conquistador-like figure from the time of the Iberian expansion expresses his loyalty by holding the crown just above the monarch's head. The millionaire Fuentes, who personifies the Eldorado bourgeoisie, is seen wearing a modern tuxedo at Diaz's left; he is with Silvia, the elegant courtesan, Paulo's former lover. The ceremony takes place in Diaz's baroque palace, whose monumental stairway serves as a spatial emblem of the political hierarchy of Eldorado. A number of other figures surround Diaz; between him and the camera, forming two symmetrically disposed rows, figures wearing ancient costumes hold their swords to salute the king. Close to the camera, a modern machine-gun contrasts with the assemblage of courtly figures. At the top of the stairs, a group of young women perform a ritual dance, providing a rather conventional frame for the symbolic action of the protagonists.

The strange ceremony, juxtaposing all the basic elements of Eldorado courtly life as seen throughout the film, epitomizes the film's allegorical imagery. It represents the chief of state as a king bearing the emblems of absolute power (the crown, the scepter, and the mantle), and surrounded by a motley group of courtiers who seem to represent different ages of Eldorado's history, including the land's original inhabitants, who are embodied in the idealized figure of an Indian with a white face (in fact, a carnival mask). This ceremony is a baroque evocation enacted with simple materials, a curious quotation of the allegorical style of representation typical of a Brazilian popular pageant—the annual samba school parade during carnival season. The play of masks, the display of courtly costumes and conventional imagery associated with a dead nobility, the artificial look and the mixture of styles—all of these make of the scene in *Land in Anguish* a fragment of that street festival transfigured and transported to the interior of what seems to be a baroque palace (in fact, the scene was shot in the Rio de Janeiro opera house). With its mixture of ancient and modern and its timeless image of the dominant class of Eldorado, the scene has a kind of oneiric character that is reinforced by the scene's context—remember Paulo's voice-over—and the discontinuous sequence of shots portraying it. The long shot with the overall view of the ceremony is followed by a close-up of Fuentes, isolated, laughing at the camera as if celebrating his treason against both Paulo and the reformist cause. Fuentes's histrionic laughter is followed by an image of him, Diaz, and Silvia ascending the stairs of the palace with happy smiles on their faces.

This imagery of triumphal satisfaction is broken by a shot showing the wounded Paulo crawling up the palace stairs, alone, with a machine-gun in his hands—an imaginary invasion. Again, Diaz is seen within the same composition of the coronation on the stairway; he gives a speech unheard by the spectator since the sound track is already filled with Paulo's words and the music. The camera approaches Diaz while he speaks, isolating his figure and the crown above his head. The imaginary invasion continues: In counter shot we see a man from the people pointing a gun at Diaz while Paulo, although present, remains passive, turning his back to the scene in order not to see it. The sound of the machine-gun interrupts Paulo's imprecation as a swish pan introduces the new series of images.

Third Movement: A New Alternation of Flashes

The rhythm of the alternation in the third movement is similar to that of the first movement, again intercutting the space of the highway, where Paulo and Sara live out their drama, and the space of the coronation (Figures 2.10–2.19; pages 92–93). Along with the dialogue between Paulo and Sara, we continue to hear Villa-Lobos's music and the sound of the machine-gun throughout the series. Following the swish pan, we see Diaz starting to fall as if struck by gunfire. Then we go to the outer space of Paulo's agony—the highway. Sara holds him and cries out a question over the noise: "What does your death mean?" He answers: "The triumph of beauty and justice." Question and answer occur simultaneously with the sequence of flashes so as to make the word "justice" coincide with the last image of the alternation. The image of Paulo and Sara holding each other is intercut with fragmented views of the disorder in the palace: Silvia screams and falls backwards; Paulo seizes the crown and looks at it intently; Paulo lifts the crown; he is seen holding the head of a worker while the worker holds a sword in his hands in a passive, ceremonial attitude (the same worker has died in a previous scene, eliminated by Vieira's bodyguards). The two last shots of the imaginary invasion show Paulo dropping the crown and falling; his move in the space of delirium converges with his move on the highway, where Sara continues to hold him as he completes his answer, shouting, "justice!" A new swish pan reinstates the sense of rupture introducing the last movement.

Fourth Movement: Final Messages

As in the second movement, a new stabilization of images follows the series of flashes (Figures 2.20–2.22; page 93). However, for the first time in the sequence we have silence, broken only by the voices of Diaz, Paulo, and Sara. The segment begins with Diaz in close-up, the crown still above his head. Again we see his moving lips, and this time we hear his words. While speaking, he looks intently at the fixed camera. His speech is vigorous, as one might expect from a severe father-sovereign: "They shall learn! I shall subdue this land and impose order on all its hysterical traditions. By force, by the passion of force, by the universal harmony of hells we shall attain Civilization!" His face becomes a mask of possession, the ecstasy of power turns into sheer madness. As he finishes his message with his eyes wide open, the light on his face intensifies, the overexposure almost dissolving his image. We then cut directly to Paulo and Sara, who, still in the same position as in the previous flashes, repeat their last dialogue. Question and answer are pronounced in the same tone. This time we follow the entire action in a single shot. Having pronounced his last message, Paulo moves away from Sara, who feels incapable of helping him. Continuing the same take, the camera begins to move along the road, distancing itself from them. Sara decides to abandon Paulo and walks resolutely toward the camera. The poet stays alone in his agony.

The epilogue of *Land in Anguish* shows the poet isolated in the dunes, a small figure in the corner of the frame, almost dissolved in the uniform brightness of the setting (Figure 2.23; page 93). The long take brings back the irritating aural overlay of the sounds of gunfire, sirens, and Villa-Lobos's music. The poet, machine-gun still in hand, slowly doubles up, and the film ends before any visible final expiration, as if in a desire of continuity or a suggestion of umbilical linkage that the narrative refuses to cut off, an instance of pain that is obsessively extended in the final shot.

When these events are first presented at the beginning of the film, we cut abruptly from the car—immediately after the first outburst of Paulo's speech—to his solitary agony in the dunes, where he begins his recollection, a long shot of the defeated poet to which an epitaph is overlapped:

> He could not seal the noble pact
> Between the bleeding cosmos and the pure soul
> . . . .
> A dead but intact gladiator
> What violence but what tenderness.

The citation of this fragment of a Mario Faustino poem at the beginning seems to announce a romantic reading of the poet's death by suggesting a pure interiority in opposition to the world.[1] The opposition between the two series—bleeding cosmos–gladiator–violence and pure soul–intact–tenderness—is an enunciation of the discontinuity between the outer world, the world of action, and the inner world. The last is suggested as the home of the poet's being, the irreducible core of his truth in opposition to the unstable universe of his engagements in reality. The interior–exterior cleavage, elaborated in the epitaph, is essential in the structure of *Land in Anguish*. However, during the film there is a clear displacement by which the romantic matrix and the idealism suggested at the opening give way to unmistakable forms of marking the contradiction between the poet's action and his inner drive. My analysis of the film's last sequence allows for the revelation of the final term of this displacement: We will see that the film, in its whole development, imposes another epitaph, one whose terms are not identical to those expressed in the text-epitaph shown on the screen and which is expressed in the final verbal and eloquent message of the protagonist as well.

The Free Indirect Subjective: A Principle of Coherence

Sergey Eisenstein, in his 1932 essay "A Course in Treatment," speaks of the interpolation of "the feverish race of thoughts" with "outer reality" in terms appropriate to the interweaving of image and sound in the sequence of shots described above. Eisenstein's specific concern at that time was with interior monologue: He contended that cinema might give full expression to a specific method of representation first proposed experimentally in literature. The last sequence of *Land in Anguish* evokes Eisenstein's observations: "Only the film element commands a means for an adequate presentation of the whole course of thought through a disturbed mind."[2]

The interpolation of the processes of the "disturbed mind" with "outer actuality" is carried out by the combination of Paulo's voice-over, sound effects (music and noise), synchronous sound, the images of the coronation in Diaz's palace, and the images of Paulo and Sara on the highway. Each of the movements of the sequence combines these elements in a specific way. In the first three stages there is a split within Paulo's mind, and the simultaneous development of two lines of "thought" is represented in the vertical relation of image and sound. The sound evokes the poet's indignation and his lament, his long imprecation addressing the continuity of the past that is embodied in Diaz's victory; the images evoke the celebration of that victory and Paulo's ultimate fantasy of disrupting the coronation. The images of Paulo's imaginary seizure of power coincide with his words to Sara exalting his death as a triumph of idealism. This simultaneous presentation of his self-dramatizing final speech and the visual realization of his fantasy has the effect of an unmasking. The montage renders explicit the nature of Paulo's words as a Freudian case of denegation. The proclamation of sacrifice in the name of ideal values is a mask that conceals the desire for power, the deepest motivation for his political struggle.

This strategy of confrontation combining outer speech and inner thought occurs in other sequences of the film. Paulo's recollection of the political process of Eldorado presents similar unmaskings. One relatively early sequence, for example, shows a drunken Paulo talking with Sara in his apartment after he has abandoned his position within Vieira's administration in the Province of Alecrim. The context of this dialogue is clear: the confrontation between Vieira's staff (including Paulo) and the peasants. The governor had failed to fulfill his promises to the people, giving priority to his agreements with the landowners. As a moral protest, Paulo resigned. In his apartment he recapitulates the whole political episode to Sara and vilifies Vieira. A medium shot shows him walking back and forth in the living room as he says, "He will repress the agitators." He stops moving and repeats the phrase, as if obsessed; the camera moves closer to him. At this point, a sudden interpolation reveals the "repressed" image: Paulo, with his arms wide open, his back to the camera, is seen as if repressing a group of peasants who move back under his command. He controls their anger at the governor's treason and at the assassination of their principal leader. An episode of direct confrontation between the peasants and Vieira's staff had been previously seen, and there too Paulo had displayed a hostile attitude: "to defy the peasants' leader and test his strength," as Paulo says. However, the interpolated shot that interrupts the dialogue in the apartment is an image of repression unseen before. Does it evoke a real occurrence, or does it show Paulo's present imagination inflected by his guilt? Whatever the answer, the voiced accusation addressed to Vieira is reflected back on himself. His words to Sara acquire a new meaning when confronted with this interpolation, revealing, once again, how the vertical relation of image and sound unmasks Paulo's contradictions.

Throughout the film, Paulo's recollections are hardly organized along a conventional pattern of conscious reminiscing. Like the last sequence, the long flashback presents an ambivalent flux of images generated by a conflicted mind. Instead of seeking retrospective self-redemption, the agonistic narrative of the past exposes Paulo's bad conscience. Together with the didactic representation of the antipopular interests and maneuvers of his enemies, the entire flashback represents a radical criticism addressed to Paulo and his companions. The overwrought emotional tone of the recollection and its fundamental ambivalence are linked to the poet's experience, but not to his experience alone. To deepen my discussion of the structure of *Land in Anguish*, in terms of narrative perspective and ambivalence, I must explore other aspects of the relation between narration and diegesis.

My discussion so far of the alternation between inner thought and outer reality presupposed a clear separation between these two levels of representation; it may therefore have given the impression that the final sequence is composed of an interpolation of subjective images and words within a linear, "natural," continuous sequence of "objective" events. However, certain features of this sequence render the nature of specific shots somewhat more ambiguous. For instance, certain repetitions of shots and actions do not result, as repetitions, from Paulo's disturbed state of mind. The temporal structure of the sequence comprises a number of moves back and forth in time that are independent of Paulo's mental process. The overall design of the narrative comprises a pattern of double representation.

The opening and closing sequences of the film deal with the moment of Vieira's resignation, a gesture that symbolizes the end of the populist dream, and with its effect on Paulo's behavior. Twice we follow the poet when he, enraged, leaves the palace and, contrary to Sara's advice, confronts the police. Twice we follow the beginning of Paulo's delirium after being shot. In both instances, his initial words and exterior actions are exactly the same. But the treatment of the event is significantly different. In the first representation, image and sound are synchronized; we follow Paulo's reaction in the car as exterior observers, and we soon move away to the image of the poet in the dunes, when the epitaph confirming his imminent death prepares the account of the past introduced by Paulo's own voice: "Where was I three, four years ago?" In the repetition of the critical moment at the end, Paulo's delirious speech becomes inner thought, and the visual montage gives free reign to oneiric imagery. The offscreen voice has its own temporal development independent of Paulo's and Sara's implied actions; at the same time, we experience visual associations that have so far been assumed to be Paulo's fantasies. The images of Diaz's coronation, however, imply the intervention of a narrative agent other than Paulo himself. Implicit in the whole development of the sequence, such an intervention becomes clearer in the passage from the third to the fourth movement, when the final messages—Diaz's speech as chief of state and Paulo's answer to Sara—are repeated. Together with such a replay, the images of the coronation deserve a more detailed consideration.

I have already described the awkward central image of the coronation, with its display of masks and disparate elements. I have commented on the oneiric structure of the combination of shots following the initial image of the ceremony, reinforced by the sheer fantasy of Paulo's assault and Diaz's death. In all this we were presumably following Paulo's mental process. In fact, in a first approach, the events in Diaz's palace seem to be purely products of the poet's imagination. The ceremony cannot be a recollection because it could not have occurred before Vieira's resignation. The coronation celebrates and consolidates a political definition implying a set of events that include Paulo's own death. In terms of his agony, it is a future event or, at least, a "fact" he could not experience directly. If the coronation forms part of his delirium, it must be taken as something generated by his agonized mind.

Yet we must refuse such an apparently logical conclusion, for it fails to account for the transition from the third to the fourth movement of the sequence, from the "feverish race of thoughts" to the fixed, stable, and continuous shots that replay, in an orderly manner, the same actions. In the new representation, the two actions seem to be completely independent facts, close to each other in terms of the film's editing strategies but belonging to different contexts in the diegesis. In that transition, silence replaces the irritating noise; continuity contrasts with the series of very brief shots; synchronized sound replaces vertical montage and disjunction. Diaz's speech, when repeated, acquires a matter-of-fact status that it shares with Paulo's and Sara's last moments together on the highway. The style of representation in this fourth movement separates it from the others, making it clear that Diaz's speech during the ceremony cannot be reduced to Paulo's subjective process. The paradox is that Paulo's sheer fantasy just represented is visualized within the same parameters, exhibiting identical figures and the same overall configuration. We do not have two coronations clearly distinguished; we have a single ceremony being disrupted by Paulo's invasion and providing the context for the solidly factual speech by Diaz at the end. Thus, Diaz's coronation, which presumably belongs to Paulo's imagination, paradoxically demands to be seen as a concrete fact within the political life of Eldorado, a fact independent of Paulo's subjectivity.

In the search for the formal principle governing the work of narration in *Land in Anguish*, we must abandon all hypotheses that consign Paulo's inner thought and the outer reality to clearly separate narrative levels. They are distinguished one from the other, but they partially overlap. The detailed description of the final sequence enables us to discern an exterior narrative agency at work together with Paulo's own split mind. The images generated by Paulo and by that agency are entangled; they are at work upon the same materials and exhibit the same style. In other words, there is a partial identification of these narrative agencies, and the form of their interaction is very specific; it does not allow us to say exactly where and when Paulo's imagery begins and ends.

My reading proposes *Land in Anguish* as a typical example of the *free indirect subjective* discussed by Pier Paolo Pasolini in his article "Le Cinéma de poésie." In his own particular terminology, Pasolini, commenting on Bernardo Bertolucci's *Before the Revolution* (1964), observes the "contamination entre la vision du monde de la névrosée et celle de l'auteur, qui étant inévitablement analogues, ne peuvent être facilement différenciées, se mêlent l'une à l'autre: appellent le même style."[3] For Pasolini, the common stylistic feature encountered in the work of modern filmmakers is this contamination, this indirect free discourse that allows for research toward poetic cinema.

Some of Pasolini's contentions concerning film language are disputable, but his conception of modern narrative cinema is illuminating, and I borrow his formula as an operational descriptive category. The crucial fact is that Rocha's film fits the pattern of the free indirect subjective. In *Land in Anguish*, whether a scene is explicitly subject to the poet's interior monologue or not, the entire narration is contaminated by the poet's state of mind. If the last sequence presents that interpolation conveying a "feverish race of thoughts," the "disturbed mind" is not only the character's but also that of the invisible narrator. This strategy is central to the entire film, as I will demonstrate.

In the very beginning of the film, the first enactment of Vieira's resignation displays the same dramatic, baroque style that later dominates the flashback and is epitomized at the end. Paulo and the exterior narrative agency act as mediations sharing the same attitude toward the facts represented as well as the same language and class codes. The two agencies mirror each other. Mediation in *Land in Anguish* transcends Paulo's own identity but assumes the pattern of his own experience. Technically, such a strategy allows for a more direct presentation of the character's inner experiences while keeping open other channels of information concerning the ambient reality. Paulo's mediation allows more poetic freedom to the representation, and his own behavior provides the immediate motivation for the problematic reflection on politics, for the oneiric and obsessive imagery that decisively contributes to the passionate tone of the discourse. The structural ambivalence provided by this decentered narration creates an unresolved dialectic of attraction and repulsion, of an identification with the protagonist and a critical view of his behavior. The poet's journey consists of a display of exaggeratedly dramatic episodes, obsessive repetitions, melancholy poetic diction, and spectacular emblems. At the same time, the film presents many graphic expositions of political mechanisms, sections of didactic prosaism and Brechtian lucidity. The recollection results from the physical impulse of a resentful poet after his political and existential failure; but from beginning to end, it obeys a linear general design, too organized for Paulo's state of mind and too didactic, as if contaminated by a sense of order and conceptualization foreign to such a particular agonistic experience. It is this sense of order and symmetry that is clearly expressed in the emphatic contiguity of both final messages: that of the victorious Diaz and that of the defeated Paulo. In the development of the last sequence, a privileged place is reserved for Diaz's royal speech on the future of Eldorado and for Paulo's last claim for ideal values. Separated from the previous "feverish race of thoughts," they exhibit a rigorous symmetry that forms the final commentary on the specular relationship between rebel and father figure.

As does its final sequence, *Land in Anguish* as a whole presents al-

legorical schematizations and symmetries that interact with heightened distortion and an eccentric texture of handheld camera movements, jump cuts, and barely tolerable sound overlay. My task, now, is
to characterize this interaction, analyzing its basic components.

Inner Conflicts: Circularity and Repetition

The agonistic state of mind permeating the narrative expresses
itself very clearly in the constant disequilibrium created by a tense
combination of camera movements and actors' gestures, verbal saturation and music. This basic tone of the representation dominates the
very first scene, with its multiple associations that are difficult to unify.
Paulo has not appeared yet, has not taken upon himself the responsibility of telling the story, but the images and sound already echo his
attitude.

The introductory long take has taken us from the ocean to the allegorical country of Eldorado. A slow aerial displacement from sea to
land forms the background for the film's credits. Once given this conventional data, we are suddenly plunged into the agitation of Vieira's
palace. The image of ocean and coast has characterized Eldorado as a
sunny tropical land permeated by African-like rhythms marking this
fragment of the world as a particular site within a cosmic order. The
scene in the palace changes the scale and places Eldorado within the
context of contemporary history; political agents are experiencing a
moment of crisis and decision, of victory and defeat. The sound of per-
cussion punctuates the scene, giving a martial connotation to every
gesture. A confused, nervous sequence of dialogues and discussions
shown in a series of handheld camera movements depicts the convulsion in Vieira's palace just before his resignation. Within the purview
of the circling camera, the image of Vieira in a tropical white suit stands
out. While Vieira walks about, looking extremely tense, he drops some
documents handed him by his assistant, Sara, as if papers had no value
at this critical moment. Searching for significant details within the
general disorder, the camera calls our attention to a machine-gun in
the hands of a political leader who follows Vieira. The possibility of
armed struggle that this evokes is subsequently proposed more explicitly by Paulo when he comes into the scene. On the terrace, the governor of the Province of Alecrim joins his staff, now a group of disori-
ented men moving back and forth on the tessellated floor like chess

pieces. The film cuts away to show Paulo arriving at the palace, a pro-cedure that displaces the central focus from the governor to the poet. He arrives in the manner of a messenger, but he neither brings news nor sheds light on the situation. He brings, rather, a firm proposal: Confidently, he seizes the machine-gun already seen in the preceding images and urges Vieira to resist, to fight against Diaz. But the gover-nor refuses armed struggle, and the potential embodied in the sym-bolic object is not fulfilled. Its destiny is to remain in Paulo's hands throughout his agony, as a fetish, up to the final shot of the film.

Having made his decision, Vieira prepares the scene for his political message to the people of Eldorado. Suddenly all is silence and immo-bility. The circular movements of the camera are now transferred to Paulo's agitated circling of the scene. While Vieira dictates his resigna-tion to Sara, Paulo moves geometrically in front of the camera, dis-turbing the historical tableau suggested by the other figures involved in the episode: Vieira looks off, gazing solemnly at an obscure vanishing point as if convinced of the transcendental nature of his gesture ("I leave the destiny of Eldorado in God's hands"); Sara respectfully tran-scribes Vieira's speech; the others compose a background of sober wit-nesses. Paulo, while circling around the scene, questions Vieira's ges-tures and the general hesitation of the progressive leaders of the country. His words, addressed to himself and to the audience, resemble a Brechtian commentary performed here by an overheated and very much involved narrator who cannot repress his strong feelings of re-volt and indignation.

Throughout the film, Paulo and the camera continue this duet, which is composed of a mixture of analytical comments and eloquent transports, emphatic gestures. The sound, usually loud and aggressive, brings a sense of exasperation, sometimes through explicit references to opera: Carlos Gomez and Giuseppe Verdi provide the film with the amplified sound that contributes to and comments on the dramatic scenes involving Paulo and Diaz and their love–hate relationship.

The rule of the film is to exclude all possibility of relaxation. Within the overall strategy of the free indirect subjective, the narrative style, expressing the narrator's attitude toward the events portrayed, does not result from "extravagant researches"; rather, it conveys a "judgment of a phenomenon," as Eisenstein would say. Permeated by revolt and resentment, Paulo's recapitulation alternates extremely rapid cause–

effect metonymic associations, presenting a linear development, and segments marked by a circular movement. In these segments, the action begins at a specific point, ranges outward, and returns to the point of departure reflecting the emotional charge linked to it. When such a ringlike structure occurs, it is usually punctuated by offscreen sound relaying Paulo's poems or an interior monologue. Let us examine some instances of obsessive repetitions related to traumatic experiences.

At the very beginning of his recollections, Paulo asks himself where he was "three, four years ago." The answer brings the memory of Diaz—"the God of his youth." The first image of the flashback, instead of being the representation of a specific fact in the past, corresponds to an emblem concerning Diaz's figure, which is repeated in other sequences of the film. This timeless image of this central figure in the film is the first manifestation of a rhetoric typical of the allegorical mode. Justice has her scales and Cupid his bow; Diaz, in his frozen image, representing the forces of darkness and repression, has a crucifix in one hand and a dark banner in the other. Immobile like a statue, Diaz enters the scene as if on a pedestal, transported by a car in a kind of solitary triumphal parade. The low-angle view in close-up isolates his figure against the sky, and the agitated dark banner resembles a wing (Figure 2.24; page 93). The conservative leader of the coup d'état, the guardian of the traditions of the aristocracy of Eldorado, is thus announced as the God of Paulo's youth and is visually introduced as a dark angel of evil.

Diaz's emblem punctuates the flashback. It is the first image and the last, in a symmetrical repetition that frames the entire recollection of the past, taking us from and leading us back to the hour of decision, to Diaz's own victory and to Paulo's impulsive decision to die. The poet's memory is dominated by his relation to this authentic father figure. Paulo begins as Diaz's protégé, and his leftist engagement implies a personal fight with him, a painful liberation from his tutelage. A significant detail in this oedipal relationship is the fact that the emblem—besides framing the flashback—appears once more in the film, exactly when Paulo launches his strongest political and personal attack on Diaz.

After his first break with Vieira, the poet wanders into a luxurious and apolitical life in Eldorado (the capital of the country). Sara, functioning as symbolic mother, comes to rescue him from this world of decay by bringing social consciousness and political struggle back into his life. Convinced by Sara and the leftist leaders, Paulo accepts the task of destroying Diaz's political career. His attack begins with a critical TV biography of Diaz. Authorized by Fuentes, Paulo directs the show made to denounce Diaz's association with foreign interests and his political corruption. On the TV screen, the same emblem seen earlier introduces the program, which is called "Biography of an Adventurer." The TV program is experienced by Paulo as an act of treason against his symbolic father. In a revealing displacement, Paulo gives too much emphasis to treachery in his account of Diaz's political career. The fixation on this theme of treason, although appropriate to Diaz, also suggests Paulo's bad conscience and that his act is some kind of repetition of the very style under attack. After all, Diaz also began as a young leftist leader.

Because of its place in the development of Paulo's emotions, this sequence of definitive rupture with Diaz presents a more dramatic use of the poet's voice-over. His words dramatize the whole episode by conveying personal doubts and inner conflict about his gesture. Immediately prior to the TV program, he comments on the power he received from Fuentes and expresses his doubts concerning the legitimacy of such a step, which makes more explicit the sense of irresponsible adventure that permeates his political engagement. Just after the TV program, his voice evokes the remorse that made him visit Diaz for a last time: "Like me he was suffering, and before he asked I went to see him feeling hatred and remorse."

The repetition of the emblem at key points reinforces Diaz's central position within the allegorical design of the film. At the same time, it represents a clear instance of obsessive imagery charged with Paulo's feelings. It is once more guilt, together with a feeling of ambivalence and an obsession with treason, that permeates the circular compositions in the film, wherein episodes are organized around a traumatic point of origin. In fact, this very episode of treason against the father figure entails a symptomatic breaking of the linear evolution, so that the scene in which Paulo is pressed by Sara to attack Diaz is repeated twice. When their conversation is presented a second time, it appears in such a way as to reinforce Paulo's feeling of being the victim of strong persuasion; his memory emphasizes the exact moment when Sara, as a dominant mother figure, kisses him to celebrate his recovered loyalty. The same circular structure dominates an earlier sequence of the film, a sequence in which Paulo has his first crisis after political engagement and accuses Vieira of betraying the people. I have described how Paulo's open accusation against the populist governor is followed by the image of Paulo himself behaving as an agent of repression. Paulo's and Sara's farewell scene is articulated around a back-and-forth movement between past and present that weaves Paulo's verbal narration to Sara with the direct presentation of the conflictual episodes that placed him in such an uncomfortable position. Guilt, ambivalence, and the fear of treason are once again associated with circularity and repetition.

The ringlike structure recurs, finally, when Paulo recalls how he became aware of Fuentes's treason. Persuaded by Diaz, Fuentes shifts his political allegiances and aligns himself with the conservatives, withdrawing his support of Vieira. On two occasions Paulo evokes that moment, and on two occasions his friend Alvaro is seen entering the newspaper office to bring the news of the right-wing pact between Fuentes and Diaz.

Along with these repetitions that are connected with those events having a strong emotional impact on Paulo, we also become aware of his feelings—love, hate, disgust, passion—and inner conflicts through the voice-over soliloquies that, at specific points, convey his poetry. Together with political engagement, poetic creation is the major concern in his life, and many of his personal crises are engendered by the frustrated attempt to reconcile the two. When he leaves the Province of Alecrim to go back to the capital and its courtly life, Sara's farewell message, meant to comfort him, is that "politics and poetry are too much for one man." This statement is highly ambivalent. Like its protagonist, the film deals with politics and poetry at the same time. Sara's words cannot be taken as a legitimate aphorism summing up the film's "message." Addressed to Paulo, they manifest an attitude of comprehension coming from this lover–mother substitute who understands his difficulties in reconciling his multiple concerns. The essential problem faced by Paulo is, in fact, the divorce between his poetry and his social engagement. His poems display an anachronistic eloquence and usually betray a pessimism that seems to undermine all his gestures of political commitment. The verses bring melancholy, disgust, and a sense of decay. When he first leaves to search for his own path, the theme of his verses is death, not confidence or a sense of discovery. Disgust and exasperation float over his poetic commentary when, once back in Eldorado, he loses himself in neurotic orgies and in a tedious life with the "mute" Silvia. Once back to political struggle, we see him detaching himself from the ambiance of Vieira's rally to entertain his mind with a lyrical proclamation of skepticism about the revolutionary potential of the people and the kind of collective adventure in which he is involved.

In all these circumstances, his voice obsessively evokes death and decay, and a baroque view of time as progressive destruction and disillusion, of man's body as the locus of a Darwinian struggle for survival, and of society as the amplified arena of the same struggle. His commentary manifests ambivalent feelings deriving from his distorted sense of the "tropical diseases" that invade his mind and body and that contaminate his feelings and his very existence. Thus his desire for idealistic purification is counteracted by his underlying conviction of the futility of realizing those ideals. Whereas the progression of the narrative conveys his visible actions, social engagement, and political discourse, the strategy of the free indirect subjective reveals Paulo's bad conscience and innate skepticism flowing as a continuous underground current throughout the film.

The sound–image vertical montage has a central role throughout the narrative, and it is impossible to separate the impulse of analysis from this kind of doomsday that the poet establishes in his agony. There is knowledge, love, hate, and perplexity in going back to the past. On top of this combination of didactic schemes and obsessive structures, the allegorical figurations search for synthesis and try to create a sense of wholeness where the power of the contradictory fragments seems to prevail.

Having dealt with the obsessive structures, let us examine the other pole of the story: the pedagogy that makes a strong critique of populism as a left strategy and prepares a deep dive into the mythical structures that are related to Eldorado's own origin, the point at which the national allegory is consolidated.

Didactic Play: The Analytical Impulse and the Critique of Populism

Despite its atmosphere of crisis and despair, *Land in Anguish* follows a conventional circular pattern of present–past (recollection)–present. Within the flashback, there is the play of an agonizing memory and certain instances of symbolic action without clear chronological references, but in its overall progression, the account of the past moves along a linear track, revealing a schematization typical of horizontal allegory.

The film exposes the logic of the coup d'état by a simplified interpretation. Many of Paulo's apparently hysterical reactions become a pretext for theatrical exaggeration and explicit commentary in the didactic mode: He interrupts the action to address some question to the audience. Throughout the film the poet acts as a double figure: a character within the fiction and a narrator explaining things and provoking the spectator while looking straight at the camera.

Two decisive sequences show him explicitly taking on this out-of-fiction role and leading the spectator to an analytic frame of mind. On both occasions, the montage provides the blockage isolating the entire scene as a synthetic lesson concerning the political process under discussion.

The first didactic sequence offers a lesson on the contradictions between the national bourgeoisie and imperialist monopoly capital. Paulo and Alvaro take on the task of convincing Fuentes to support Vieira in order to defeat Diaz and the forces representing foreign capital. Their conversation is not depicted as a conventional fictional dialogue. Both Paulo and Alvaro address the audience directly, explaining in detail the mechanism of capitalist competition. Like teachers in a classroom, they turn Fuentes (who is physically present) into an illustration of a social category and its correlative form of consciousness. The camera follows their lead and reinforces the pedagogical tone of the representation. Fuentes's perplexity in face of their lesson confirms their contentions. The following scene, a pause for reflection, enacts Fuentes's decision-making process up to the moment in which he accepts their proposal.

The second example leads us to the most significant interruption of action performed by Paulo in the film. It takes place in the sequence entitled "The Leader Meets the People," the major synthesis of the populist festival in *Land in Anguish*. The stage is the terrace of Vieira's palace—the locus of historical decisions from beginning to end. Paulo, addressing both the participants of the political rally and the audience of the film, introduces Vieira as the "candidate of the people." The handheld camera moves away from Paulo as it might in a documentary film, but here this documentary style is used as a strategy to theatricalize what takes place in front of the camera. As the space is opened up and made visible by the camera movements, we face a display of symbolic figures composing an awkward tableau of historical agents: a senatorial figure behaving like a provincial politician, young leftists stirring up the masses, a priest wearing a colonial cassock, journalists, students, bodyguards, Vieira, Sara, Paulo, a group of samba school performers, poor women, workers, and peasants, all moving and acting simultaneously. The senator proffers clichéd rhetoric in praise of progress and education, the leftists mobilize, the priest preaches, the police monitor, the journalists observe, and the samba school performers sing and dance before the camera. The noisy and agitated scene, confined within the limits of Vieira's controlled space, evokes the administered popular spectacle, the controlled "spontaneous" manifestation of popular will typical of populist campaigns: the well-known simulation of the candidate's identification with the people.

More specifically, this tableau develops an allegorical representation of Brazilian populism as carnival, as a grotesque juxtaposition of incongruous figures, a display of dancing masks miming the unity of forces and interests that are in fact incompatible. Exuberant festivity provides the ritual cohesion that disguises the lack of substance of the political message brought by those in power who manipulate everything (in the political rally, people hold placards with no inscriptions, completely blank). The first stage of Vieira's career had already emphasized the carnivalesque tone of the Brazilian political process. Vieira's campaign for the governorship of the Province of Alecrim was revealed as the gradual assumption of a popular mask—Vieira as a self-conscious clown—and the constant background playing of a carnival song punctuated his progression toward provincial power, lending a connotation of make-believe to the efficient populist spectacle. Now, with Vieira's second electoral campaign, the rally amplifies the lesson on populism.

All the social agents are assembled in a single space to perform their typical act within the general ritual. Even Paulo, unseen in the first campaign, is now present as a catalyst (within the diegesis) and as a commentator. These two functions are at first separate: The rally moves along until the introduction of music by Villa-Lobos bids the diegetic sounds of samba to recede in order to make room for Paulo's voice-over. Paulo's interior monologue expresses his skeptical view of the whole scene. In the second interruption the two functions go together, and Paulo intervenes to make his direct comment to the audience. At one point in the rally, Sara becomes uncomfortable with the chaos around her and Vieira. Trying to bring order back to the scene, she interrupts the samba and invites Jeronimo—the union leader defined as "the people" by Vieira's supporters—to give his message. The senatorial figure offers him the space of the scene with an emphatic gesture. Jeronimo addresses the camera directly and confesses his own bewilderment, making clear that he must wait for orders from the politicians. Suddenly, Paulo comes to the foreground and, his hands over Jeronimo's mouth, prevents the union leader from saying another word. Paulo then looks intently at the camera and throws out his major challenge: "Now you can see how the people really are—illiterate, idiotic, depoliticized; can you imagine Jeronimo in power?"

Reacting to Paulo's words, a man in rags emerges from the crowd and wins his own space within the scene. His speech exposes and demystifies the union leader as a false representative of the people: "Jeronimo carries out our supposed goals, but he is not the people; the people is me, with seven children and nowhere to live." That is, outside of the political representation, the real people can only be named on the basis of extreme poverty, and when the man in rags is set loose among the mob, he is killed on the spot, with all the symbolic strength of a montage typical of the "aggression theater"—a security agent ties him up and tucks a gun into his mouth while the priest covers his face with the crucifix and we hear cannon shots. The overall development of the scene is a graphic object lesson on the political game of ersatz democracy played by the leaders of Eldorado. Paulo's challenge calls our attention to a major populist fallacy: its creation of a fictive supposed "people" active within the political arena. On the one hand, Paulo's aggressive commentary enacts right-wing clichés about socially dominated classes; on the other, it aims to shock the film's progressive middle-class audience, which is here invited to examine its own conception of the "people," its own idealizations and prejudices.

Such an interruption and other instances of direct speech could be seen as typically Brechtian strategies. The interaction of drama and commentary has many variations in the film; at times its disjunctive editing provides a schematization able to express a conceptual view of the process enacted, placing the spectator in an analytic frame of mind. One should not overestimate, however, their immediate explanatory effect. As we have seen, these strategies are mingled in a tapestry of a self-contained recollection in which clarity is not a basic concern. In *Land in Anguish*, the pedagogical impulse is contaminated by passion and hysteria. A rhetoric of shock works together with step-by-step argumentation. Paulo functions as a kind of teacher, but a teacher who is overly involved and passionate, relying on the intensity of his voice and gesture, on the force of his provocation, rather than on the serene wit of that poet who assumes the posture of a sage. Most of the time, instead of arguing and explaining, he aims to shock; instead of seducing, he prefers to irritate. Artaud's spirit contaminates his Brechtian discourse. His weapon is not irony or implicit rhetoric inducing a specific line of reasoning; rather, it is explicit indictment, a passionate language of revolt, ambivalent in its love–hate relationship with self and the world. His manner, in its deliberate lack of temperance, is thus painful for the audience.

In fact, the lack of temperance is contained by a larger temperance; the outbursts of emotion form part of the specific manner in which *Land in Anguish* depicts Paulo's long agony—that is, through conventions highly reminiscent of opera. As an antinaturalist representation of a man's death, the agony in the film is enhanced with pomp and ceremony. Paulo does not simply die; he has to sing an interminable final song before dying. His poem, the core of the film, constitutes a kind of psychic encyclopedia in which he concentrates all of his life, his feelings, and his knowledge. Like opera, the film combines schematization of plot and amplification of gesture with passionate language. Ambivalence emerges again: Some scenes explicitly associate opera with Diaz and the Eldorado aristocracy, and at the same time, opera sets the tone, expressing the heightened sense of revolt permeating the entire film.

At specific points, the music of Verdi's *Otello* or Carlos Gomes's *O Guarani* comes to the foreground to lend a particular connotation to images involving Diaz. This strategy is displayed in the scene in which Diaz makes a definitive rupture with Paulo after the TV program. Here the amplification of gesture and the very tone of the dialogue between Paulo and Diaz produce estrangement, an effect intensified by the commentary brought by the musical pieces. The combination suggests that opera is akin to the pompous rituals of ornamental nationalism that function as a mask of grandeur for an aristocracy hoping to conceal its own lack of tradition, identity, or heroic past (Eldorado-Brazil is not Italy; Carlos Gomes is not Verdi). The Rio de Janeiro opera house is Diaz's realm in *Land in Anguish*; there he lives alone with his particular sense of mission. It is significant that Paulo's final liberation from Diaz and Diaz's definitive solitude are represented in an operatic scene, the place of domestic resolution being amplified by both characters' individual mythologies and mutual attraction. The film proposes the drama of separation lived by its protagonists as a melodramatic coup de théâtre.

The National Allegory: Symbolic Action, Paulo's Quest

Land in Anguish, read as an allegory of the right-wing military coup carried out in Brazil in 1964, presents a conscious reduction of the real political process. Such a simplification is essential to the film's purpose because it allows for the personification of the basic forces involved in the struggle. Minor factors, nuances, and internal contradictions within class or social groups (intellectuals, for instance) are forgotten. Each human figure condenses many attributes, embodying different segments of society. As personifications, the main characters represent syntheses of political stances and psychological inclinations, remaining faithful all the while to their basic attributes.

Diaz embodies the ascetic, conservative, Christian tradition. His life is dedicated to the preservation of Eldorado against the domination of "savages" (the people). Authoritarian and powerful, Diaz is certain of what he wants for himself and for the country, deploying a rhetoric permeated by racial prejudice in the overt defense of the privileges of aristocracy. He personifies the ruling class, which above all else preserves tradition and purity; he keeps himself aloof from tropical nature and society and lives alone in his palace. For Paulo, he is the father figure, as he is, in a sense, for the entire country.

Fuentes represents the progressive bourgeoisie. He is the modern face of the ruling class of Eldorado. A dynamic entrepreneur, he owns the country's most important factories and mines; he controls its cultural industry and animates the high society of the capital. Surrounded by women, an organizer of bacchanals, he is associated with immediate sensuous experience, with alienation and a lack of political concern. Despite his social position, Fuentes is not a political leader, and his lack of perspective results in a display of cynical opportunism. Psychologically weak, hesitant, empty-headed, he is unable to conceive of a project for his country.

Vieira is the populist leader of rural origin, a typical Latin American *caudilho* ("chief"). A reformist, he is the father figure whose major weakness is a lack of consistency. A good actor, he promises much and does nothing. Within the political spectrum of Eldorado, he is the agent of compromise who tames the potential for revolt within the dominated classes. He is seen by the leftists as a prerevolutionary leader with a historic vocation. For Paulo, he is the disappointing paternal surrogate who fails to fulfill the collective aspiration and who misses the revolutionary chance.

Sara is the self-aware political activist totally involved in the dominant leftist strategy (that is, the support of populism as the channel leading to social reform). She personifies hope, perseverance, sacrifice, and rationalized militance. Though emotionally involved, she is very realistic, trying always to act under control. Firm in her decisions, she is open to discussion and sincere in her personal commitments. Like the other personifications, she presents a rigid political face that functions as a kind of basic matrix encompassing other personal attributes. As a figure of equilibrium and comprehension, she is Paulo's counselor, protector, lover—a mother substitute.

Alvaro is the other bearer of political message within the poet's life, a friend who has preceded Sara in this role but who is much weaker than she is. Personifying a sentimental youth devoted to political reform within legality, he vacillates and is finally manipulated by Paulo. His action is recalled through constant references by other characters, even though his visual presence is downplayed. His single strong scene occurs only at the end, when he commits suicide—a suicide that mirrors Paulo's voluntarist resistance.

The EXPLINT (International Exploitation) is the all powerful "structuring absence" that stands for foreign capital and multinational corporations. There is no trace of its physical presence in Eldorado—no image, no sound—or of its overall control of the economy. Its decisive intervention in the political process is something mentioned only in explanatory dialogues. It is a word in Paulo's mouth, the evocation of the principal enemy in leftist discourse, the reference to an acknowledged supporter in Diaz's conspiratorial speech in which he convinces Fuentes to align himself with the most powerful. Nothing happens in Eldorado without the sanction of the EXPLINT, including the coup. It is an invisible, godlike agent that recalls the preeminent role of foreign corporations within the schemes elaborated by the nationalist Left in its constant—and often justified—denunciation of right-wing conspiracy.

Each of these allegorical personifications has its specific site within the linear action and the cosmic order of *Land in Anguish*. Diaz has, in the baroque palace, the architectural projection of his own condition: the remnant of a Christian, European culture adapted to the tropics. We do not have any external view of his palace; it is depicted as pure interiority, insulation. Vieira lives in a kind of hacienda, and his governmental palace asserts a theatrical space with an emphasis on the terrace, a stage surrounded by a luxuriant, apparently primitive vegetation that downplays the relation of its architecture to any other urban context and reinforces the idea of a cultural system that has its ventilation points driven to a provincial, rarefied urbanity. Fuentes is associated with closed spaces in the city or terraces in inaccessible penthouses surrounded by fog and TV towers, suggesting technology, modernization, and privacy for plotting. His interior environments bring a divestment and a geometry that contrasts with the ambiance of Diaz and Vieira. The people are sometimes mixed with the landscape and are sometimes gathered as a mass around Vieira; within the quadrangle of power, their presence is accepted to say what is to be said; the unexpected invasion is exemplarily punished. Paulo is the only element allowed to move freely, thereby establishing the existential and political commerce between these opposed spaces that position the different agents within the rigid hierarchy of the allegorical representation. In fact, we can speak of a ritual dimension in the line of action—not to mention the role played by imagery at key points—that suggests a magic causality at work in the political process and embedded within the schematized enactment of class struggle. As allegorical personifications, the characters of *Land in Anguish* act as though they are possessed by a single mission or idea. Here possession can be assumed in both psychological and religious terms, and I must now comment on the film's specific style in connection with its plot development for an understanding of the way in which the double line of causation works.

The Brechtian lessons embedded in specific scenes suggest a materialist frame of reference, revealing the material interests and the corresponding ideology of each social agent. Reinforcing this frame of reference, the events in Eldorado follow a script that recalls the Latin American coup d'état paradigm of the 1950s and 1960s. The industrial development of Eldorado, a country still immersed in a neocolonial structure based on the exportation of raw materials, brings new contradictions. The growth of the working class creates a new front of class struggle. Industrialization only sharpens the social tensions in the countryside with its continuous frustration of the peasant's demand for land. The old agrarian structure remains untouched. Within the general opposition of country to city, the progressive national bourgeoisie is seen by the Left as being allied to the people in the struggle against a rural aristocracy that fights for the preservation of semifeudal conditions in the countryside. Within the international capitalist order, the analysis made by the Left privileges the conflict between the national forces—including the industrialists—and imperialism. In its stage-by-stage conception of the historical process, the orthodox Left sees the compromise—the social pact—expressed in populism as a tactical advance, a first step in modernization that, by creating an industrialized capitalist society, prepares for the advent of the authentic socialist revolution. In *Land in Anguish*, the agents act according to this general scheme. We follow Sara and the Left in supporting Vieira, with Paulo and Alvaro explaining to Fuentes Vieira's historical mission in the liberation of the country. We thus follow Fuentes's first move toward the left, when he accepts the opposition foreign–national as the main political contradiction, and his turn toward the right, when he is persuaded by Diaz that class struggle is the true axis of the political game. He ends up accepting that to survive as a capitalist, he must take international capital as his ally against the pressures of the working classes, whose ultimate purpose is power.

The coup is staged as an enactment of this script, and in *Land in Anguish* its logic corresponds, in a general manner, to the critical view of populism also to be found in the sociological output around the mid-1960s. However, the crucial information in the film is its unique way of articulating the representation of the political intrigue with other dimensions of the process. In Rocha's allegory, the process is also cultural, social, economic, psychological, and religious. Rocha wants to make a general diagnosis of the country, the synthesis of all its aspects, even if a journey into history is necessary. The agents acquire the condensed figuration that hinders a term-to-term relation to referents found in Brazilian reality. The range of types refers to something more than the specific characters of the political life in the 1950s and 1960s. Here the style has a causal effect and the reading of the actions involves aspects of experience that are beyond those explained by political-economic categories. We go beyond the sheer denunciation of the forces that carried out the coup or the elucidation of its immediate mechanism. The film places itself as a blunt expression of a state of mind and conveys a totalizing feeling of the crisis. In order to totalize, Rocha does not hesitate in imprinting a fundamental mythical sense on the analysis of the political events, and these are assumed as part of a larger system, understandable only through his way of representing peculiar styles of political action. At the center of the figuration—which wishes to totalize and reach deeper orders—there is the *transe* metaphor that characterizes the national crisis.[4] Within this mythical characterization of social experience, the logic of material interests finds itself articulated by dint of a world of symbols that seem to fight for hegemony in leading gestures. Overdetermined, the social order becomes a cosmic order, and the actions gain a ritual dimension as if programmed. The style of the film suggests other effective forces that point outward to the magic-religious sphere. This effectiveness is emphatically expressed by the "possessed" face of the characters, who display an awkward identity of style that in fact prompts all the political actors in Eldorado to perform their role in such a program, particularly at the moment of the *transe* in Eldorado. They expose their faith in a fixed idea, and this faith damages their illusions of freedom and shows the force of repetition in their attempt to create history.

The central question of populism and of Paulo's attitude toward Vieira allow for some considerations on this double line of causation (historical materialist–magical religious) present in the film. The story line and many dialogues develop a critique of populism as a mistaken tactic for the Left. Populism's success depends on Fuentes's support, and the hope for a nationalist position on his part is demonstrated as naive. Moreover, in specific sequences, the role of populism as a controlled inclusion of the people in the political game receives a graphic demonstration, as already explained in my analysis of the scene entitled "The Leader Meets the People." Besides the specific strategy of attack embodied in Paulo's challenge at the rally, the film underlines another aspect of populism whose consideration leads us back to Paulo's subjective process and to a more precise definition of the "magical causation." The political alliances made by the Left imply that since they do not have the ideological conditions to choose the "correct perspective," the people of Eldorado must be induced to follow a man—a father substitute—and his promises of a better future for all. This attitude corresponds to a form of consciousness far from the high level of structural social awareness appropriate to a truly revolutionary attitude. Instead of class consciousness, the populist way reinforces a familial spirit of cohesion. Within this context, political leadership is legitimated through charisma rather than through effective programs of reforms and solid principles. The socialist idea is seen as too abstract and analysis as too demanding and complicated. A man capable of such a specific kind of leadership is more appealing because his command is based on an unconscious substratum. Assuming such a strategy, the Left supports a type of interaction between leader and masses that is far from reflecting those rational categories informing its view of history.

The resort to passion and charisma is usually explained as a tactical move, and reason continues to be seen as the ultimate guide of history. However, in the context of the allegorical country Eldorado, the ritual of mass mobilization and the magic of political leadership seem to lose their metaphorical sense. Many decisive steps in the intrigue leading to the confrontation between right and left and the victory of reaction are represented as a battle in which effective praxis is replaced by symbolic action and in which material forces are eclipsed by spiritual powers.

Instead of placing the army in the foreground of the political scene, the film enacts the coup d'état as a battle of speeches, as a struggle for domination performed by two different political discourses. When the moment of confrontation between the isolated aristocracy (represented by Diaz) and the popular forces (represented by Vieira and his followers) comes, parallel editing alternates Diaz's ascension to power with the images of the defeat of the populist spectacle. Diaz is seen climbing the hills completely alone, reaffirming that his road to power completely bypasses the people; meanwhile Vieira is seen in a rally making a last speech and followed by the masses. While Diaz's discourse, demanding law and order and the salvation of the sacred traditions of Eldorado, grows stronger as the sequence progresses, Vieira's stereotyped speech on the rights of the people and the liberation of Eldorado from imperialism becomes weaker. His voice becomes fainter and fainter as he tries to compensate for the weakness of speech by resorting to a grotesque kind of mimicry, his gesticulations trying to imbue his words with a strength alien to them. Diaz ends his journey on the top of the hill, with the happy exaltation of the eternal dawn waiting for him and Eldorado; Vieira ends up kneeling to kiss the priest's hands, exhausted and unable to speak. In *Land in Anguish* the hour of decision is the hour of *transe*, and the turning point is acted out as collective possession, a cosmic convulsion punctuated by the Afro-Brazilian religious song that marked our first approach to Eldorado in the opening sequence of the film.

Diaz's victory is not only a matter of fact and deed but also a matter of discourse, a matter of symbolic causation, as if words had power over fact. Diaz's ascetic life and his missionary attitude resulted in the "salvation" of Eldorado, a fact that he celebrates by immersing himself in an ecstatic religious drunkenness typical of the ascetic mind.

Diaz's absolute joy contrasts with Paulo's desperate and self-destructive appeal to violence. Paulo's personal resolution seems to reflect a feeling of disgust typical of a self-centered character. At the same time, his resolution is something more, reflecting the logic of personal and collective sacrifice. When he calls for armed resistance against the reactionary forces, his concern is not with tactics. Whereas Vieira calls the armed resistance an "adventure" (meaning irresponsibility), and the Left follows a rational line of self-preservation for future action, Paulo refuses a pragmatic view of the present. He is not concerned with immediate victory or preservation. He wants bloodshed as a ritual, as necessary for the evolution of the people of Eldorado from their present amorphous state as a group to an organically structured nation capable of expressing its cohesion and aware of its own values. In the scene of the major populist rally, Paulo's voice-over advances this view:

> I wander through the streets and see the people
> Skinny, apathetic, defeated
> This people can believe in no party
> This exhausted people with its lifeless blood
> This people needs death
> More than one could possibly think
> The blood that stimulates a brother pain
> The feeling of nothingness that generates love
> Death as faith rather than fear.

Paulo's final delirium at the end of the film returns to this idea and develops it. Given the country's ever present inconsistency, violence—whatever its immediate consequences on the political level—would in his eyes constitute a redeeming factor, an act of collective purification. His call for bloodshed is the demand for a collective ritual in opposition to the aristocratic "ritual of the elect." For Diaz, the sacrifice of the other (the people) redeems the noble man in power: "Politics is an art for the privileged; in the people's blood we wash our souls." Diaz's metaphysics of sacrifice is constructed to legitimize the exclusion of the people from the political scene. For Paulo, bloodshed and sacrifice have an antithetical meaning: They represent a leap to a new quality, the means through which people acquire political consciousness and force their way into the political space. (It is no accident that the representative of the people in the oneiric imagery, conveying the desired invasion of Diaz's palace, is the man killed in Vieira's rally on the terrace.)

In his meditation on the inherent violence permeating social life, Paulo reserves the expression "sleeping barbarians," to refer to the dominant classes of Eldorado. The expression, which includes himself as a petit bourgeois intellectual, synthesizes a basic idea differently expressed throughout the film: the Westernized ruling class of Eldorado carries within its own body those "savage" attributes projected into the people's mind. The "civilized" minority inherits that original violence essential to the colonialist enterprise led by Europe in tropical lands. Beneath the surface of scientific rationality, the "civilized" minority's own mind is immersed in that ocean of magic thought, superstition, and mythology that the dominant ideology conceives of as exclusive to a "primitive" consciousness. In the sequence "The Leader Meets the People," we have the most explicit manifestation of Paulo's intuition concerning this specular relationship between the dominant and the dominated. On the terrace-stage, the carnival goes on; Sara urges Paulo to do something to call the people to order. She says: "Look at this chaos; Vieira cannot even speak." And she says: "You threw Vieira into the abyss." He answers: "For a century nobody will be able to speak. . . . the abyss is out there and we all march toward it." Then he refers to the populist adventure as a "*transe* of mystics," making clear the key role played by irrational faith in history, a role below the rational surface of leftist tactics. Although active, Paulo remains skeptical most of the time. His basic motivation for action is his love for Sara and his conflict with Diaz rather than a clear ideological identification with the Left, especially the young militants.

As the film progresses, Paulo's apparently chaotic mental processes gradually reveal their pertinence to the social evolution of Eldorado. He seems to be a privileged figure able to grasp the larger order within things and the basic inadequacy of the interpretation constructed by the Left in an effort to accommodate fact within its theoretical model of history. Paulo joins the "adventure" but senses the ambivalence embodied in its ritual dimension. The progress of the allegory shows that the symbolic order established by his obsessions and poetic insights cannot be reduced to a purely subjective process accounted for by psychological explanations. The strong correspondences between what had been assumed to be oneiric imagery and real events reveal that my account up to this point is only partially adequate.

The emblematic image of Diaz with crucifix and dark banner in hand has been associated thus far with Paulo's own feeling toward this strong father figure. Its symptomatic position at both the beginning and the end of the long recapitulation is accounted for by a psychological framework. Within the film's larger play of symmetries, however, the repetition of the emblem involves the connection of the remote past with present events, a connection strongly suggested by the allegorical evocation of the origin of Eldorado. The first appearance of the emblem is followed by a dreamlike scene that introduces the theme of origin. Coming from the sea and walking on the beach, Diaz is seen carrying a black banner and a crucifix. He has company: a priest in an old Catholic habit, a figure resembling a sixteenth-century Spanish conquistador, and a "symbolic" Indian; they are all clearly imaginary figures, carnival masks (except for Diaz, who wears his normal twentieth-century suit). The scene presents the same awkward mixture of elements and the same characters as those encountered again in the coronation at the end of the film. A huge cross is fixed on the sand, and Diaz approaches it to kneel and perform a ritual recalling the first mass celebrated in the new land "discovered" by Catholic Europeans. The same Afro-Brazilian music is heard over this ceremony as was heard in the first shot of the film and over the magical confrontation of speeches involving Diaz and Vieira. This African religious music punctuates the Christian rite led by Diaz as if the scene required its presence in order to fully represent the very foundation of Eldorado. A curious detail of the scene is that Paulo is also there on the beach to witness the original act. He is far from the camera, in the background, and he stays immobile, assuming the same posture that he will again assume before the imaginary killing of Diaz at the end: He turns his back on the scene, looking downward, repressing the direct view as though facing a taboo.

This oneiric imagery gives spatial representation to Paulo's unconscious drives while simultaneously projecting present experience onto a mythic level: It connects the conquest of the New World and the sanctification of the new land—the arrival and triumph of Christians over the natives—with Diaz's seizure of power in the present. Diaz's emblem introduces the representation of the original act and recurs exactly when Diaz wins the battle of speeches that stands for the coup d'état. The baroque ceremony after the victory again unites past and present. Diaz, surrounded by the tokens of royalty and absolute power, delivers his message as if his words were the proclamation of the very foundation of the country: He behaves like a conqueror talking about a civilization to be built rather than preserved. The similar imagery associating the foundation in the beginning and the coronation at the end (in fact, a new foundation different from that of Paulo's utopia) suggests that they form part of a continuum, an underground current that binds past and present as instances of the same victory, the same removal of possibilities in history.

The present coup d'état is thus represented as a *repetition* of the same act of domination-domestication-repression by which the Christian values claimed the right to define the specific colonial order, regulating, for its own material and symbolic profit, the combination of cultures typical of Eldorado. Essential to this strategy is the film's representation of Christian domination as something regulated by those very magic powers officially rejected by the Westernized dominant classes. It places Diaz's victory within a specific order of events developing along causal parameters completely alien to a secular view of history. A reenactment of the primordial violence, the present political struggle is conceived of as a moment of *transe*.

The entire film is permeated by the feeling of an all-embracing turmoil, as if hidden forces are leading the characters to the performance of a rite of passage, to a traumatic experience that will take the country to a new stage in its historical development. The recurrent African religious music reinforces this feeling as it stresses the ritual dimension that permeates the populist festival involving the masses and Diaz's doctrinal soliloquies. At the precise moment of the coup, the battle of speeches, performed in the parallel between Diaz's solitary ascension to ecstasy and Vieira's ineffective gesticulation, is again punctuated by the African religious music, the historical event being represented as an orchestration of *transes* lived by possessed characters. Within this sacred order, the confrontation between Vieira and Diaz is a battle of charismas in which Vieira's defeat results from a lack of magical power.

Diaz wins not because he is on the side of reason but because he has charisma and is thus the most effective agent.

Through its various allegorical strategies, *Land in Anguish* suggests a causal system that converts class struggle into a visible order of events through which, at a particular historical juncture, a latent process of a different nature finds its expression. The organization of imagery through Paulo's mental processes, the role played by baroque-style symbolic representations, the constant intervention of voice-over commentary—all suggest that behind the coup there are other determinations that do not eliminate the class struggle as a frame of reference but that do make it less absolute. The strategy of the free indirect subjective, turning Paulo's mental process into a basic mediation, is not meant simply to give expression to the worldview of a disturbed mind; it is there to give expression to an ambivalent order of things that finds in Paulo's mind its subjective counterpart.

In *Black God, White Devil*, a similar structural ambivalence marked the peasant's quest for justice in a film that turned the *sertão* into a kind of allegorical site of man's present suffering within the context of underdevelopment. In *Land in Anguish*, Eldorado—ironically distant from any Golden Age or Promised Land—is the new allegorical site of underdevelopment and neocolonial order, a tropical arena for the convergence of contradictory cultures, dominant and dominated. In this conflict of different symbolic systems, the central role played by Paulo's quest for justice and for power within the film results from the parallel, of which Paulo is not conscious, between his mental process as a poet and the problematic identity of Eldorado as a confluence of cultural codes. In the agonistic recapitulation of personal and collective past, the passages of oneiric imagery suggest the convergence of myth and dream. Paulo's mental processes rehearse many substantial elements of memory and the collective experience of Eldorado, which are repressed even by the project of an orthodox Left that tried to confine such cultural data in the space of "popular excesses" with no effective role in the process leading to revolution.

Although the overall design of the film follows erudite patterns, decisive moments—like the evocation of Eldorado's historical past (the first mass celebrated by the Christian conqueror), the victor's parade, and the ceremony of Diaz's coronation—are instances of carnivalesque allegories that introduce the mediation of a popular imagery linked to a sacred view of social life. They are explicit manifestations of a crisis by which the intellectual's approach to social experience renounces its internal coherence, its homogeneity and order, making room for unconscious drives that are seen as the best way to grasp essential and concealed aspects of collective experience.

As a discourse derived from deep anger, *Land in Anguish* dives into kitsch, into the aggression against good taste in a search for coherence and unity. Placed on the threshold of incoherence, the representation of politics in Rocha's film combines an impulse toward totalization with the agonistic consciousness of the paradoxical nature of reconciling dominant and dominated codes. Acknowledging the crisis of available representations, the film expresses a deep exasperation with the play of appearances that contaminates all aspects of national life: the illusions, the distortions, the clichés that affect even the most rational and critical views of the historical process. Within this vertiginous play of appearances, an allegory of hope, or the teleological view of history, have no place. *Land in Anguish* is a baroque drama, in Walter Benjamin's sense.

As an experience of disenchantment, Rocha's work enacts a progressive distancing from power. Paulo's quest is depicted not as an epic conquest or the fulfillment of tragic destiny but as an ambivalent journey into the abyss. From Paulo's first break with Diaz, there is a gradual twist by which his leap toward freedom becomes a leap to defeat and death. His progressive fall is the axis of a representation of the political life of Eldorado as a baroque courtly intrigue (with the people excluded). Seen through the eyes of the dominant classes, the struggle for power is a courtly affair. The poet unconsciously accepts such a view, and his political engagement on the people's side keeps the principle of authority untouched. He wants to replace Diaz by a different kind of leader, one sensitive to popular demands and national interests. Nevertheless, Diaz is the only agent who is able to assume the fate of the baroque despot-martyr figure, a powerful man whose ambivalence includes the sacrifice of the task to be achieved (with the weight of history on his shoulders) and the arbitrary exercise of his will that enslaves all (the prerogative of evil without appeal). Facing failure, Paulo moves toward a melodramatic conception of this despot-martyr figure, separating the martyr (himself) from the despot (Diaz). However, the editing process clarifies Paulo's and Diaz's relative identities, as two faces of the same authoritarian principle. In this double figure, the film works over the continuity among the successive generations involved in national organization projects framed from above. Although he presents some restrictions to Eldorado's political theater, Paulo's open proposal is of a war *decided upon from above* to shake an amorphous crowd mired in inertia.

The court politics of *Land in Anguish* condense a whole national tradition of elite compromises and coups under the name of revolution. This is the tradition that the film critically presents in this baroque piece in which the fight for power is reduced to a game of individual passions and endless treachery. In this tradition, the role of the scholar is to aspire to become the prince's counselor, to accept the rules of the game, as does Paulo, who reaffirms, in the allegorical Eldorado, a vocation that the political culture in Brazil has taken as natural from 1930 to the 1960s. The poet, once defeated, enacts the agony of his illusory status, maintaining at the same time an obstinate narcissism in a discourse that is obsessive and self-indulgent in its pomp and ceremony. Rocha's film expresses the political collapse of the courtly pattern and offers a kind of allegorical epitaph for a particular aesthetic consciousness, blending criticism and homage as if the epitaph were written by this same consciousness in the very moment of its death.

Rocha's aggressive style criticizes leftist (and Cinema Novo) involvement with populism—a political strategy that privileges the movement from the top to the bases—and demands a radical revision of the pedagogical assumptions and methods of revolutionary art. *Land in Anguish* is the courageous cinematic expression of the acute, painful reflection on a political failure that triggered a shock experience capable of providing a new impulse to artistic practices in Brazil. The responses to such a seminal work define the basic lines of Brazilian political cinema and culture in the late 1960s.

Figure 2.1

Figure 2.5

Figure 2.2

Figure 2.6

Figure 2.3

Figure 2.7

Figure 2.4

Figure 2.8

Figure 2.9

Figure 2.13

Figure 2.10

Figure 2.14

Figure 2.11

Figure 2.15

Figure 2.12

Figure 2.16

Figure 2.17

Figure 2.21

Figure 2.18

Figure 2.22

Figure 2.19

Figure 2.23

Figure 2.20

Figure 2.24

3

Red Light Bandit: Allegory and Irony

The Absolute Ironist: Fragmentation and Intertextuality

Like *Land in Anguish*, *Red Light Bandit*[1] ends with the representation of the protagonist's death. Its tone, however, is entirely different: irony and self-mockery replace eloquence and drama. Death comes as the last gesture in a personal pantomime enacted by an antihero, whose adventures provide the material for a picaresque narrative. For ninety minutes we follow a series of loosely connected episodes in the life of a famous outlaw mythologized by mass communication— the so-called red light bandit: his robberies, murders, and affairs. A series of the protagonist's trivial adventures functions as the pretext for the depiction of a specific milieu that is proposed as the paradigm of Third World experience: the realm of crime and corruption crystallized in a red-light district—the zone of prostitution, illegal drug traffic, and organized violence. This depiction is achieved through a process of gradual expansion whereby the integration of new elements does not depend on the protagonist's action; it results, instead, from an apparently arbitrary intervention of the narrative agents. In *Red Light Bandit*, commentary prevails over action.

In its overall design, the film is symmetrically divided into two halves roughly corresponding to the rise and fall of the hero. The first half is dominated by action and commentary on a local duel involving the Red Light Bandit and his major rival, the chief of police Cabeção ("Big Head"): the small-time outlaw versus the small-time guardian of private property. The second half amplifies the scope of action and introduces J. B. da Silva, the so-called King of the Boca do Lixo.[2] He is the grotesque politician, at once capitalist and gangster, who controls and profits from all kinds of illegal activities.

The social milieu depicted in *Red Light Bandit* had been a traditional subject of serious naturalist fiction, but Sganzerla's treatment is characterized by the ironic avoidance of illusionist dramatic representation and passionate social denunciation. His film exhibits a deliberate lack of concern with consistent plot, psychological coherence, or social determination, opting instead for the ludic arbitrariness of collage. Its depiction is humorously irreverent, consciously "cool" with respect to the human misery implied in the depicted world. This effect of indifference is created by the fragmentation of the image track and by the interaction of two voice-over narrations, one by the bandit himself and the other by two radio announcers. In *Red Light Bandit* the hero's first-person commentary is decentered by the accompanying radio narration. The imaginary world of the bandit's criminal activities thus becomes a mass media construct that inflects his image. The interplay among the bandit's monologue, the announcers' interventions, and the action depicted by the images creates throughout an ambiguous play of reality and appearance that constantly subverts our assumptions concerning the character's identity and his social relevance. The numerous quotations and parodic references to diverse filmmakers and genres project this play on identity beyond the level of character onto that of filmic structure and style. It is impossible to rigorously determine the locus of the bandit's narrative voice, his point of anchorage in time. There are some residues of the classical circularity of the flashback, but we arrive at the last sequence without any specification of the focus point (where does the voice come from?)

Basically, *Red Light Bandit* goes back to the film noir tradition in its narrative form, combining voice-over and flashback. The hero places the past in perspective, underlines his solitary journey in a dangerous world, and tries to organize his experience and reset his own identity, just as does O'Hara, the Irishman in Orson Welles's *The Lady from Shanghai* (1946) who typifies the act of telling a story as a self-evaluation, with a special penchant for self-depreciation. However, in this retaking of Welles's disenchantment, Sganzerla radicalizes this image of a fragmented identity—the crisis of the subject—that stems from the U.S. filmmaker, that has its place in the noir tradition, and that has received a new meaning from Godard on.

The last sequence synthesizes the basic strategies of *Red Light Bandit*: The representation of the bandit's death highlights both the fragmentation of the image track and the essential role of explicit intertextual references and the sound track's parody of mass media discourse. The film's last movement opens with a symbolic commentary on the bandit's identity, raising once more the question that dominates all of *Red Light Bandit*. He looks at his own portrait on the front page of a newspaper. Under the prominent composite portrait of his face is the caption: "This is the Red Light Bandit" (Figure 3.1; page 121). This composite portrait suggests an identity constructed from a collection of verbal descriptions whose fragments are combined to form a single representation. This device, designed to trigger visual recognition, metaphorizes the whole process of image making enacted by the multivocal narrative of the film. In fact, at this point, the bandit's portrait is far from being clear. It is merely a collection of ill-fitting fragments emerging from random actions and a verbal commentary that is both profuse and diffuse. The actions have been repetitious and disconnected; the commentary has been contradictory and unreliable. We have not followed the progressive revelation of a coherent personality, a trajectory that leads to an understanding of his present behavior and opinions. Like the composite portrait, the bandit's identity has, throughout the film, been created mainly by the voices of others, particularly the voices of the radio announcers.

When the bandit looks at his own image created by others, he seems satisfied. He says, with a certain indifference, "It is not bad, after all." And he adds: "but all this will have an end." He has frequently announced the end of his career, sometimes specifically referring to suicide. At this point, the viewer is used to expressions of self-destructiveness in his monologue and does not attach great significance to these remarks. His words are followed by a shot of a poster whose inscription reads "under the sign of death." This is another apparently misleading premonition, given the film's frequent use of posters and advertising materials to introduce images of death and violence. As we see the menacing words, we hear the voice of a strange male from offscreen who, after presumably recognizing the bandit, considers informing and ironically invokes his starving children as a legitimate motive for playing the role of informer. This elicits no real suspense; the game has been played before.

The sole hint of an approaching death is offered in the subsequent scene, when the Red Light Bandit (both the film and the character) completes a circle returning to the point of departure. We are back, for the first time, to the shantytown that had been announced in the beginning as the hero's birthplace. This return to the origin produces a symmetry linked to the *Red Light Bandit*'s allegorical design and to its central emblem of garbage. At this point, the view of the shantytown does not present the cliché of poor children playing with guns and training for their future criminal lives; this cliché had been presented at the film's beginning with ironic emphasis, while the bandit's voice explained that he came from "there," pronouncing the words as though he were seeing the images of the shantytown along with the audience. In this end sequence, his return is the occasion for contemplative melancholy. Jorginho—this might be his real name—plays the guitar and sings "Mi corazon te llama," a camp example of Latin American nostalgia (Figure 3.2; page 121). As we hear his sad voice, a series of long shots depicts the shantytown as a calm, idealized realm of quiet far from the city lights. Unlike in the rest of the film, the camera does not move in these shots, and the immobility of the setting takes us far from the images of violence and corrupted childhood depicted in the beginning. It is as though in its extremes the film plays with the basic and antithetical clichés for this kind of milieu: the lyrical idealization that equates it with a bucolic life and simple feelings and the naturalist representation that equates it with hellish existence.

The quiet atmosphere of this digression is interrupted by the arrival of the police. The camera movements return, along with the chaotic noise of cars, sirens, and gun shots. Despite the agitation of the images, this last chase follows the normal pattern of *Red Light Bandit*: The relation between the actions of the police and the actions of the bandit is highly tenuous. As in other sequences, the awkward spatial displacement of the policemen is buttressed by dialogue referring to a confrontation not actually seen (Figure 3.3; page 121). To make things even more bizarre, the fragmentation of diegetic actions is juxtaposed with strange images of flying saucers and planetary battles borrowed from a TV science fiction serial. The images of flying saucers often flash as the supposed chase pursues its "normal" course (Figure 3.4; page 121).

The bandit's voice-over again announces his end—"I am finished, but another like me will come"—reminding us of Corisco's phrase in *Black God, White Devil* expressing his consciousness of death and his theory of revenge through the perpetual renewal of the people's warrior saint. The reference is reinforced throughout the film by the recurrent images of Saint George and the dragon; these images possess no clear diegetic purpose and return at the very end only to be burned rather like the sled (Rosebud) in *Citizen Kane,* an ironic reference to the consumption of identity (Figure 3.5; page 121).[3]

After Jorginho's words, which clearly expose the gap between the supposed chase enacted by the police and the bandit's action, we have a symbolic scene focusing again on the question of identity. The hero is seen on his knees near the bank of a river. Beside him is an open suitcase; the word "I" covers its entire internal surface. The contents of this ego-suitcase are a collection of old newspapers and magazines, a book, old clippings, and other personal effects (Figure 3.6; page 121). He appears to throw away material published about himself, the vestiges of a socially constructed identity. Once again, the image of the self is suggested as being a mosaic of disparate elements. When the ego-suitcase is almost empty, he casts it into the water and concludes, "Of one thing I am sure. . . . There is no God." The ego-suitcase drifts downstream like abandoned trash, residue peripheral to the order of things (Figure 3.7; page 121). The sentence, "There is no God" and the image of the suitcase synthesize philosophical ideas treated mockingly. If there is no God, then there is also no man at the center of a created universe. The identity of the self is an illusion. Subjectivity is emptiness; man is trash.

The suitcase drifts away; Jorginho's life drifts away with the same lack of ceremony. He represents his own death as a self-conscious farce, as the end of a comedy—something that provides a way out of that "madness that will not change anything, not even the color of your tie," as the hero himself says. We then hear the sound of a *berimbau*— the African instrument that is introduced as to recall a Third World context, both here and in Rocha's work as well—while Jorginho's voice-over recalls the somewhat prophetic lines heard at different points in the film: "The Third World is about to explode; those who wear shoes will be killed." This formula is repeated throughout the film and parallels the metaphor *sertão*–sea of *Black God, White Devil.* The allusion to Third World revolution is made here without any concern for poetic diction; the ugly statement of an urbanized slob ironically contrasts with Rocha's *cordel*-like poetry.[4] Aside from the crudeness of their formulation, Jorginho's words form a detached, almost schizophrenic commentary that punctuates his private theater. He then rehearses his own death and laughs, as the offscreen sound brings a postmortem commentary reminiscent of *Sunset Boulevard* (1950): "So that's how I rehearsed my own death" (Figure 3.8; page 121). The whole game reaches its awkward conclusion when he wraps himself with electric wires, which have been absurdly pulled into the situation out of nowhere. This wrapping of himself in the clumsy mechanism of suicide is an allusion to the death of Godard's Pierrot, a reference that permeates the entire film, from the theme of identity and fragmentation to minor plot devices. Again, the elevated world of poetic references is evoked and replaced by cheap lyricism and calculated ugliness immersed in black-and-white trash. We are far from the audiovisual juxtaposition that closes *Pierrot le fou* (1965): Rimbaud's verses heard over the image of blue sea and sky. Whereas Godard recapitulates the dissipation of the aura and the split of the subject in the world of technical reproduction, Sganzerla underlines the peripheral experience in which fragmentation and the crisis of the subject have their own style.

The development of Jorginho's theater leads to another intertextual reference: a reminder of the interruption of action at the end of *Black God, White Devil*. In Rocha's film, Antônio das Mortes's gestures first suggest realistic representation but later negate it, so that the whole scene is inscribed within the symbolic order established by the legend. In Sganzerla's film, the bandit first rehearses the expected and plausible death—a heroic bandit is usually shot while trying to escape, fighting to the end. Jorginho mockingly simulates this dramatic end, laughing and making us wait for subsequent gestures, but next comes his peculiar suicide inscribed in the film's network of intertextual ironies.

The mechanism that will set off the discharge is under his feet waiting to be triggered. The last moments of hesitation are filled by the sound of "Que bonitos ojos tienes," a song taken from *Enamorada*, (1946), a Mexican melodrama directed by Emilio Fernandez. This song is completely out of context, reinforcing the strategy of dedramatization. The consummation of the suicide coincides with a news ticker announcement of an event unconnected with Jorginho: a military invasion. The interpolated image brings the news that "thirteen thousand Marines are invading the Brazilian Northeast," and a second flash shows the passing words "to protect" The parallel editing alternates the bandit's last gesture with the introduction of a fact of broader social dimension (Figures 3.9–3.13; page 122).

It is only after Jorginho's death and these announcements that the police are brought to the scene for a final display of opportunism and professional incompetence. A long take shows two detectives routinely chatting alongside the bandit's freshly discovered body as chief Cabeção approaches the scene. One of the detectives—the chief's assistant—distracts his colleague, preventing him from warning their chief of the danger. When he reaches the corpse, Cabeção is surprised by a fatal electric shock, dying comically and lying down next to his "partner" (Figure 3.14; page 122). This common destiny equates the two rivals—Cabeção and Jorginho—in their inglorious and irrelevant demise. Jorginho's suicide consummates a self-conscious demystification; Cabeção's accident confirms his own delusion concerning his heroic social mission and competence. Their devaluation is completed by the intervention of the radio announcers, who for the first time during the entire sequence return to narrate these events as a minor detail within the apocalyptic invasion represented at the film's conclusion. While the African music ironically reminds us of the sacred overtones of the "cosmic" *Land in Anguish*, the announcers refer in passing to the bandit's death and return to the theme of the military invasion, inscribing it within a disconnected but all-embracing set of events: "While the national bandit was ending his criminal career, a short circuit in the Tatuapé *favela* announced that they were arriving from the East. . . . [pause] yes, that very afternoon, the mysterious flying saucers."

The expression "national bandit" has a clearly ironic intent, and the reference to the short circuit displaces the theme of the electric charge, now announced as a social fact simultaneous with the multi-level (that is, by marines and by Martians) invasion. And "they" in the sentence "They arrived from the East" connotes both "they, the Reds . . ." and "they, the Yellows . . . ," in an allusion to Cold War paranoia. Both puns playfully displace the epithet "red light." The reference to Rocha's work goes on: While we hear the African music, we see the people from the shantytown dancing on the garbage dumps in an apocalyptic atmosphere, surrounded by smoke and fire (Figure 3.15; page 122). From this point on, this image is incorporated into the sequence of flashes that establish vertical relationships with the announcers and with the music on the sound track. The combination of the news ticker (informing us that the marines' invasion is meant for Brazil's protection), flying saucers, radio tower, and apocalyptic dancing creates imagistic chaos, punctuated by the speakers' announcement in which terrorism, the Reds' arrival, and the Martian fantasy are overlapped. The image of the "survivors of the Third World" conducting their Afro-Brazilian carnival in the realm of trash—which appeared in the beginning of the film—marks this closing sequence, turning itself into an emblem, a kind of nightmarish vision threatening the conservative mind.

The thematization of tragic destiny in modern times, such as one finds in film-noir, is developed through an exaggerated dramatization with parodic effect. As the visual alternation continues, the alarmed tone of the radio announcers culminates in an enumeration of irrelevant events forming part of the general disorder: "A strange noise and a red color in the sky motivated the suspension of a Chinese wedding in Los Angeles, a heart transplant in Acapulco, and a street demonstration in Porto Alegre, Brazil." For the last time in the film, the "event" narrated is not actually depicted but only suggested through the juxtaposition of verbal descriptions and disconnected images of irrelevant details; the diegetic fragmentation reaches the point of dissolution. The flashes assembled from heterogeneous materials (residues of different film genres) supplement the radio announcers' narration with a transparently false visual evidence.

The radio voices announce: "The barbarians' invasion is imminent. . . . they are ten seconds away from Brasilia. . . . everything is suffused with a terrible red light, no one can tell what is going to happen. . . . the people are invading the public parks. . . . only a miracle can save us from total extermination. . . . it takes only one obscure individual in the crowd to shake the foundations of power in the world." It is, ironically, just as they announce this planetary disaster that they interrupt the flow of information to call attention to their own identity within the broadcasting system; the sound comes from a provincial radio station in Itapecerica da Serra, a small Brazilian town. The planetary scope of the event reported ironically contrasts with the extremely modest status of the source of information, a provincial station whose verbal logo reads "Continental, your station and ours."

In a first movement, the final sequence displaces the individual destiny of the protagonist, reducing it to a peripheral detail within a planetary convulsion. In a second movement, the radio announcers, already discredited by their own self-aggrandizing style, are subjected to a similar trivialization, thus projecting onto the narrative agent the irrelevance already attributed to the protagonist. The dramatic tone elicits laughter, and the distorted imitation of paranoid conservative discourse offers a parodic representation of the end of the world. This end of the world is observed only by a lonely moon in center frame of the final shot of *Red Light Bandit*—a shot whose stability and equilibrium sharply contrasts with the agitation of the preceding apocalyptic images (Figure 3.16; page 122). However, in their final statement, the radio announcers undermine this touch of dignity in the visual conclusion. The male voice says: "Moral of the story: Alone we are worth nothing"; the female voice responds: "So what?"

That question gives a final turn of the screw to the devaluation of things, casting a shadow of irrelevance over the whole process. The narrative, having progressed through an endless play with unreliable statements, carries its game to the very end, enacting its inconclusive conclusion with good-natured irreverence. The film is talkative, it has an opinion about everything, yet in the end it refuses to give advice, to provide a moral of the story. Its irony is absolute.

The discourse of *Red Light Bandit* is that of black humor projected as a pageant of failures. Confronted with the irony that envelops the filmmaker and his own work, one is led to ask: How does the film articulate its radical irony with its equally apparent project of social and political allegory? How does the "crisis of identity" express a sense of dissociation from past illusions even as it reveals the same (albeit displaced) impulse toward the grasp of totality, the search for meaning, that informs Rocha's allegories?

The Ruins of Self-Identity: The World Theater as Farce

"A guy like me had to degrade everything." So says Jorginho's voice-over at the very beginning of the film, before his image appears. Given my account of *Red Light Bandit*, this statement might easily be the filmmaker's, for the voice has not yet been identified as Jorginho's; hence, the possible reading—partly false and partly true—of that voice as authorial. This ambiguity about the subject who utters is elaborated again much later in the film. A title, superimposed over the image of Jorginho's ego-suitcase, announces, "my last bomb." Since this image is contextualized by the radio announcers' alarmist discourse on terrorism, the "bomb" can be diegetically interpreted, with "my" referring to Jorginho. Although this interpretation is plausible, we must remember that Jorginho is never, except in this passage, seen to be involved with terrorism. At the same time, the general design of *Red Light Bandit* solicits another reading, a reading in which "my last bomb" is understood as an authorial statement—"my" referring to the film itself and "bomb" to a novel aggression to be launched by the narrative's jagged development. This proposal of protagonist and film as ironically interchangeable subjects who utter, of Jorginho as metaphor for the filmmaker and *Red Light Bandit* as a common name celebrating the suggested collapse, is the procedure that I now intend to analyze.

Explicit self-devaluation, a recurrent attitude on Jorginho's part, is usually expressed by his offscreen monologue at different moments in the film: "When you are alone you become ridiculous; self-debasement is the only choice"; "I can say it out loud: I am an idiot"; "I wanted to be smart, to have power, to do something important, but I spoiled everything." These comments on his life refer to a past that is never explained during the film. The disconnected narrative combining random episodes concentrates on present actions, on his repetitious assaults and violent gestures, which lead nowhere. None of his present actions suggests even the slightest hint of anything like an ambitious project. The idea of doing something important (in the past) is only expressed in his commentary on his present frustration in a context of tedious routine. This apparent lack of motivation does not prevent him from extending his self-recrimination beyond verbal complaints. In an awkward way, he performs gestures connected with the idea of suicide. For example, when he goes to the beach with Janet Jane he talks about killing himself, and we see him spraying an insecticide on his body. His voice-over repeats the theme of suicide, and we witness inept and inefficient gestures of self-destruction (drinking oil paint, jumping into shallow waters). His routine as a bandit and his self-destructive thoughts as a third-rate philosopher have a certain arbitrary, unconvincing tone. In each move, we face the idea that the deepest dimension of what was said is held beyond the reach of the one who says it in order to keep a double meaning: of a serious effort and of a comic distance. Isolated, lost in the metropolis, Jorginho's inexpressive figure does not seem to be attached to any life or object, rather like the film itself, which refuses to take seriously its own representation: *Red Light Bandit* is a collection of loosely connected small episodes with no apparent role in the progression of the narrative; Jorginho's own constant thievery fails to provide for an administration and a practical use of the stolen goods. Accumulation, the simple piling up of things, seems to be his rule—or vice—just as it governs the film's narration. Jorginho's actions are the result of immediate impulse, apparently unplanned. His random violence and expropriation assuage a fickle appetite; the objects of his violence and thievery are arbitrarily determined: a birdcage, an Encyclopaedia Britannica, or the ordering of an omelet right in the middle of an assault on one of his victims. His attitude is usually that of indifference, expressed in his face and gestures during an incoherent voice-over commentary. Immersed in a world of undifferentiated perception, he seems unable to distinguish the essential from the inessential. Here and there he demonstrates and even proudly displays an acute sense of himself as a failure, a feeling that at times projects a shadow of melancholy on his face. As noted in the foregoing analysis of the film's final sequence, a flip philosophical tone infiltrates some of his remarks along with the ongoing display of bad taste. Placed within a context of incongruous actions and references, Jorginho cannot be taken as a character in the full sense. Lacking psychological coherence, he functions as a repository for a collection of different attributes, arbitrarily combined: He is an ego-suitcase, as is explicitly affirmed at the end. And *Red Light Bandit* is a kind of film-suitcase, with its narrative piling up images and sounds that could be the trash of the editing process: film clips, second takes of the same scene, fragments of street actions, shots of passing light. The density of the drama—the supposed conflict between the project of the ego and the resistance of the world—is crossed by the movement of farce, the presence of a mechanical principle organizing an amazing universe in its intersections and faults.

Sharing a common label and exhibiting similar styles, film and protagonist mirror each other. The discussion of Jorginho's (lack of) identity implies the discussion of the film's (lack of) identity. Such a discussion is acknowledged as a central concern by the film itself, which insists on playing on the ambivalence of Jorginho's questions concerning himself.

The question "Who am I?" raised at the very beginning of *Red Light Bandit* already involves both the protagonist and the film. The bandit's voice, superimposed on the image of a cheap magazine illustration, introduces the question of identity, while the illustration itself evokes enigma, colonial wars, a film genre, and a philosophical cliché. It is the first image of the film, and it is constituted by a drawing that juxtaposes the figure of an Egyptian sphinx and the figure of a soldier of the French Foreign Legion, a juxtaposition commented on by the legend "the destiny of man." Identity and fate: the articulation of the issues is abrupt and concise in this kind of ideogram that opens the film. But the editing style does not give us time to think; we jump rapidly to the film credits, which are combined with news ticker lights and broadcasting voices. The film is introduced as though it is an event among others—the radio announcers refer to it with the same tone used for other diegetic elements, providing a first identification: "a western about the Third World"—while the news ticker raises another question concerning the protagonist (and by implication the film-maker): "genius or idiot?"

This ironic self-questioning and the reference to the western as a film genre and to the Third World as a symbolic space give continuity to the themes of the first drawing, evoking adventure, romance, and violence within the context of an imaginary frontier struggle. The assumption of colonialism as a basic reference and the ironic self-definition of *Red Light Bandit* as a film aligned with that tradition of adventure and exoticism denied by Cinema Novo will be reworked in the sequence that divides the film symmetrically into two halves (before and after the emergence of J. B. da Silva, the King of the Boca do Lixo). This sequence, placed in the middle of the film, gives total emphasis to reflexive strategies. It is immediately preceded by an explicit comment on Jorginho's identity and followed by a long sequence dealing with the theme of suicide, paralleled by J. B. da Silva's introduction.

In the sequence that ends the first half of *Red Light Bandit*, the question "Who am I?" is heard again in an extremely suggestive context. Jorginho awakens and goes to the bathroom of his dwelling—a red-light district flophouse—to shave. He looks at himself in the mirror, then spreads the shaving cream on its surface so that his own image becomes totally blurred. As he turns to leave the bathroom, he squeezes the tube of shaving cream all over the floor; his gesture clearly reinforces the sense of dispersion and lack of form given by the mirror scene. At this exact point, the "Who am I?" is heard offscreen. The ironic answer to this question comes with the following image, which again equates film and protagonist. We are shocked by the eruption of a noisy sequence from an adventure film; the whoops and the cavalcade evoke a western. As the scene clears, we recognize a North African landscape and the uniforms of the Foreign Legion. This quotation returns us to the first image of *Red Light Bandit*, to the opening magazine illustration, embodied now in a C movie. A counter shot shows an almost empty theater in which we see Jorginho relaxed in his chair watching the film. Before the end of the movie, he leaves the room, goes to a bar to have coffee, and walks on the Boca do Lixo streets. Leaving him, through tracking shots and pans, the camera offers a panorama of the neighborhood marked by posters, billboards, theater facades, and other visual displays, all touching on themes of sex and violence. Comments by the radio announcers include *Red Light Bandit* in a fresco of sex and violence, ironically suggesting that it too is a cultural product—or a piece of merchandise—originating in the same social and commercial context displayed by the image track. As the camera moves, offering sights typical of the Boca do Lixo, the voices speak of a film full of "crime, poetry, agitation, adventure."

This sequence inscribes the film within the context experienced by Jorginho in the fiction, suggesting the red-light district as a paradigm of film transactions and the isolated bandit as a metaphoric surrogate for the film-author, completely involved and manipulated by the network of gangsterlike relationships imposed on him by the milieu in which his work has to be carried out. The affinities between the film industry on the one hand and brothels and drugs on the other are graphically represented in the very architectural structure of the Boca do Lixo; they are given further emphasis by the way in which this film's cinematic references are anchored in the social tableau composed around Jorginho.

Using a specific strategy of quotations, Sganzerla combines diverse references associated with opposed cultural contexts. After many references in exterior shots to pornographic film, there is another fragment of a cheap adventure film in a projection room. Back in the streets, we hear Jorginho's offscreen voice talking about *Gringo* (1967)—an Italian western with anticolonialist overtones—in a way distinct from that of the intellectuals concerned with the allegorical meaning of the story. For Jorginho, the protagonist of *Gringo* is a good role model because he is strong and tough, coarse, as life in the Boca do Lixo requires. Here, the anti-intellectual feature and the pattern of the tough guy recall Michel Poicard's attraction to Humphrey Bogart in Godard's *Breathless* (1959).

One more step and we go back to the dialogue with Rocha's works, one basic leitmotiv within intertextuality. The next murder committed by Jorginho is punctuated by the African drums from *Barravento* (1962), Rocha's first feature, while the handheld camera moves, as it might in a Rocha film, over the body of the victim lying on the asphalt. The murder scene is followed by another reference to the universe of film distributors in a shot of an elegant woman telephoning a newspaper to provide Jorginho's biography and a diagnosis for his "disease." The sequence of the phone call evokes a film-distributor's office; the wall behind the woman is covered by a huge poster referring again to sex and violence. In an ironic reference from the radio announcers, the woman is introduced as the "mysterious lady" calling from Araraquara, a small town in the state of São Paulo; she is said to be the wife of Jeronimo, the "hero of the *sertão*." The combination of data concerning this woman is completely incongruous and the allusion to the "hero of the *sertão*"—a reference to a famous radio soap opera—adds to the film's playful juxtaposition of country and city. Later in *Red Light Bandit*, when Jorginho's "fortress" is invaded by the police, a *cangaceiro* is seen in front of the house; an unexpected presence that leads to intertextual references in a typically *tropicalist* juxtaposition of urban and rural elements.

The radio voices situate the lady's phone call as if it were a historical event. Jorginho's biography, as related by this femme fatale, is completely different from the data given by his own voice-over in the beginning of the film. She informs us that he came from a "golden cradle," that is, from a good family, well-educated—"He could be a lawyer." She attributes his criminal actions to an outburst of violence in a pathological state of despair. Jorginho himself introduces the theme of his "sick mind" in the opening sequence of *Red Light Bandit*, when he talks about his abnormal mind in a way that implies an allusion to Cinema Novo. The radio announcers start defining the film as a western about the Third World as the music from *Land in Anguish* is heard for the first time. This results in an ironic combination of western, urban life, and the practice of the "tricontinental filmmaker." After saying "I failed, a guy like me had to degrade everything to see what could result from all this," Jorginho says that he is "that way" (we infer "weird and stupid") because his mother tried to have him aborted, fearing that he might die of hunger in childhood. The reference is to that *cangaceiro* ideology expressed in *Black God, White Devil*: "I kill people to prevent them from starving." The statement, paradoxical but integral to Rocha's symbolic system, is transformed into a caricatural piece of nonsense. The reenactment displaces the paradox from the level of an epic, ceremonial representation to the debased level of the "news in brief" and the underworld chronicle of a big city.

The sequence following the woman's phone call extends both the biographical references to Jorginho and the "profanation" of Cinema Novo. The bandit's voice-over, accompanied by visual illustration, recapitulates his sexual life, describing the women with whom he was involved. The collection of types depicted once more offers a display of bad taste and the kitschy enumeration of incongruous data. All those evoked have "professional names"; many are foreign-sounding, as is usual in Brazil, where the foreign is associated with the seductive. One is "very Catholic and works for an airline company"; another is the "solitary type of Mooca" (Mooca is one of the Italian quarters of São Paulo, which could hardly be associated with the idea of a "solitary type"); still another is a "practitioner of free love and family-oriented." There is, as well, the "intellectual type," a college graduate who likes Cinema Novo and graduation balls. Cinema Novo, as part of this list, is converted into another item in an agenda of false erudition, in a random collection of cultural elements reduced to mere signs of a modest social distinction. This ironic view of Cinema Novo crowns the succession of minor jabs made throughout the film. Until this point, displacements expressed an irreverent view of the basic strategies of Rocha and Third World themes. The target is no longer a stylistic or thematic element; it is Cinema Novo as a cultural and social phenomenon. Taking as its specific example the movement led by Rocha, *Red Light Bandit* expresses its skeptical view of the destiny of critical, dissident film production within the capitalist system. Cinema Novo is here proposed as an example of the absorption of critical discourse as fashion, as an ephemeral event—an object of taste equivalent to graduation balls. The revolutionary impulse is seen to be condemned to impotence by the process of reification—the commodity form neutralizes any revolutionary content—and Cinema Novo is reduced to a minor detail in the media kaleidoscope.

Sganzerla assumes an ironic stand toward the dominant political cinema in Brazil, and, pushing irony to its ultimate consequence, *Red Light Bandit* includes itself in the circle of impotence. Jorginho twice repeats the axiom of self-devaluation—"When we can do nothing we make asses of ourselves"—and the film, from beginning to end, assumes this basic premise. Dissolved in the cinematic strategies of quotation, Jorginho's deeds and "messages" end up functioning as displaced representations, as mocking allusions to the experience of independent cinema in Brazil.

This network of allusions contaminates even the intrigue involving Jorginho and Janet Jane, isolated within the context of fragmented scenes. Its development is clearly inspired by *Pierrot le fou* and *Breathless*. Rehearsing the idea of woman's betrayal, it presents some specific parallels with the ends of both films. As already described, Jorginho's suicide, a quotation of Godard, closes a dialogue developed throughout the film. Before fulfilling his promises of self-destruction, Jorginho kills Janet Jane. She is *dégueulasse* ("disgusting"), not as ambiguous as the *petite bourgeoise* played by Jean Seberg and lacking the poetic aura surrounding the figure of Marianne in *Pierrot le fou*. Janet Jane is a caricature of the femme fatale, a patently bad character. A ridiculous prostitute and an unreliable lover, she tries to involve Jorginho in the enigmatic operations of J. B. da Silva's gang and ends by betraying him. He kills her in a sequence just before the scene of the composite portrait that opens the final sequence of *Red Light Bandit*. With Janet Jane dead, the bandit's voice says: "Now it is my turn." Conjoined with this fragment of plot taken from gangster movies and mediated by Godard, Sganzerla offers still another metaphor of Cinema Novo as *Red Light Bandit*'s cinematic past. When Jorginho has killed Janet Jane, the handheld camera circles over her body, imitating Rocha's tactile style, as we hear again the music from *Land in Anguish*.

The killing of Janet Jane constitutes a symbolic action of aggression toward Cinema Novo, as represented by the actress Helena Ignes.[5] The film returns to the shantytown—an adequate setting for a requiem for the dead character related to Cinema Novo—and Jorginho sings a mournful song. This reading provides another key to Jorginho's opening phrase: "I was born there" (that is, in the shantytown). *Red Light Bandit* proclaims its origin in Cinema Novo, which in fact had one of its principal settings in shantytowns in the early 1960s. Jorginho's return to the shantytown to die is the film's return to its origins, closing its circle of reflexive statements.

Throughout the film, the comments on Cinema Novo convey an attack on the political aspirations of the "aesthetics of hunger." Its self-respect and dignity are seen as contradictory stances within the trashy context of a peripheral capitalist country and within the gangsterlike universe of film production and distribution. Although the target is Cinema Novo's so-called pretenses, there are statements of clear affiliation with that movement, and Sganzerla's film displays the typically Cinema Novo attempt to grasp the totality, the impulse to embrace all that can be said of Third World experience, an impulse that places *Red Light Bandit* within the allegorical tradition set by Rocha, despite its paradoxical texture and its self-denegation.

The film's allegorical design is apparent in those instances already stressed in my analysis. Jorginho's behavior is obsessive in its single-mindedness; he performs a kind of compulsive ritual of violence and self-destructive quest. *Red Light Bandit*, with its principle of juxtaposition, places the radio announcers at the center of its narrative, their voices providing a heavy load of commentary and digression. The fragmented action is absorbed within a network of symbolic references to the Boca do Lixo, the accumulation of details, gestures, and commentary functioning as a kind of anatomy of Third World experience, a satirical form that collapses the allegorical and the parodical aspects of the film. Through the radio announcers' dominant presence as narrative agents, *Red Light Bandit* enacts its own implication and dissolution in a specific machinery: the machinery of cross-cultural references socially articulated by the commercial discourse of mass media. Dealing with this hegemonic discourse in society, *Red Light Bandit* appeals to parody, a typical "anthropophagic strategy" in the spirit of *tropicalismo*. It brings to its cinematic texture the hidden logic of mass media, reworking the basic features of an urban folklore, imitating with exaggeration the process of fragmentation and displacement by which other messages coming from opposing and critical sources are neutralized. Interestingly, the film, while incorporating this process, suggests a parallel between the language of mass media—as a discourse of clichés and residues—and that incongruous "syntax" of a life typical of the Boca do Lixo that, in the film, stands for Third World experience. A closer analysis of the radio announcers' performance will complete my consideration of the film's allegorical design.

The Media Voices: Allegorical Site and Parodic Agency

In *Red Light Bandit*'s all-embracing mechanism of fragmentation, the enumeration of disparate attributes, as a process of ironically composing a caricature of identity, plays a key role. The radio commentary is the basic source of this process, which subverts hierarchies and the organic consistency proper to authentic characters. Two voices, male and female, join in the special prosody of a duet—sometimes with echo chamber effects—addressing the audience whenever any new agent is introduced. They present lists of past activities and present features, which reduce personal identity to an awkward series of social abstractions and kitschy references. A murder victim is presented as the so-called Flower of the District and identified as the "flying" Japanese's lover, as an ex-housewife, ex-midwife, ex-student of law. Janet Jane is introduced as "scandalous," as being in spiritual retreat in the Cordillera de los Andes, and as obliged to return to Brazil to be present at her sister-in-law's delivery in Belo Horizonte. The conjectures concerning the identities of Jorginho and of J. B. da Silva elicit the longest enumeration, piling up alleged demonstrations of irrelevant expertise in past activities and awkward connections in the present.

Jorginho is said to be an ex-champion of table-soccer;[6] the grandson of the Brazilian who killed Francisco Solano Lopes, the Paraguayan chief of state, in the nineteenth-century war between the two countries; an heir of the Aztecs and of the Tapuias (Brazilian tribe); a savage figure from the seventeenth century lost in the asphalt jungle; the idle Brazilian in the wave of the last stage of capitalism, an opportunist and a rebel, an unwilling bridegroom, a stupid dancer, and a former sexual tourist.[7] The news ticker calls him the "poor man's Zorro," and the announcers ask the press to refrain from making a hero of him, adding that the Robin Hood story is a lie because "he is only an illiterate thief, an asshole, a liar." Affecting mystery, the voices ask: "Who is this marginal creature of legend? a sex maniac? a mere provocateur? a magician? an eccentric searching for truth? a nobody fascinated by his own success? or a poor slob who emerged from Freud or the Boca do Lixo?"

This enumeration finds its visual counterpart when Janet Jane discovers Jorginho's "true identity" by opening the trunk of his car. From her inspection of its contents, she recognizes the Red Light Bandit. As she empties the trunk in a series of disjunctive shots, the voices proclaim this crucial fact in a tone of alarm. From the trunk she takes clothes, toilet paper, weapons, beach mats, a religious image, the suitcase with the inscription "I," books, an insecticide can, necklaces, a volume of Antoine de Saint-Exupéry's *The Little Prince*, and other miscellaneous objects. The sound brings several attempted accounts of a life story: Jorginho has seven different names and identities, including Ari Galante, a false capitalist; Jorge Vargas, a false bookseller; and Peres Prado, a false farmer from Rio Grande. He is an ex-waiter in Campo Grande; an ex-runner; an ex-street vendor who used to sell nail clippers on São João Avenue; an ex–ticket taker in a third-rate movie theater; an ex-bank clerk in the Amazon. The bandit is said to be Mineirinho's cousin and a godson of Dom Helder Câmara.[8] The idea of identity concealed in a junk-filled trunk anticipates the notion of ego-suitcase and the "I" already projected in the chaos of his dwelling, with its awkward collection of disparate objects.

In the definition of character, the film uses a similar strategy when dealing with the most powerful of its imaginary constructs: J. B. da Silva. He enters the film in a sequence at the São Paulo airport, supposedly arriving from Spain. He is introduced as the King of the Boca do Lixo, a versatile gangster involved in smuggling, right-wing terrorism, bootlegging, and counterfeiting; he is an unreliable car dealer, a pimp, and the Boca do Lixo candidate for the presidency. His biography is later given on the sound track, as we see him for the first time alone, examining his face in a mirror. While he squeezes his pimples, the announcers begin their enumeration, illustrated by photographs of his religious childhood as in a conventional documentary film. He is said to be an ex–billiard champion; a smart figure who invented many things, including a correspondence course in mastering the viola and a generally applicable method for bypassing obstacles; the composer of *chorinhos*; a champion marksman; and famous for wealth acquired as a smuggler of cans of "rotten sardines."

Through this process of enumeration, the mechanical and arbitrary dominate the organic and motivated; the piling up of ruins from the past parallels the development of present actions. Both are regulated by a principle of juxtaposition. At the same time, the very content of the enumerations and the nature of the episodes display stupidity, corruption, cynicism, and futile competence that contaminate the storytelling itself, foregrounding the unreliable character of the narrators and the gap between what is said and what is seen. As a result, the film is populated by imaginary beings structured as random collections of features. In the core of the comic effect, there is a structural principle: *the contradiction between the repeated idea of a possible wholeness and the required incongruence of its components.*[9]

At the center of the film's structure and decisive in the general process of devaluation, the media voices outstrip Jorginho and other characters in the demonstration of stupidity, incongruity, and cheap philosophy, tempering their sententiousness with the taste for melodrama and fearful advice typical of lower-middle-class morality. While

Jorginho's remarks are short and attached to specific issues concerning himself, the mediation of the radio voices is effected through long discursive passages of a more general sort. Their privileged status as source of information gives them an ambiguous position, for they function both as radio announcers within the fictional world and as a narrative agency exterior to the diegesis. As radio announcers, they ask questions and make conjectures and prognoses concerning the Red Light Bandit to their implied audience. We see Jorginho buying clothes, driving through dark streets, resting at home, walking like a normal citizen, lying on the grass in a public park, invading a house, and escaping from the police, all while we hear the radio announcers' commentary. As narrative agents, they make comments on the film itself and define the nature of Sganzerla's work, radicalizing their role as an anti-illusionist factor within the film. In the final sequence, the voices close the circle of irony and take over the enactment of the awkward apocalypse, subverting the idea of conclusion in the enunciation of a moral that they themselves immediately question.

Besides referring to the film as film, the voices distance the spectator by undermining cause-and-effect sequencing while seeming to respect it, exaggerating the gravity of the subject. When Jorginho refers to his childhood in shantytowns and a group of dirty kids are seen playing with guns, the seriousness of the image ("education for violence within poverty") is subverted by a shot of the boys smiling, gesturing, and exhibiting directly to the camera a comic book dealing with violence and superheroes. This ironic reference to the "bad influence" of cheap literature, films, and comics is reinforced by the radio announcers' play on cause and effect: They interrupt Jorginho's recollections with the abrupt announcement "Some years later," introducing him for the first time as an adult bandit burglarizing a house. The leap from childhood to criminal life is so obvious and the cause-and-effect relationship of shantytown to crime so cynically posited that the announcement functions as a humorous commentary on the commonplaces of crime in urban society, as though these assumptions are too banal to deserve serious elaboration or discussion. And the irony of arbitrary assumption of naturalist causation is increased when Jorginho describes his own fate: "I was bound for the electric chair." (There is no electric chair or capital punishment in Brazil.)

Amplifying the play on cliché in their fatalist evocation of crime and punishment, the voices later explain, "Nobody knows how many assaults, larcenies, and rapes he has already committed. . . . Aged twenty-six and having killed twenty-six, he was condemned to 167 years, 8 months and 2 days in jail, not to mention the fine of ten dollars. . . ." Later, they add that "should he be sentenced again he will get 400 years. . . . he can be released only upon proof that he is completely . . . nuts!" (The last word is given a rising, slurred intonation.) Placed between these two ironic references to his offenses against law and society, Jorginho's confession ("I am proud to say, I am an idiot") displays a stupidity incompatible with the celebrated dangerous figure constructed by the discourse of the media. Jorginho's images, gestures, and speech undermine the media commentary on him, highlighting the disproportion between verbal and visual information.

Apart from Jorginho and the radio announcers, the display of nonsense and stupidity pervades every image, every action, and every line. All the characters in the fiction reveal themselves to be as stupid and inconsequential as Jorginho himself. At one point, a maid indignantly refuses to talk with the bandit when he invades her employers' house, offering in excuse the proud statement: "I have to prepare coffee, I don't talk to foreigners [meaning strangers]." The chief of police constantly displays his ignorance—in protesting against a modern picture hung on the wall of the house, when he says that he prefers Brazilian cigarettes because American cigarettes "give you cancer," and when he calls artists and intellectuals a "bunch of queers." Janet Jane is the underdeveloped vamp who feels she is in Heaven when she is taken by Jorginho for the typical lower-middle-class weekend on the polluted beaches of Santos.

The stock of corrupt figures inhabiting an imaginary society of urban crime is derived from fiction constructed by the mass media, with the specific difference that in *Red Light Bandit* they are caricatures; the film openly states what is generally more subtly represented. From the minor figures to the narrative agents, the basic rule is the display of one's imbecility and cynicism, exposing the gap between performance and pretense, between the ceremonious tone of speech and the irrelevance of the subject. The essential point is to make the marginalized figure assume an exhibitionist attitude, parodying his or her subaltern condition, making a caricature of an identity built by the other. Defeat and impotence are assimilated by means of a self-demoralization that puzzles because it refuses to deal with failure on a moral register. The affirmation of garbage and ignorance becomes somehow an aristocratic affectation, a rejection of the rule, a parody addressed to people in power and simultaneously to the serious intellectual who intends to be society's saving conscience.

In the world depicted in *Red Light Bandit*, the dominated are stupid, the dominant are cynical. As the figure of power in the realm of garbage, J. B. da Silva epitomizes this general process. The overtness of the *Rei da Boca* ("gang chief") is the opposite of the bandit's clandestineness. A character who deals with drugs in several spheres, J. B. is the underground world in its extroverted version. Through his behavior, the scandalous cynicism and dishonest maneuvers of politicians are brought to the literal surface of text and gesture. His sheer nerve allows him to acknowledge publicly what is usually concealed as the secret desire of a selfish scoundrel. His corruption, as populist leader and mafioso, is limitless. Compared to this urban gangster, the country-based Vieira in *Land in Anguish* is a saint and an idealist. In *Red Light Bandit* the political dispute lacks clear borders because the main interest is in showing the style of making politics as a central theme, correlated to a cultural style in which extravagance and incompetence predominate. The agenda does not really focus on efficiency but, rather, on the charm of a way of being that is identified with a series of frustrated experiences that, no doubt, constitute a world with "personality."

J. B. da Silva presents his platform in a TV interview, making clear that there is none: "I myself am the platform." He then advances some social concerns, proposing specific solutions: He offers chewing gum to the starving; electric hoes to the peasants (instead of agrarian reform); for the solution of family problems, a Home for Unwed Fathers. He later explains to a journalist: "A country without poor people is a country without folklore; without folklore, what would we show the tourists? So, long live poverty!"

All his interviews are spectacles of self-assured, good humored indecency. The press seems to show his political and illegal affairs as two legitimate and connected sides of his public life. They question him on both sorts of issues—murder, burglary, smuggling, his financial activities, his candidacy for the presidency, his friendship with Juan Peron, his bank, the supposed Nazi who belongs to his gang—switching easily from one area to the other. At times he stages a showy claim for honesty that invariably has the opposite effect, and his explanations of past operations and future plots merely confirm his reputation as the

dangerous chief of a national organization with international connections. At the airport, on his first appearance, he refers to his trip to Europe as a visit to Juan Peron, the ex-dictator of Argentina, and the occasion for the inauguration of a branch of his bank. In many scenes,
we see beside him the mysterious "German"—an allusion to a Nazi
refugee hidden in Brazil. This figure embodies that ironic mixture of
genres found in *Red Light Bandit*, here fusing the serious and political
with cheap media legends about dangerous conspiracies among Nazi
refugees in Latin America.

This allusion to the Nazi friend, together with the reference to
Peron and J. B. da Silva's public actvity, make his figure a set of signs
condensing diverse leaders of an ambiguous populism in Brazil. Leaving the plane upon his arrival, he shouts, "*O petróleo é nosso*" (The
oil is ours), Getúlio Vargas's nationalist slogan during the oil campaign of the 1950s. His hat and dark glasses complete the reference to
the Brazilian dictator, who committed suicide in 1954 in the middle of
an acute political crisis. J. B. da Silva's overall behavior also recalls
Ademar de Barros, the São Paulo-based right-wing populist, one of the
supporters of the 1964 coup d'état.

Introduced by the radio announcers as the king of the Boca do
Lixo, J. B. da Silva completes the positioning of that specific section of
the metropolis as an allegorical site, condensing the essential aspects of
Third World experience as posited within the film. The narration begins with the awkward depiction of Jorginho, the Red Light Bandit, an
isolated criminal figure actually insignificant but rendered important
by the sensationalist press. A first expansion of the fictional world represents corruption, sketched in a series of night scenes involving pros-
titutes, pimps, drug addicts, gangsters, car thieves, and the police. In
the first half of the film, the Boca do Lixo is made a self-enclosed cosmos, exhibiting its routine and small illegal operations, which take
place in symbolic spaces: nightclubs, cheap hotels, porno theaters,
bars, flophouses, dirty streets, and stolen cars. The visual panel illustrates the notion of "realm of garbage" referred to by the radio announcers: "the empire of disorder and of gangsters; realm of drugs, of
child prostitution, of industrialized crime; Boca do Lixo, where the
gangsters are everywhere, in the pool halls, in the nightclubs, in politics, in sports, in assassination attempts, in the family, in the monas-
teries, and in jails, contaminating peace and war—the garbage without
limits."

This expansion of the realm of garbage and its equation with the whole society is reinforced in the second half of the film. We reach the figure of power, the symbolic father of this microcosmos, the chief of organized crime, the big shot whose operations, diffused within the social order, contrast with Jorginho's isolation. The introduction of J. B. da Silva is the first step in the displacement of our hero, reducing him to a peripheral status, to a kind of blank sheet filled by the traces and masks designed by media discourse. Unknown and without address, he is a kind of asphalt-jungle outlaw. J. B. da Silva is the established lord of crime, complete with sect and fortress. His actual fortress is described by the radio announcers as a typical medieval castle: the mysterious "blue mansion" with its own source of energy, its trapdoors and secrets, a place that nobody can get into.

J. B. da Silva, his sect, his fortress, his public discourse and political affairs—all constitute the institutional support for the microsociety depicted in *Red Light Bandit*. They form the "establishment" that reinforces the status of the Boca do Lixo as a paradoxical self-consistent world based on inconsistency. They politicize the allegory.

Throughout the film, voices and actions suggest the intimate connection between the exhibition of some basic attributes and the condition of being peripheral, dominated. The announcers comment ironically on the inhabitants of the Boca do Lixo, saying that "they are not from this world, they belong to the Third World." J. B. da Silva laughs and suggests that the Third World does not have inhabitants, just survivors. Jorginho asks, "Who am I?," sprays insecticide on his body, looks at the camera, and, seeming perplexed, runs away to jump into the sea. In the scene, the announcers say: "The bomb and the famine separate the Third World from the rest of the Earth," evoking external menace and internal disaster. Such a disaster is also supposed by the bandit when, with apocalyptic overtones, he foretells social violence against those "wearing shoes." The Red Light Bandit's apocalypse displaces the kind of totalization present in *Land in Anguish*, replacing *transe* with a great explosion. This imposes a terminal connotation— the end of the world—on the collection of follies of this universe set apart from civilization by the bomb (theirs) and the hunger (ours), such as the film promulgates. The *Red Light Bandit*, a parallel canto to Rocha's film, is an allegory that keeps some thematic constants linked to a nation's general diagnosis. The terms are changed, as is the iconography; there is even this texture of paradoxical statements that seem to deny everything, but the impulse to figure a totality is not eliminated.

In this "western about the Third World," the Boca do Lixo is structured as the diegetic allegorical site of underdevelopment, and the media voices are the parodic narrative agency of this allegory. The site provides the major emblem for underdeveloped urban society. The narrative agency provides a synthesis for the hidden logic of mass-culture ideology. Establishing an isomorphism between discourse (of the mass media) and its object (Boca do Lixo), the film performs a two-pronged attack on two contexts: One represents a powerful instance within social discourse; the other represents a peripheral province within social experience. The first attack is intended to reveal the disproportion between the media's claim to universal authority—as the source of a new paideia—and its pathetic inconsistency, fragmentation, and narrow-mindedness. The second provides a new metaphor for Brazilian society, trying to absorb the "inconvenient data" not found in the Cinema Novo approach to underdevelopment: those coming from modern urbanized society in Brazil. Sganzerla does not assume the opposition between national authenticity in the breast of nature (the mythic dimension) and the urban decharacterization (the historical dimension) because modernity is seen as an insurmountable framework, an unavoidable second nature, a space of intersection and plurality where it does not make any sense to ask for the origin. An essential feature here is that the problematic of the migrant is absent; there is not the usual linear path from the rural area to the urban area, from the archaic to the modern, as an allegory of the identity crisis.

Incorporating the "inconvenient data," *Red Light Bandit* builds a mosaic of episodes in which the juxtaposition of modes of discourse, the mixture of modern urban and archaic elements (a favorite *tropicalist* emblem), and the interaction between local and international references create the basic effects: a disorganization of the usual order of things in the representation of Brazilian society—a subversion of hierarchies, a dazzling interpenetration of what is usually seen as separate.

Together the Boca do Lixo and the discourse of the media present, in the mode of black humor, the reflexes of capitalist development in a dependent country whose history is seen as a progression of inescapable changes determined by a world order in which its experience and desire are peripheral. In this context, the filmmaker refuses legitimacy to established representation, devalues social codes, and dissociates himself from the "illusions of the past" embodied in Cinema Novo. At the same time, he is aware of his insertion in a dialogic process in which the language of the other is very strong. He cannot radically refuse this language, and he wants to recycle it because its destruction would imply the disruption of his own identity. Trapped in his peripheral condition, the filmmaker embraces this paradox so radically that his discourse becomes the expression of self-estrangement, of the radical split within the self, and of the lack of consistency in the exterior world.

Like *Land in Anguish* and its character-poet, *Red Light Bandit* and its protagonist make a speech out of impotence, with the difference that irony and self-mockery replace eloquence and drama. In Sganzerla's film, impotence bedecks itself with humor because a splitting of the self allows for an exterior view of its own fall. Within the context of the "aesthetics of hunger," the *sertão* in *Black God, White Devil* is taken as the allegorical site of a teleology, and the prophetic evocation of Third World revolution places the national experience in the center of a universal order. The distinctive trace of the present against history would be this Third World vocation to fulfill a universal task, to aid the essential transformation of humankind on its path to freedom. *Land in Anguish* is Rocha's version of the crisis of these historical purposes; it is a dramatic version of this removal to the periphery that reasserts, however, the sacred side of violence as the answer of the oppressed. *Red Light Bandit* completely separates time from any supposed sacred realm, composing the allegory of a world deprived of teleology. The "aesthetics of garbage" finds its dwelling in the vacuum generated by history and reaches the allegorical drawing of Brazil as a comic province far from the civilized world.

Figure 3.1

Figure 3.5

Figure 3.2

Figure 3.6

Figure 3.3

Figure 3.7

Figure 3.4

Figure 3.8

Figure 3.9

Figure 3.13

Figure 3.10

Figure 3.14

Figure 3.11

Figure 3.15

Figure 3.12

Figure 3.16

4

The Levels of Incoherence; or, The Mirage of the Nation as Subject

"I am a leftist." The tone of voice is assertive; it is the tone of someone who wants to be taken seriously; the circumstance is pathetic, but Fuentes insists. Nevertheless, Diaz controls his impatience and even smiles, lenient, before giving the final touch in his lesson on power and class struggle. Fuentes's words state an identity that, to the ears of any coherent conservative, sounds like nonsense.

Paulo Martins's sense of humor has never been his strong point, but the young militants's religious faith in disclosing Vieira's historical qualities makes Paulo smile in order to enhance the superior look he gives the students who, minutes ago, were vilifying him while trying to win him back to Vieira's side. In the future, the poet's lack of coherence will make him act as if he had assumed this same faith in Vieira, but his participation in the final delirious political campaign does not prevent him from signaling the "general mess" that surrounds the populist leader. The faith of the youngsters is the noblest face of the movement that surrounds Vieira, but this virtue does not exclude them from the lack of consistency, which is one of Paulo's obsessions in his narration. In *Land in Anguish*, the characters' speech and gestures are almost always on a serious, dramatic level, where the urgency of the situation validates the extravagance and prevents it from being comical. Fuentes's statement, in this sense, is one of the few moments in which the nonsense in Rocha's film assumes that specific comic nature that will be the rule in Sganzerla's film. In *Land in Anguish* we have amusing images of Vieira holding a child on his lap while making a speech, but this kind of political hypocrisy has its electoral logic and is not ultimately disturbing. Its humor is not based on that aggression toward word syntax that will become systematic in *Red Light Bandit*, transforming the lack of consistency into a kind of omnipresent feature in society.

In its national crisis, Eldorado can have its fate defined by the Left

123

or the Right (both embodied by clearly identified figures); its issues are specific, and at the moment of confrontation, the cards are laid on the table. There are effective actions and the incoherent gesture is a problem of the defeated: The coup is full of logic. It works out. People talk about crisis in the context of the Boca do Lixo, but they specify neither its terms nor its agents; a hectic world is adrift, triggering a merciless mechanism that leaves no space for a confrontation of forces that can lead the process in other directions. The cards are out of sight. However, the narrators state at the apocalyptic ending: "Nobody knows what will happen: fascism? communism?" Although this happens amid a series of weird statements, it makes an oblique reference to the 1968 political polarization, which is also echoed in the film by the use of sound recorded in students' demonstrations—a political action never named by the narration nor seen on the screen. Such a resonance is curious because it incorporates the contemporary fact in the form of noise, alluding to an atmosphere of social unrest that remains diffused through the experience of the characters, although they themselves know, after all, that they are framed by a social crisis. The radio is the narrative instance that describes the processes, but its trademark is ignorance, alarm, and cliché.

In *Land in Anguish* the 1964 factor prevails; the pain is generated by the coup. Rocha's baroque drama expresses the crisis of a whole political theory at a time when the historical decisions discussed are already a fact from the past (pre-1964). His way of underlining the mistakes of the orthodox Left is typical of the 1966–67 debate, especially in the emphasis given to the strategy that was not used in 1964: armed struggle. In the film, armed struggle is linked to Paulo Martins's sacrificial-metaphysical program, which, in fact, does not delineate a clear hope for victory; instead, it asks civil war to perform a fundamental function, whatever the result: to eliminate the formless character of the nation (the nation could not sustain, at this time, any consistent program). In any case, people paid less attention to Paulo's theory and more to the obvious call to arms evoked by the weapon hanging on the poet's arm. Rocha's film, in dramatic terms, was saturated with a feeling of mourning because of the realization that the delay of radical confrontation meant a long-term defeat, making the present unbearable. This same present experience was discussed by Rocha in the experimental film *Cancer* (1968), a dramatic laboratory made to underline the distance between the organized society (in the center, the intellectuals) and the huge and amorphous ground of the excluded, people whose world seemed to follow another logic. The armed struggle that did not take place in 1964 would come later in the form of guerrilla combat that remained a circumscribed gesture of a self-proclaimed political vanguard whose project encountered neither its proper moment nor its effective historical agent. The guerrilla was bred in the 1968 unrest, a moment of radicalization of the middle classes—especially the student movement—that produced mass demonstrations commanded by the young generation.

Placed in that context, *Red Light Bandit* does not provoke any discussion of political alternatives; this is not its way to allegorization. The film internalizes, in its own way, that critical moment. The social crisis, although external to the protagonist's journey, is constantly suggested on the fringes of the film and affects its structure. The "anarchic" option translated into this attention given to the individual "alone against all" is the film's way of expressing its connection to its political context. Its antiauthoritarian verve satirizes the established order, depicting it as its opposite—whence the sense of disorder that dominates the film. It is a tabula rasa stance that, structured as the expression of an identity crisis, exhibits the jovial trace of a confident good humor but, at the same time, the melancholy trace of failure. Near the end, J. B. da Silva, the King of the Boca do Lixo, is dead; people celebrate as in a classical comedy (with fireworks), but the affirmation of life does not last; the hero is condemned to death, and soon signs of suicide dominate the scene. That is, the irreverence of the representation, linked to the students' unrest, coexists with bitter premonition. This is condensed in the protagonist's fate, but it clearly is an allegory of the nation as a whole. We will see this melancholy again in all the rest of the films discussed in this book.

Both *Land in Anguish* and *Red Light Bandit* work deeply on the double register of the narrative, placing the voice-over at the center of the process, juxtaposing interior life and exterior world. In Rocha's film, everything is processed in the same serious, dramatic tone. In Sganzerla's film, a picaresque movement comes to dissolve pathos, added by the disqualifying work performed by the narrative agency embodied in the radio voices. *Red Light Bandit*'s characters are not placed at the center of the political struggle. The tendency is to move away from the social agents to whom the revolutionary vocation had been imputed (students, workers, peasants, intellectuals). Rocha's film is the one that really embodies the so-called decisive historical agents, and his view of them provoked scandal because he "touched the wound" by disqualifying such agents or, at least, their idealization. The union leader in *Land in Anguish* is clearly confused and co-opted, and the young militants represent a portion of the new generation that accepted social responsibility but that was not free from dogmatism. Judging their peers, they also expose themselves to judgment. In *Red Light Bandit* the young militants have no place, but their energy returns in the form of a coded noise that alludes to a crisis not mentioned in the film; in the last sequence, the music of Jimi Hendrix, juxtaposed with the *candomblé* (Afro-Brazilian beat), alludes to a portion of the new generation whose social engagement involved a rebellion that was globalized via the electronic culture of the media—pop music lived its moment of antiauthoritarian utopia at the end of the 1960s. At that juncture, political militancy and rock music were not mutually exclusive, but the students shown in *Land in Anguish* cultivate their alterity to the youth culture promoted by the media. In *Red Light Bandit*, this youth culture inspires the irreverent representation of national incoherences, but the ending reenacts Rocha's tone of disappointment with Brazilian political destiny. In his confrontation with social power, however, Sganzerla moves away from Rocha's drama and serious political debates. For him, reality is inscribed in a frame of more mundane disparities that are interesting to observe by eyes and ears not influenced by any doctrine of history. Not by chance, he focuses on those who do not have a known tradition—the ignorant, the excluded, the underground population that, for him, offers the best image of the whole nation; he has fun with their reading of the world (which is ultimately catalyzed by the media). Attacking conservative paranoia (which equates modernity and communism), Sganzerla tunes in to *tropicalism*, to the declaration of obsolence of the "grannies culture." For him, kitsch is like "second nature"; it is a trace of a national being observed with good humor. For Rocha, kitsch is the visible manifestation of evil, the sinister; a display of diabolical masks of power that when exposed produce uneasiness rather than fun. As figures of a nightmare, those masks are a product of politics and can never be accepted with that self-mocking stance found in Sganzerla's satirical view of "Brazilian misery." In *Red Light Bandit* kitsch has its own élan, its own grace, before being a visible face of repression or a sign of a precocious decadence of the oppressed. So the moral system of visibility that Rocha placed at the center of his representation of history dissolves. The "We can't take it any longer" uttered by Paulo Martins, in respect to the alienating game of appearances, expresses the exasperated disillusion of someone who wants to go deeper, supposing that thus he will find a more consistent ground. It is this dramatic search for national truth after defeat that marks *Land in Anguish*. Inverting this drama, Sganzerla takes the path of desacralization, dismissing any reverential attitude toward the nation. A typical strategy of the 1968 parodies was to explore the corrosive power of technical modernity in relation to the "Brazilian misery," which was taken as a social and an aesthetic feature, a stigma affecting rich and poor, permeating a national lifestyle that resented its distance from the advanced standards it tried to imitate. For the parody that sees the international standards in their positive role, any distance in relation the technically advanced has no nobility, and its representation requires a lowered tone that, critically, demoralizes the elites (by the aesthetic side of their misery) and refuses the direct expression of solidarity with the oppressed. The latter no longer form any ideal figure. The populist deformation that Rocha's cinema had already dismantled in serious dramatic terms, now in 1968 had to be attacked with a corrosive humor. The thematization of "national incoherences" did not aim only at criticizing the military regime; it was also the negation of leftist orthodoxy, especially the political culture of the Communist party, seen as inscribed in a closed game that had to be broken before one could see face-to-face the mass of the excluded. Even before 1968, Cinema Novo itself, together with a large portion of the politically engaged students, was already engaged in the critique of the traditional Left, seeking a new political culture. In fact, there was that strong impulse coming from a young generation that demanded a new interaction between culture and politics, a fact not easy to evaluate within the global process generated by the print and electronic media. The political struggle faced setbacks because of the transformation of its symbols into merchandise. The multiplicity of the images of revolution, on the one hand, problematizes its content; on the other hand, it provides a channel by which information travels, bringing to the new generation the sense of the simultaneity of multiple social and cultural movements—in the university, in the movies, in the theater, in music.

In Brazil during the 1960s, the critique of paternal provincialism had a psychological and moral dimension that perhaps had little effect in terms of the structural social changes demanded by political activism; however, this critique answered a demand for democratic social values that kept alive the idea of social justice and freedom. Critical texts written in those times already worked on the idea that the student movement could not be simply understood as the expression of a classical conflict of generations but, rather, was linked to specific features of the world juncture. The demands of the new generation involved a critique of both conflicting social systems: There was a rejection of the idea of a "good world" either in the so-called socialist systems or in the capitalist welfare society. And there was a rejection of the barriers placed by the imperatives of social organization, a stance that led to an increasing attack on science, technique, and instrumental reason (although this was not the jargon then used). There was May 1968 in Paris, the Spring of Prague, the antiwar movement in the United States, the emergence of the ecological movement, the counterculture. It is not surprising that it was in the cultural sphere of the young that one could find a reincarnation of the anti-institutional movements similar to those of the historical avant-garde of the beginning of the century. It is also not surprising that such movements faced sophisticated processes of neutralization in the media; and the sheer development of consumer society created new forms of control linked to the new dispositions of the so-called culture of narcissism. The romantic rebellion joined the market of images; much of what was a promise of rupture ended up as a replacement of dilemmas. But there was something more than just illusions and cynicism in the creation of the utopian moments, festivals of freedom that were quickly broken up by the police. As with the aesthetics of the avant-garde, the young militants had a political anxiety about the "radically irretrievable gesture," that could not be absorbed by the system; whence the theme of violence so decisive in all social spheres. This anxiety generated a radicalization that did not produce the desired changes but that at least set a new scenario and created new social roles within the imaginary of revolution.

In the Brazilian cinema, different artists found different ways of allegorizing the experience of the 1960s. The 1964 coup and the subsequent military regime gave a unique inflection to the cinematic approach of the different aspects of the juvenile subversion involving the tense interaction among political parties, university, family structure, and mass media. Cinematic allegory, while discussing the identity crisis also brings to the foreground the generation gap, the representation of private dramas that were already a theme in *tropicalist* songs. The wish to have a general diagnosis of the nation and the theme of failure were linked to the representation of new dilemmas faced by young artists. The filmmaker, especially, needed modernization, but he saw it at the same time as a menace because of its specific role in Brazilian society. Cinema Novo sought professional stabilization without putting aside the strong primacy of authorship, but it consciously avoided radicalizations that would lead to its isolation. The demand of authenticity had to find a new answer in a cinema that was more concerned with communication even though it was national and, if possible, modern. Among other films, *Macunaíma* and *Antônio das Mortes* expressed the major tensions implied in this alternative. On the other front, the avant-garde answer to those times came in films like *The Angel Is Born, Killed the Family and Went to the Movies*, and *Bang Bang*. These films were committed to the performance of the "irretrievable gesture"—by a certain order of things, of words, and of images—which, in politics or in aesthetics, acquired a central role in the perspective of a generation marked by the feeling of the inauthenticity of the established culture. In this sense, they in fact answered *Land in Anguish*, keeping on the agenda the idea of violence, of taking action with or without ideological inspirations, as the strongest weapon for undoing the unbearable game of appearances that permeated the entire nation.

In the diagnosis of the overall incoherence of politics and of national culture, the irretrievable cinematic gesture ended up being performed through the observation of figures of transgression. The new heroes were looked at while living extreme experiences, but in a context where the dissolution of history itself as teleology no longer allowed for the imaginary return of that nonexistent historical subject in Brazil: the people-nation consciously prepared to face revolution.

Part III

Allegory and Melancholy

5

Macunaíma:
The Delusions of Eternal Childhood

The Parameters of the Hero's Journey

Macunaíma's credits are superimposed on a large greenish-yellow screen and are punctuated by Villa-Lobos's "Desfile dos Heróis do Brasil" (Brazilian Heroes' March). Such a combination forms a well-defined prologue that stands apart from the rest of the film. A black screen and silence create a zero point from which the voice-over starts the narration: "Deep in the rain forest, there was a moment when silence was so striking while listening to the Uraricoera murmur that." The visual scene intrudes on the sentence and fulfills this special moment of expectation: We see the face of the actor, Paulo José, disguised in the role of a parturient mother, followed by the image of Grande Otelo, a veteran actor, falling on the ground as a newborn baby, screaming.

This is the narration of Macunaíma's birth. In these two shots, the film epitomizes its carnivalesque approach. As we will see repeated further on, the grotesquerie of the images brings a special sense to the "neutral" storytelling of the voice-over. The tone of voice indicates an omniscient narrator, whose trustworthy speech clarifies the scenes, exposes the hero's thoughts, and introduces new characters. Combined with other aspects—such as the journey's geography—this voice-over is a key tool that certifies the legendary dimension of the story. Throughout the film, the authority of the voice-over is unquestioned in the conveyance of the legend. The verbal enunciation and the scene are complementary; they split the job; the passage from one register to another optimizes the comical effect of each episode through calculated ironies, usually created by the occultation (in the speech) of what is obvious (in the image). The role of the voice-over—the partial presence of Mário de Andrade's text in the film—is to leave the spectator at ease to enjoy the journey, leaving the judgment of Macunaíma's attitude to other channels of the cinematic narrative.[1]

Though adapting Mário de Andrade's book, the film updates some of its central questions, concentrating on the discussion of the terms of the primitive–civilized opposition as framed by a critical observtion of contemporary society. The argument develops in connection with the performance of the protagonist, whose victory or failure signals the supposed virtues or faults of a collective being. Macunaíma performs as a syncretic figure standing for a "Brazilian" identity in its mode of insertion into modern society and its political conscience. By articulating the issues of identity and modernization, Joaquim Pedro offers a new reading of the "national character" in its interaction with the technical world.

Within the polarity rain forest–big city, we can see in Macunaíma's journey a spatial disposition of time that has as its pretext a territorial occupation. Settlement, economic expansion, migrations, extraction fronts, constant conflicts between natives and invaders, interracial crossing—everything has already happened, and these processes have left traces in the forest where the hero is born and in the composition of his family. In the film his birthplace remains visually undefined, with no features that could specify it as the arid *sertão*, the Amazon, or the High Inland. In fact, it is a semi-isolated site (there is contact with the distant world, as evidenced by its traces in clothes and objects). The hero comes into the world in a poor hut where the family lives under severe conditions. The effect intended is of a symbolically "rural Brazil" living in a time after that of the autochthonous tribe, despite keeping some traces of its material culture, its relation with nature, and its mythology. The ethnic plurality of the family group, the living conditions, and Macunaíma's baptism as a "hero of our people" identify this initial archaic space as "national," as a point of origin set in opposition to the space of migration, "God's world" that spills him into modern urbis.

In this place of origin, the early development of the hero is not properly set up. In the end, Macunaíma does not grow; he shows natural inborn talents that guide his behavior in the country or in the city, from beginning to end, in a process of a continuous repetition of himself that prevails over all changes. The important challenges are in the city, the space of adventure that remains, from the hero's point of view, a nucleus of an alterity with which he lives successfully but with no definitive engagement. At the end, he returns to his birthplace and confirms it as the source of his identity. However, this homecoming displays an unexpected rupture, a divorce between the hero and his old world. For Macunaíma there is no possible homecoming. The question remains to be answered: What has changed? the hero or the origin space?

The answer varies according to the terms that organize the journey. In the film Macunaíma's migration has a completely different meaning from the one proposed in the book. Things change in the film's narrative, and the word "journey" does not refer to a quest—as was typical of the Romanesque tradition that Mário de Andrade parodically incorporated in his rhapsody. The medieval novel and the work of the Brazilian writer assume an allegorical time-space, a disposition of facts that gives full sway to magical causality and to prodigious events. They have at their center protagonists who are half common man, half myth. Joaquim Pedro's film considerably alters the hero's relation to the Romanesque marvelous.

First of all, the film takes Macunaíma's magical powers away; he suffers miraculous changes, the world shows supranatural causal links, but the hero does not have any power on this ground. In fact, Macunaíma—born in a space that evokes the marvelous—is not shown as someone with more powers against natural laws than any other common mortal. His achievements are produced exclusively through his mental acuteness and by chance, in the manner of the trickster. When the marvelous interferes, its source is external to his will. The urban world in particular, changes its nature in the film. In spite of the improbability of the clashes, the asphalt jungle is not a place for total wonder. So there is no place for the book's farewell gesture in which the hero transforms the city into a sloth. Nature, for its part, is no longer a kingdom organized around Macunaíma, with its procession saluting him on his arrival and departure from the Uraricoera basin. The tissue of the united cosmic order—where, in its origin, the hero's life and death, the country and the city, the riverbank hut and the constellation Ursa Major were inserted—is now dissolved. There shall be no redemption in Macunaíma's solitary death, no celestial transcendence as an ultimate dwelling of the hero, who is tired of this world. His annihilation is complete.

Second, and even more conclusively, the film displaces the *muiraquitã* ("amulet") theme. Ci is the urban warrior whom the hero finds in the garage scene. The very place of this meeting dissolves the nature of the search, depriving Macunaíma's movement toward the city of its own ultimate purpose. In the book, Ci is the "forest mother," the great hero's passion, the owner of the *muiraquitã*. After her death, Macunaíma loses the amulet while fighting against Boiuna on a riverbank. Later on, the bird *uirapuru* whispers into the hero's ears the news that the stone was in the hands of the giant Venceslau Pietro Pietra, in São Paulo. The reason for Macunaíma's trip, as in the Romanesque tradition, is well defined: to search and recover a precious gift. In the film, the wandering of the hero and his brothers Jiguê and Maanape—undefined in the beginning—does not necessarily have the city as its goal. Since the quest dimension is not present, the film has to give the move toward the city new meaning, which it does through dialogue with another tradition: the fictional realism that takes us back to the cinema of the 1960s itself and to the literature of the 1930s. Macunaíma's move to the city receives the treatment used by Cinema Novo for the migrations of rural workers. He and his brothers arrive in the urban setting as migrants piled up in trunks, as anonymous figures who add to the daily quota of expatriated poor, images commonplace in Cinema Novo films. The linkage between the two worlds—the forest and the city—no longer has to do with myth (the search for the *muiraquitã*); it now has a sociological basis, reinforced in the film by the image of the arrival, by the driver's speech about the fate of unemployment and begging that awaits them, by the intervention of the voice-over that, ironically, defines the fate of Iriqui (Jiguê's mate) as a prostitute. With this displacement, the film does not leave the universe of the allegorical novel (there are magical metamorphoses), but it reinforces new circumstances that frame a "more real" space for the journey.

This switch of reasons is linked to the project of presenting a more critical view of the character, assumed by the film director and pointed out by the critics.[2] I prefer not to explore here the higher or lower degree of critique in de Andrade's book; my aim is to observe how the film treats the story, showing the logic that reigns, on the screen, over the representation of Macunaíma's adventure. In the film, there are new motives generated by the genre of representation, and as the analysis reveals, they are directly linked to issues raised in the 1960s, particularly the vicissitudes of the political conscience and the engagement with the context of modernization.

Macunaíma's route keeps its circular structure of leaving the land and returning home. Nevertheless, the displacement of the *muiraquitã* theme alters the meaning of nature's interference and the reasons for Macunaíma's fall at the end of the journey and for his divorce from a space that, at the beginning, was his ground par excellence. When the hero decides to come back home, the film compensates, again, for the lack of the original motivation with psychological explanations for his behavior. When he leaves the city and goes back to nature, he misses Ci—who now represents the city—and this feeling acquires a new sense in the hero's process of decline. The film emphasizes psychosocial relations and reduces the mythopoetic dimension, thus "shrinking" the polymorphic nature of the text in order to turn our attention to the interaction between Macunaíma, as a psychological type, and the urban society.

The world could be an antagonistic place that could cause the hero's collapse or his change. This does not occur, and Macunaíma achieves triumphs in the city simply by repeating his typical behavior, which is characterized by laziness, astuteness, and selfishness, all previously shown in his family life and in his interaction with nature. His competence in deploying this selfishness and seduction is never questioned when the impact with the city occurs. Macunaíma is polymorphic in his appearance: He is subject to impressive metamorphoses (he is transformed into a prince while puffing a cigarette; he undergoes ethnic change at a fountain); he shows, without any previous notice, what arises as a "natural gift" (the precocious lust, speech, reading). While in the city, the same gifts and the same behavior, molded by nature, assure Macunaíma's victory in the interaction with the context of the modern machine. This is an index of a familiarity that the film deals with on different levels.

Macunaíma and the Machine

The hero's relation to the machine is the central theme of his arrival in the city, when the brothers face the street, the red tape, the skyscrapers, the crowd. The voice-over comments on the group's arrival and explains the hero's "concern" while we see the series of shots that disclose the urban space as it might be observed by a pedestrian. The image tries to reproduce the immigrant's view (Macunaíma's, in this case), and the only scene that is more defined in the series emphasizes Jiguê's and Maanape's bewilderment when listening to the incomprehensible instructions they are given for legalizing their documents. Macunaíma is just sight and silence. The narrator expresses his reflection: "Now he did not know who was machine or who were people in the city." All emphasis is given to his perplexity and lack of action, to the theoretical and contemplative aspect of his questioning and anxiety before the new order of things. A night image accentuates Macunaíma's figure on the viaduct watching car lights passing by. This is the only shot in which the electric world of the urban night is shown in the film as an emblem of civilization. Joaquim Pedro's choice was not to emphasize the electricity, the cars, and the machine in the daily life of the city, although technology is a fundamental theme. Macunaíma's path is tuned in to the imaginary of the trickster and his small-time daylight swindling: lies, seductions, cheating those who either work or have some money.

While Macunaíma is watching the cars, the narrator explains his concerns: "The hero has spent a week without eating or wooing, just thinking about the machine." From this night shot we go to an image of the three brothers in a bed with several women. Macunaíma remains seated, pondering. This image underlines the reference to "a week without wooing," thus expressing a higher concern with the progress of the sexual comedy instead of a visuality that could underline the structures of this new space. Over this image of the group in bed, there is a comment: "On Saturday night, his thoughts became clear: Men were machines, and the machines were men in the city; Macunaíma felt free again and went for a walk with the brothers."

The hero's relation to civilization is not defined by that comic chain of failures in which the provincial shows fear, incompetence, or a lack of synchronization with the movement of the machine. The moment of arrival is taken as a pause for reflection, and at the end of a week Macunaíma's insight is philosophical. The film explores his surprise, and for us, as urban people, it proposes a new critical perception of the habitual and well known. It uses the hero as a mediator for a sin-gularizing process, for a rupture in the automatized relation of the audience to its own environment. In this reversibility between man and machine, the film follows the hero's point of view, observing modernity from the outside and seeing the technical world as a de-humanized environment. That is, there is a partial identification be-tween the "naive" perspective of the premodern and the film narrative when judging civilization. I say "partial" because the narrator talks about the hero's thoughts with his usual good-humored appeal, creating a context that shakes the seriousness of the reflection and underlines the playful information about his sexual abstinence. Progress and technology, for their part, are shown critically, thus losing their status as a higher ideal, as a standard of measurement. The observation of the technical world is placed on a level that pushes aside the issue of national competence.

Consequently, from the beginning the "primitive" is the one who focuses critically on technology and the urban man, and not the other way round. To understand the urban mechanism as alienation seems to be Macunaíma's way to freedom in his confrontation with the city as second nature. The tone of the interaction will immediately make it clear that Macunaíma's problem is not his performance before machines. His first contacts with the urban environment already promote Macunaíma's decisive encounter with his most typically modern experience during the entire journey: his relationship with Ci, the warrior. Here the technical world has an ostensible presence as a dynamic space for conquest (the garage elevator), as a living place (Ci's house is full of gadgets), and as a key factor in the event of Ci's death (the time bomb). The hero's affair with Ci is the condensation of the new in the film *Macunaíma*, in opposition to the old as represented by the modest boardinghouse to which the hero's brothers take him after the disaster, by the various street meetings in the hero's perambulations, and by the giant Venceslau's palace. These are places less marked by the more recent technology, spaces in which we meet characters of a Brazilian life "fauna." In no other moment in the film does technology participate in the development of the action as in the elevator scene, where we observe a production of a thorough orchestration of machine and man.

When the hero meets Ci, he not only dives into the advanced pole of modernity but also meets the archaic magical stone, the *muiraquitã*. This lucky token emerges in the film associated with urban woman and will become his heritage, the reason for fighting against Venceslau Pietro Pietra. Joaquim Pedro's film has its particularly inspired moment of mise-en-scène in the elevator scene, characterized by elaborate long shots that follow action continuity, with the precise use of two flashes when humor effect demands a rapid montage.

In the beginning of the whole sequence, the hero "smells" trouble in the middle of a desert street and a complete silence. We hear gunshots, and Ci appears, handling a machine gun, being chased by a car crowded with guards. A confusion is triggered and Roberto Carlos's music supports the introduction of the "tough-talking" woman, a musical sequence with a discontinuous succession of images (the woman kills her pursuers in a kind of Grand Guignol action, with mutilated arms and scattered blood). When this introduction is over, Macunaíma and his brothers help the warrior escape from the police by giving her pursuers misinformation. Once the policemen are gone, the hero gets excited at the prospect of a chase and walks toward the garage where the woman has hidden herself (Figures 5.1–5.2; page 153). When he gets closer, the camera puts us within Ci's point of view; she waits for him inside the elevator and observes him "smelling" her trail on the ground as if his one sense was that of smell (Figures 5.3–5.4; page 153). The hero now changes roles: Instead of chaser he becomes the chased, and Ci commands. She accuses the hero and threatens him; he explains the situation and expresses his desire. While they talk, the elevator goes up and down (the camera inside shows us the dialogue). Back on the ground floor, she is ready to leave but the resourceful Macunaíma triggers the door switches and closes the door before she has a chance to escape (Figures 5.5–5.6; page 153). She protests and they fight. The comic battle is depicted in a series of shots that conduct the up-and-down movement of the elevator with cuts and angles that give us an enhanced view of the histrionic side of Macunaíma's defeat (Figure 5.7; page 153). Higher in the building, while Ci is still beating him, the mechanism for getting the cars out of the elevator reaches Jiguê. Stone in hand, Jiguê hits the woman on the head and she falls. Macunaíma gives instructions to his brother and sends him down to guard the space while he starts to paw the unconscious Ci. Our attention is drawn to the brother's move and we are led away from the hero and his transgression; when we come back to the couple lying on the floor, we watch Macunaíma fidgeting with the *muiraquitã* hanging on Ci's neck. Ci wakes up and tells him to take his hands off, explaining the meaning of the stone. Next, the elevator arrives with the brothers. Ci's energetic attitude, once she is awake, frightens them, but her final gesture is surprising: She hugs the hero and takes him back to the elevator to "play." While the elevator goes down and the two embrace, the camera remains above to emphasize the couple's plunge while a contrastingly sentimental song associates an imaginary elevator (that never comes) and a frustrated hope for the "cursed woman."

Once the sequence is over, the hero's rite of passage into modern space is accomplished. The verticality of the elevator replaces the hammock swing as a seasoning for sex, and Macunaíma shows his seductive power facing the modern young woman, and his ability to command the machine. The elevator shaft is the conveyor that launches Macunaíma into the city's breasts (Ci) and transforms into a shelter what was once a threat. As in other moments, Macunaíma's talents and skills contrast with his brothers' clumsiness. The hero's contact with the technical world proceeds at Ci's house, where the modern signs come from electronics, weapons, working tools, and leisure gadgets that entertain Ci when she is not fighting in the city. The hero's hammock placed above the double bed is the instance of the archaic–modern opposition that follows the process of allegorization, typical of the period, in which the environment is a museum collection housing an incredibly broad spectrum—from the oscilloscope to the urtica leaf, from the TV on the ground to Ci's bombs—to all of which Macunaíma is completely indifferent. Except for the telephone, he does not touch anything; he is not interested in exploring the household machinery (Figure 5.8; page 153). When alone, he chooses total idleness rocked by the guitar's melancholy chords, resting with no further curiosity besides enjoying the benefits of Ci's den and her only demand, inserting his sexual potency, his desire, his pleasure, into a forced labor relation where he gets something in return that he really appreciates: money.

Everything in Macunaíma's later course will clarify the special nature of his relation to Ci—she is his highest achievement, his "Paradise on earth," a fulfillment figure with whom he will establish an unprecedented relationship. Ci is his major passion—a soft uterine prison. That is why she is also the loss par excellence, a loss that is configured neither in his mother's nor in his son's deaths but only in this feminine figure that demands only his penis and provides everything else. Ci and the *muiraquitã*—which becomes her symbol after her death—motivate Macunaíma's sole project: the struggle against Venceslau. This struggle is the only segment of the hero's life with a teleology, a definite quest. In the film, the stone is not portrayed as a real good-luck charm (after all, it does not protect Ci), a fact that reinforces its psychological dimension as a precious gift representing the hero's craving to recover his mate. Ci, as Paradise, was not only a shield against the world but also an instance of the hero's complete alienation even from her own battles. Macunaíma didn't pay attention to the specific nature of Ci's fights, a subject outside his agenda (the hero's indifference, quite consistent with everything else about him, is well adjusted to the vague-ness necessary at that time, 1969, because of censorship). In any case, the vagueness of the battles belongs to the image of Ci as a condensing figure. She simultaneously embodies an archaic myth (the domineering warrior woman of the Amazon) and allegorizes the modern woman. She condenses female militancy on the historic level, alluding to urban guerrillas and to clandestine life under the dictatorship in the city jun-gle; in addition, she is a sex symbol with a modern body that sports the insignia of the youth culture: consumption and advertising icons, blue jeans and white sneakers, no bra, loose hair. As a synthesis of these mass-culture elements, Ci collapses rock and roll and urban guerrilla culture, alienation and militancy, liberation from the capitalist order and market attachment. In a noisy and hasty way, she explodes into Macunaíma's life as the ultramodern, concentrating in the same figure the opposing faces of a consumer society that threatens the patriarchal moral code, giving a new rhythm to things and human beings, to pro-duction and the articulation of desire. Young and free, Ci is also the image of modern violence; she acts in a world dotted with ticking-clocks, the same ticktock that punctuates Macunaíma's reflections on men and machine. She moves in a space that requires acute calcula-tion, a distribution of energy according to the watch's hands' regular-ity, where a slip, caused by the "dispersion" imposed by desire, can be fatal. Voracious, Ci is the utopian reconciliation-of-opposites figure. As a curious affirmation of Macunaíma's jovial and lazy spirit in the universe of speed and time bombs, she is the mother-machine-lover who exposes herself to the maximum.

With Ci's death, the time of the time bomb disappears, and the hero's fate is to interact with idle people at the slow rhythm of occa-sional meetings in the park or near the canal, in the square where people gather to watch and listen to gossip, or on a desert island: that is, spaces outside the mechanical movement of the city. Venceslau Pietro Pietra, although an industrialist, is shown to us in his leisure and party mode, in association with environments that are far from symbolizing the modern even if the scene takes place in the factory. His speech refers to imported machinery, but the axis in this case is the irony toward dependent capitalism. His house, in spite of a few mod-ern objects, carries a heavy nouveau riche symbolism that undermines his modernist pretense. At the decisive battle, he threatens the hero with a bow and arrow, and, as usual, he is surrounded by an atmosphere that promotes a kind of correspondence between his city world and Macunaíma's Romanesque origins.

The film deals discreetly with the dynamism of the city world, without any emphasis on technology (except for the elevator scene). There are no more affinities between *Macunaíma* and a whole montage cinema tradition concerned with signaling the urban dynamics by a quick combination of images, by simultaneous effects, by a plurality of focus, and by speed. The alterity of this space in relation to the hero does not bother him: When meeting Ci he succeeds in practical terms. Almost always indifferent to the technical world, he is effective in the improvised use of objects that are placed in his range of action. His desiring look and interest are attracted to the magical, the prodigious, something that can bring benefits without any effort, whether a provider-mother or promises of easy wealth (note the duck he buys expecting it to "defecate" wealth). His performance in relation to technique is not his most serious problem.

The Hero's Victory and the Defeat: The Identity of the Archaic and the Modern

The modern space per se does not defeat Macunaíma or reveal any supposed incompetence of the hero. He is neither expelled nor swallowed by the city. His stratagems allow him to handle problems and face the exploitative impulse that dominates all the characters. Social Darwinism is central to his trajectory. In the middle of the jungle, where he is born and dies, or in the city, where he spends his days, Macunaíma moves in a universe in which the law of the hunt prevails: Devour or be devoured. This is the law of his first relation to the world outside his family—in his encounter with the monster *currupira*—and also the law of his tracing Ci when they first meet. In his war against Venceslau, the "giant who eats people," in different moments he is the victim of a grotesque hunting, and he eventually saves himself from being cooked in the caldron.

The law of the hunt finds its most complete expression, close to the end, in the wedding party given by Venceslau Pietro Pietra in his mansion: There, high society meets and shapes its carnival—its moment of excess, of play and derangement—as a death pact, as an instance of literal anthropophagic realization, as a self-cannibalizing lottery, a rite through which a class radically commemorates its predatory vocation.

The anthropophagic feast crowns Joaquim Pedro's metaphor of society: The technological world and civilization only define the sophistication of the weapons at play in a process in which, everywhere, the same logic prevails, equating the "primitive" and the "civilized," the jungle and the city, the struggles of nature and cultural competition.

Macunaíma—the film—asserts anthropophagy as the principle of interaction between the characters, as the rule of society. Having leveled the archaic and the modern, history as progress becomes sheer illusion, a bourgeois construct that conceals the modern barbarism. This is the imperative of "assimilation of the other," a kind of general law to which the film draws our attention. Within this imperative, all the characters' relations become acts of limitless consumption. Each encounter immediately defines a horizon of vampirism (either consensual or imposed), and the private space of the characters exhibits the signs of voracious accumulation typified by Venceslau's collection. Macunaíma, with his consumerist urges, is no exception to the rule. A congenital parasite, he feels at home in the small world of excesses he finds in the city. His figure is not surrounded by the emblems of privation that are usually associated with the oppressed and that are typical of early Cinema Novo's austere stagings. The *tropicalist* drive is present in the composition of several locations and even in the hero's facade (clothes and ornaments) and mutations (pimp, hippie, trickster, and rock singer). His goal is immediate gratification, a propensity to excess that turns him into the central piece in the kitsch that marks all personifications of this allegory. Sentimentality and a *nouveau riche* style of consumption define a general atmosphere permeating different class positions, thus making grotesque consumerism a kind of national trait.

Macunaíma, the personification of laziness, is outlined as a paradigm for such an undiscriminating consumption that receives its final expression in the collection of household electric gadgets—quite useless in the jungle—that he takes back home as booty after triumphing over Venceslau and rescuing the *muiraquitã*. Work having been eliminated, it is through consumption that Macunaíma touches the modern and establishes his adhesion to the mechanism of predatory appropriation. His adhesion to the universe of consumption only reinforces inclinations that he already had and that are stimulated in the urban environment.

When Macunaíma and his brothers leave the city, they take a young woman, ironically called "the princess," as part of the hero's booty. Surrounded by bits and pieces of his new treasure, Macunaíma tries to look like a teenager, wearing a cowboy outfit with sunglasses and playing the guitar like a rock singer. Juxtaposed to the idea of consumerism, his image in the canoe going back to the Uraricoera brings back the old theme of the "primitive" buying exotic baubles that he will not be able to use. The film reinforces such an effect when it eliminates the Romanesque universe of Mário de Andrade's book. At the beginning of the book the hero celebrated his fusion with nature as the Rain Forest Emperor surrounded by his vassals in a completely structured cosmos. In the film he has no kingdom, and the gadgets taken in the canoe will not become museum pieces with a symbolic value in a new cultural context. Once the hero's kingdom is dissolved, the vision of his collection as mere baubles prevails, and his gringo image is just one more of his assumed appearances. Back in the forest, he is the same Macunaíma—egocentric, irresponsible, and parasitic—and his laziness acquires a seasoning of melancholy with fatal overtones.

The hero's "great satisfaction," attributed to him by the voice-over when he leaves the city, does not last long. In the canoe he still has a feeling of euphoria, a feeling of power and fulfillment. The long shot, showing the river and the canoe passing by, shows the peaceful landscape as receptive to the hero's good mood, despite the irony of these relics of civilization piled up in the canoe that floats down the river according to the slow rhythm of the paddle and of life prior to steam and electric power. The modest aspect of his procession and his tacky clothes and manners clearly show the contradiction of a Macunaíma who is very self-assured but who is already singing the sentimental tune "Come, Let's Go Back to Uraricoera's Shore," a song of a retired provincial hero masquerading as a young rocker. Proceeding, we have his deep longing for Ci, his same old inertia amid the electronic gadgets scattered on the ground like wreckage, his rejection by his brothers and the princess who followed him from the city. One day he wakes up alone in his rotten hut; a prelude to his death. Before his end, there is a last metamorphosis in which Macunaíma, rejected, loses his enthusiasm and assumes the identity of Jeca Tatu, Monteiro Lobato's emblematic character who synthesizes Brazilian rural poverty as an idle hillbilly, worm-ridden, sick, and toothless in his precarious hut.[3]

Many anticipatory signs can be noted from the first moment of this frustrated homecoming: in the images of broken leaves, in the melan-

choly waltz on the sound track, in the hut that is waiting for them.
Why should it be that in this context—the old stage of childhood—the
brothers and the princess lose their patience and Macunaíma his charm?
I will recall the terms of the hero's journey in order to accentuate the
reasons for this final inversion.

From his childhood to his encounter with Ci in the city, Macunaíma
is a person with no goal, an improvisatory figure clinging to the present, responding to immediate whims. From desire to desire he builds
a day-to-day life made up of availability and noncommitment. The
death of his companion and the headlines about the whereabouts of
the *muiraquitã* trigger a first project—to recover the stone—and establishes a teleology within Macunaíma's temporal order, which was for-
merly mere succession. Although there are some unavoidable digres-
sions until the final triumph over Venceslau, the hero lives a moment
of commitment, a journey motivated by search for a value, by the
achievement of a goal that is not immediate, that requires some sched-
uling: The struggle imposes discipline on the previously unrestricted
pleasure principle.

Macunaíma reaches, then, a commitment that implies the conflict
with a father figure, endowed with power and authority, a conflict
caused by the "stealing" of a value associated to Ci—in the film, the
"city mother." The script of the journey searching for the *muiraquitã*
shows clear traces of the oedipal scenario, and after Ci's death, Macunaíma finds in his war against Venceslau his big challenge, his opportunity to confront a growing-up crisis, when the desire for Ci is the desire for the *muiraquitã* and Venceslau is the figure of interdiction.

Since they arrived in the city, the brothers supported and protected
the hero as a mischievous infant; they showed patience and an endless
self-sacrifice when dealing with the parasite's behavior, of which they
were always the biggest victims. During the war against Venceslau,
they fully performed their role of suckers, falling into the traps set by
the trickster. Macunaíma keeps his charm just the same, and he
reaches his peak of glory in the battle against the giant, in which he
overcomes great odds by using stratagems, especially in the final confrontation when he defeats the enemy and recovers the stone. However, following the law of desire, the appropriation of the *muiraquitã*
is an illusory fulfillment. Lack and nostalgia for the ultimate object
remain. Furthermore, we see a Macunaíma for whom the victory over
Venceslau, the journey to the city, and the experience of commitment

are far from constituting a rite of passage, a challenge that launches the hero into a new phase. Victorious, Macunaíma does not make the leap in quality. The conflict is badly resolved because it reinforces the hero's attachment to Ci in a regressive attitude that brings back his well-known script of childish selfishness. He does not grow up; he refuses the status of a providing hero, in charge of a world order; he does exactly the opposite. His adventure does not have a higher, sacred meaning, and his victory only exposes his precariousness. Macunaíma does not achieve God's grace or self-knowledge, so he will not have a tragic grandeur in his agony. A figure of sameness, he does not merit the hero's stature given to him by his brother Jiguê at birth. Admittedly, everything was a parody from the beginning, but what we have in the end is a greater deflation of his status as a smart hero. If he were a picaresque hero his fate would be a continuous movement, the constant replacing of adventure and new wits. But Macunaíma, on the contrary, goes back home to his childhood world, without achieving any special goal since his return is not an act of returning the amulet to its origin—he found it in the city.

In the old family place, isolation and the absolute lack of adventure give to the magic stone the same status as the collection of home appliances: They are useless trophies of an early retirement. Macunaíma loses his charm. The eternal childhood is the hero's "bad fortune"; this is the lesson of his victorious condition, which the brothers understand in this unfortunate return. Why bear new metamorphoses if they only reach mere appearance? Once this is understood, the fate of the hero is to lose his audience, to decline. The community abandons him, and with good reason, the film suggests.

Macunaíma's fall is merciless. Rejected by his brothers, all alone, he receives nature's final coup. During his journey, the hero faced challenges and was not swallowed up by the city. Upon his return, he is swallowed by Uiara, the monster with a pretty woman's face who personifies the dangers of the Amazonian lagoon. He dies because he is unable to win the support of his own originary world, as if, through the female seduction of the lagoon, this world takes revenge for his attachment to Ci, the warrior, the embodiment of modernity: The plunge into Uiara's waters is a death symmetrical to Macunaíma's pleasant plunge into Ci's world.

The hero returns as a winner but then goes straight to defeat. In the film, the circularity around the *muiraquitã* motif is absent, and his return has a touch of arbitrariness in the sequence of successes and failures. He does not go back in search of a conscience left behind in the forest, nor does he go back to recover his domains once he possesses the magic stone. He was not expelled by the new world, nor is he looking for the rain forest as a prodigal son searching for shelter after facing life's troubles. He goes back to show that his attempt to go backward in time leaves him midway, submerged in a decayed world, resourceless, as with Jeca Tatu's idle world—no longer "primitive" but not yet "civilized." Macunaíma's journey, in the film, is a parable of a migration with no return, of the problematic contact between two worlds under similar rules, the modern being a bypass to the return to a mythical harmony that, in fact, never existed. Why, then, is there this rigid posture in judging the hero who, on the other hand, has brought all the charms to the journey?

The Rejection of the Trickster

Death takes the hero unawares, in profound sleep. The happy times were definitely over at the swimming pool scene, when he lived his glorious moment and, in the comedy, was a hero. On his path to the pathetic, he suffers a series of setbacks that turn the taste of this comedy into something bitter, although the film has used his charm to seduce the spectator and satirically comment on the nouveau riche aspects of an urbanized Brazil that, in fact, restores the jungle paradigm. Sympathetic to the hero's antibourgeois mockery throughout the journey, we have to assimilate this outcome and ponder the exemplariness of abandonment, the connotation of punishment produced by the brothers' decision to withdraw from the scene. Such an outcome seems to play a well-defined role in the incorporation, with some reservations, of the tradition of the popular comedy. In dialogue with the *chanchada*, *Macunaíma* makes use of the communicative potential of the genre but at the same time declares the symbolic death, the exhaustion of its central character: the trickster (*malandro* in Portuguese), the urban folkloric hero celebrated in the theatrical and cinematic *chanchada*, in the radio culture, and in popular anecdotes. Randal Johnson, in his book *Literatura e cinema: Macunaíma*, points out the inversion of expectations as a key strategy used by Joaquim Pedro according to the genre he employs. The hero's cruel end, after a melancholy decline, has the effect of putting limits to his trickery.

The tone given to his death sequence does not mean a change in the focus of the film's narration. Since the beginning, the film has observed the hero very closely but from an external perspective, pervaded with laconic comments that left the ironic effect for the contrast between the utterance and the situation. While everything is successful, the tone of the scene contributes to the spectator's empathetic laugh and his identification with *malandragem* ("trickery"). Near the end, the images of the lonesome hero assume a pathetic air as Macunaíma takes on a mask of a charmless *caboclo* (the Brazilian poor from the southeastern countryside). But there is no sarcasm in the voice-over; there is only that same tone of fable that guarantees affection for the protagonist. The more direct irony will come in the last scene with the repetition of Villa-Lobos's "Desfile do Heróis do Brasil," which had been heard in the film opening. This return occurs when the hero has already disappeared in the water, captured by the seduction of Uiara, the "people eater," and we only see his green jacket, the green now acquiring a military connotation. The jacket floats surrounded by blood while the Villa-Lobos march ironically evokes civic euphoria.

The image–sound confrontation underlines several contrasts: between the early promise and the pathetic outcome; between Macunaíma's inglorious death and the exaltation of the fatherland's heroes; between the poor and unhappy land of the image and the "happy land of the Southern Cross" praised in the music.

In this final composition, there is a critique of mythical regression implied in the celebration of the putative happiness of the nation. But what, after all, is Macunaíma's role within the process? A victim? In this case, the final rhetorical twist would be trying to give resonance to the abandonment and the frailty of the hero, positing Macunaíma as someone sacrificed by Brazil, by the tropics, by everything that ornamental nationalism idealizes. But it is not quite in this ideological context that Macunaíma's death occurs. There is no movement within the film that prepares us to see the protagonist as a victim. Besides, we do not really support him at this moment. On the contrary, if there is any previous preparation, it comes from the judgment expressed in the brothers' gesture—they do not leave him without reason. As the cause of their last judgment, there is the hero's final lie, and the film's final twist truly crowns their condemnation of him. However, if what is sought is the demystification of the hero, why should one use this association with a military olive-green when this figure—so far from any idea of order and progress—dies? Such an association leads the critique too far, assigning to Macunaíma all the burden of rejection of the nationalist myths appropriated by the military regime: the exaltation of nature and heroism, the myth of a tropical paradise, and the trope of national destiny.

From the beginning of the film on, the use of the march as a frame for the narration insinuates an ironic equivalence, through the signifier "hero," between the civic referent and the protagonist's identity, establishing a subterranean bridge that goes from trickery to the victory of the military discipline. Concerned with the "myth of the *malandro*" as a national hero, the film wants to highlight the bitter fate of this figure within the space of a new modernization, assuming the two apparently contradictory legends—that of the *malandro* and that of the military hero—as two complementary translations of an imaginary construction bound to offset the national sense of inferiority. Joaquim Pedro's final gesture makes us think about a hidden partnership between "our people's hero," symbol of a "national" refusal of the work imperative, and the patriotic hero, symbol of order and discipline. Facing the ambivalence of the *malandro* as an individualistic hero, the film takes from the beginning a sympathetic stance toward its anarchist opposition to order; later it moves to diagnose its limitations and even suggests its conservative function: Might trickery, in the end, be a trace of established order?

Not by chance, the film identifies the worst aspect of Macunaíma's childishness as refusal to work: his lack of solidarity with his peers, his refusal to collaborate with the community. The hero's laziness, in the end, does not place him in opposition to an alien power, which might legitimate him by association with the historical gesture of the indigenous culture facing the colonizer. Considering the context of the brothers' rejection, there is no space for an eulogy to laziness as cultural resistance to domination. The critical view prevails, addressing laziness as a purely individual feeling. The values of an anthropology of work as a humanizing practice prevails over other stances. The film refuses to foster the symbolic and the feast as society's major structuring forces, just as it refuses to associate Macunaíma with the praising of the counterculture. Economics and politics form the basis of the critique, one addressed to military conservatism and to consumerism as a trace of modernity.

In its criticism of consumption as a value, the film struggles against the nation's illusory modernity, which is pegged to the dependence embodied in the figure of the opportunist industrialist Venceslau, the parasite who constitutes the elite *malandro*. That is to say, all classes in Brazil are *macunaímically* modern in their capacity for consumption, assimilating new waves and new products but ignoring the deeper secret of their production. The consequent progressive gesture, in opposition, would be the production of modernity and not only the hasty collection of new things. Thus the film suggests the falseness of the opposition between Macunaíma and Venceslau, given that the eternalization of the trickster pattern would be parallel to the eternalization of the reflexive, conservative character of modernization. The refusal to work is the revenge of the oppressed, which the film recognizes during the protagonist's trajectory, but only as a short-term tactic, without any broader historical horizon. The bitter ending suggests the exhaustion of the Macunaíma pattern as an ideal of national identity, despite the irreverent wisdom of the hero. Radicalizing the brothers' rejection of the hero, the narrative comes to an end with the "grown-up" perspective of condemning him as a regressive figure of an antihero. His path is recognized as dotted with victories, but in the end the film suggests a secret symbiosis between the anthropophagic order as a social rule and his individualistic whims. The insertion of the hero into mainstream society would well express the compatibility between his kind of behavior and the consumerist side of modern society, the basis for reproducing the status quo.

This is *Macunaíma*'s answer to the controversial aspects of Brazilian experience and culture. Maybe because of the conjuncture when it was framed, this response tried to ward off the self-indulgence involved in reiterating the positive dimension of the rite of national identity condensed in given values. As a result, the film ends up suggesting the negative and conservative dimensions of the hero in relation to revolutionary projects. Joaquim Pedro's film takes up again the dialogue with the *chanchada*, within the general process of recuperating the genre, a process triggered by the atmosphere of *tropicalismo*. Choosing an easily read language, Joaquim Pedro moved toward the popular paradigm, but at the same time he denied its basic premises. In fact, in its carnival tone, *Macunaíma* brings the same perplexity as do other Brazilian films to what is considered an outrage in the country's history—something went wrong in 1964—and the same desire to examine the reasons for the failure. The chosen strategy, therefore, is to involve Brazilian cinema in the old controversy about the "national character."

It is obvious that a problem was recognized: Along with socio-economic determinations, there needs to be a parallel anthropological incursion to clarify the national imaginary, to better ponder the Brazilian failure within contemporary history. The hero created by de Andrade's transfiguration of myth is treated, in the end, from a judgmental and pessimistic perspective, from a perspective interested in exorcising the naive faith in the virtues of individualism and *malandragem*, both seen by Joaquim Pedro as obstacles to a collective mobilization toward the economic and political production of a sovereign modernity.

Since 1967–68, in the cultural process fed by the Left there has been a movement toward an analysis of the specific features of the consumer society then gaining momentum in Brazil. In *Macunaíma* the urban world acquires an original representation that promotes not the cliché of incompatibility but, rather, the match between a typically modern alienation characteristic of mass culture, on the one hand, and that of the archaic "national character," on the other. In this sense, there is an affinity between the film and those contemporaneous theoretical reflections, then admittedly incipient, that create a psychosocial diagnosis of modernity pointing out the close relation between narcissism and consumer society. These theories underline the problem of infantilization within the process of mass depoliticizing, a process linked to fashion, advertising, and the empire of communication. Thus the most general issue of the social tutelage based on the consumer fetishism comes, in Joaquim Pedro's film, to show its national dimension arising from the complicity between what is presumably a Brazilian "natural" inclination and the mechanisms of reflexive modernization.

Macunaíma exhibits the sui generis model of integration of the "Brazilian way" in the world of technology and capital, a world that was previously consolidated by an ascetic and future-oriented mentality but that now requires a hedonist and *macunaímic* profile to those who wish to live under the tutelage of its consumer standards.

Figure 5.1

Figure 5.5

Figure 5.2

Figure 5.6

Figure 5.3

Figure 5.7

Figure 5.4

Figure 5.8

6

Antônio das Mortes: Myth and the Simulacrum in the Crisis of Revolution

Opening—the Past in the Present

The film that Rocha made in 1968–69 is a revision of *Black God, White Devil* hybridized with *Land in Anguish* and the *tropicalist* context. *Antônio das Mortes* (*O Dragão da Maldade contra o Santo Guerreiro*) brings back the *cangaceiros* and the *beatos*, in a reappropriation of the myth performed in a new and gloomier juncture. The representation of the peasants' rebellion reworks elements of the allegory of hope used in 1963, now with a stronger pedagogical intent: The representation of social conflicts underlines the "correct revolutionary action" to be followed. This affirmative pedagogical tone contrasts with the conscience of the crisis of revolution displayed in *Land in Anguish*. This pedagogy, though, is not all there is to *Antônio das Mortes*, and while analyzing its nature and boundaries, we can perceive in the film the same melancholy found in other films made in 1969–70. My analysis points out what is beyond the explicit classroom allegory and suggests the director's view of the country's modernization and its effects.

Once again, Rocha looks straight at the intellectuals' contradictions, and once again he uses his trademark: a mixture of didacticism and complex mise-en-scènes, now better adjusted to the standards of mass culture, as Cinema Novo's market project demanded in 1969. Combining political reflection and action film, the new iconography of the *cangaceiro* creates a show of colors far from the "aesthetics of hunger," and it incorporates the *tropicalist* aesthetics of kitsch. But we are still far from the fluency and continuity of the thriller, from shot–counter shot syntax. *Antônio das Mortes* brings again Rocha's theatricalism, the sequence shot, the handheld camera, the solemn speech, the long sequences in which the characters freeze and the tensions flow into arguments about power, myth, and history. Facing the new version of the Holy Warrior, let us analyze how the allegory of God and devil comes to dialogue with other "orders of time" that the Brazilian historical experience forced the filmmaker to take under consideration.

In the opening of the film, the triptych showing the image of Saint George killing the dragon calls forth the myth through a well-known pictograph very common in Brazilian homes. Therefore it signals a legend and its dissemination in the culture. In the following shot, the camera focuses on the arid *sertão*, the stage of another paradigmatic action—that of Antônio das Mortes. In this desert space, after a short interval of empty frames, he enters on the right, close to the camera, and slowly crosses the frame, firing away at the resolute pace of someone performing a task very deliberatedly. Shouts coming from off-screen signal the victim. Antônio goes out, and after a while, from the left there enters a dying *cangaceiro* with exaggeratedly trembling body who finally dies in the center of the frame (Figures 6.1–6.7; page 179). This long shot works as a motto establishing the icon Antônio das Mortes, setting up the action that sums up his identity: the *"cangaceiros* killer."* The modern electronic sound signals that the rule for *Antônio das Mortes* is the mixture of references and not the sheer reiteration of the materials of the nationalist tradition.

The two icons—that of Saint George and that of Antônio das Mortes—function as a mythical frame that precedes the time of action. The story begins in a little village in the *sertão* called Jardim das Piranhas (Caribes Garden), when Coirana, the *cangaceiro*, arrives. The first image of the little village brings us the figure of the schoolteacher who, in the open air and surrounded by a group of boys, recalls memorable historical dates and events. His list includes Discovery Day, Independence Day, the Abolition of Slavery, the Proclamation of the Republic, and the death of Lampião (the most famous of the *cangaceiros*) in 1938. The year 1938 is placed here as a historical date, the *cangaceiro* deserving as much attention as other heroes named in history classes. A procession, dotted with flags, of *cangaceiros* and *beatos* occupies the screen, bringing with it an Afro-Brazilian rhythm, a choir of harsh voices, and frantic dancing. In the teacher's lesson, Lampião is dead and the *cangaço* belongs to the past, but the procession forms a theater that seems to bring the archaic figure back. In the central square, the group silently lines up around Coirana, Antão—the Afro-Brazilian—and the *santa*, a white woman who wears a white gown and other adornments that specifically signal her affiliation with the Afro-Brazilian syncretic religious faith. The chief of police, Matos, passes in front of the camera that moves to catch Colonel Horácio on the right, all ears to balance his blindness. The camera goes back to Coirana who, staring at it, announces his reasons for "once again putting on the *cangaceiro* hat," all expressed in *cordel* poetry rhymes. Since the people are starving, his mission is that of the revenger, the heir of Lampião (Figure 6.8; page 179).

Coirana's challenge is cast in terms of the tradition, but the answer evokes an urban environment involved in other rituals with more civic connotations: the school fanfare in the parade celebrating Independence Day. The date was recalled in the teacher's class, but here the evocation is sponsored by the official power and expressed by the neatness and discipline of the boys in the parade: a double counterpoint—to the rebellion of the *cangaceiros* and to the messy and precarious class given in the little town to poor boys whose parents cannot afford to buy school uniforms. In the street, Police Chief Matos meets Antônio das Mortes—who is watching the parade—and leads him to a chat in a tavern, anxious to invite him to fight against Coirana. Like everything else about him, Antônio's answer is formal. In a long take of his face on the screen, he remembers the past with melancholy, but his eyes shine when he talks about Lampião, Corisco, and his fights in the *sertão*, a time that is over: "Now you come to tell me that there is still a *cangaceiro*. I cannot believe it. But I will comply with your request, sir. I want no money at all. I am going to Jardim das Piranhas to find out if it is true."

Once the situation is defined, a long shot of the region of Milagres—where the film was shot—takes us back to the dry lands, to the hills and to the little town and its square, the central stage of the battles. The musical theme for Antônio das Mortes in *Black God, White Devil* is back, punctuating the new representation of the same cultural context; this is now taken as an archaic world that reemerges in the present. In Jardim das Piranhas, the *sertão* shows traces of the new times: Antônio arrives by car and not on foot like the lonely walker in *Black God, White Devil*. The trucks, the road, the gas station, and the car-repair shop are near; we can hear the radio, and there is a tavern in the square, Bar Alvorada, whose facade has the same design as the government palace in Brasília, the Alvorada Palace. We are not in a closed, microcosmic *sertão*, an organic, cohesive world of social interactions. Now the *sertão* reckons its limits in the face of an exterior world, the source of the novelties that corrode the basis of tradition.

Colonel Horácio's domains are threatened by external forces. On the internal front there is Coirana, crying out for vengeance, throwing down a challenge that attracts Antônio to the fight.

At the opening of *Antônio das Mortes*, there is space for three speeches: the teacher's, Coirana's, and Antônio's. In all of them the central figure is Lampião, recalled as a historical figure (school memory), an old rival (Antônio's personal memory), and a myth to be revived (Coirana's attitude). Lampião is the spirit of rebellion updated. His death, in the teacher's class, is the key for a historical and evolutionary line that prepares the achievement of the telos, which is freedom. Coirana claims that his violence is performed in the name of justice, to accomplish the "unaccomplished." In these speeches there is a suggestion of time as evolution—Lampião as a step of a national history. But this suggestion is superimposed on the circular time of restitution of the Holy Warrior's archetypical battle between good and evil. So we have different "orders of time"—the mythical and the historical—placed by relationships and signs involving the main actors of the allegory.[1]

First of all I examine the new *cangaceiro* and his followers, the religious discourse, and the clamor for justice. At the center we face the collective force that is after all unable to be anything more than a show of dance, song, prayer, and death. What sense does this "past in the present" acquire within the argument about the revolution? Is Coirana a necessary link in the path of national redemption? Or is he just a faker whose insurrection is nothing but a simulacrum of history?

The Sacrifice of Coirana: The Teleology of Salvation

After his speech in the square, Coirana looks for shelter in the hills surrounding the city. Colonel Horácio feels the threat, although he does not believe the seriousness of the whole thing ("I have heard that this *cangaceiro* is pure theater"). Antônio arrives, and the conflict unfolds in two movements. In the first, we have the polarity Antônio–Coirana, as the "*cangaceiro* killer" arrives ready to shoulder his task. This does not happen immediately, and his relation to the powerful is quite confusing. Police Chief Matos shuffles business and repression, and the colonel makes it clear that he does not want Antônio: "Unpaid assassin brings bad luck." In any case, when Coirana descends the hill and once again comes to the square in the village, the duel between him and Antônio das Mortes eventually occurs. Antônio hurts his opponent but does not kill him, thanks to the interference of the *santa*. The expression in her eyes deeply impresses him, paralyzing his aggression and, from that moment on, she starts to guide his conscience. During Coirana's agony, Antônio, feeling guilty, becomes more melancholy, begs God to forgive him, and sets himself against the powerful. Moved by Coirana's suffering and affected by the *santa*'s sermons, Antônio joins the cause of the oppressed. The hired assassin Mata Vaca, who was the colonel's first choice, arrives from Minas Gerais with his gunfighters to replace a repentant Antônio.

In the second major movement, there is a new disposition of roles within the antagonism between the colonel and the starving masses. The central tension remains; there is a stoppage in the main line of action, and the scandal breaks out within the colonel's private sphere. Before his primary mission of exterminating the agitators, Mata Vaca is led into chasing Matos, whose affair with Laura, the colonel's wife, has gotten to her husband's ears. The family conflict spreads to the square, causing a pandemonium; meanwhile, in the hills, people peacefully pray around a dying Coirana. The atmosphere of death thickens: Matos is executed, and the colonel orders the massacre of the *cangaceiro*'s followers. Once Matos and Coirana are dead, Marlos Nobre's electronic music lends a special dramatic tone to the events, which accelerate after the colonel's order. The sound asserts a unity of principle, and an atmosphere of trance reigns over the whole place at the moment when the massacre against the people is carried out. This happens simultaneously with two funerals: Matos's, at the cemetery, where Laura and the teacher lie down on top of the corpse, hugging and kissing each other while the priest keeps trying to separate them; and Coriana's, in a place deeper in the *sertão*, guided by Antônio das Mortes, who atones for his sins. Both funerals are cut short by the shootout. The only survivors of the massacre are the *santa* and Antão; the latter saved by the strength of the former, who paralyzes Mata Vaca and scares him away. Marlos Nobre's music dissolves along with the paroxysmal tone of the drama. Antônio das Mortes and the teacher arrive late at the scene of the massacre, but they establish a union that, inspired by Coirana's example and blessed by the *santa*, will combine forces to act on behalf of the people and march against the colonel's hired gunmen. In the final sequence, Antônio das Mortes kills Mata Vaca and, with the teacher's help, all the hired thugs, and this justice is crowned by Antão's attacking the colonel with a spear, the Holy Warrior killing the dragon (Figure 6.9; page 180).

His mission over, Antônio das Mortes goes back to his lonely world, but now he has a new consciousness. Followed by the priest and the *santa*, Antão resumes his pilgrimage through the *sertão*, now free from the spirit of obedience that had followed him until he attacked the colonel. Once the lesson is learned, the protagonists who have fought on the people's side leave the scene. In their victory, there are signs that perhaps the achievement of the new has come closer. We cannot say that there is a new order in Jardim das Piranhas, but there are some changes that seem to be decisive for the fate of the characters in other places: for the fate of Antônio, Antão, and the priest. Such changes have at their root a basic element: the sacrifice of Coirana.

The *cangaceiro* in *Antônio das Mortes* is a fragile hero whose grandeur is questioned in the beginning. However, he acquires a posthumous density that projects onto his journey an evangelical resonance. Around him takes place the most symptomatic oscillation in the film. Much of his strength comes from the protective figure of the *santa*, but it is his action that triggers the movements and casts the challenges, as if to confirm Corisco's speech ("If I die, another will come because Saint George, the saint of the people, can never die").Wishing to repair all the injustices of the past, he wants to be a "watershed" in the order of time, a redeemer awakening, once and for all, the oppressed. Such a decisive mission echoes in the voice of the *santa*, who refers to the "endless war" about to explode. And visual signs gradually insert Coirana within the typology of Christ despite the initial diagnosis of Antônio and the Colonel that he is "pure theater."

The suggestions of Coirana as a simulacrum are strong, and in truth the configuration of the group he leads is peculiar: a self-oriented carnival procession, absorbed by chants and dances, seeming to be living in another time and space in its agitation, always refractory to the relation to the surrounding world. It is a human group that in the uniformity of its action (or inaction) embodies, first of all, a unitarian idea of "the people." At the same time, it shows a style that enhances the stereotype of alienation: chant, dance, and religion. However, everything is so radically composed in front of the camera that it creates an awkward feeling. The dynamic of the procession avoids any observation of its dance as charming folklore or illustration. Its mark is the boldness of those who invade a space where they do not fit. Those in power see the group as a menace and answer with violence. Coirana's "people" do not carry any intentionality, but they are an odd presence, out of control. Because of their performance—some would call it Dionysian—they embody a phantom of disorder that deeply affects the safety of the landowner. Not by chance, in the scene of the disturbance in the square when Antônio hurts Coirana, the colonel complains precisely about the "devil's chant," a dissonance in his world. The mass is a menace because it recalls its difference, although its presence is full of rites, not of demands, and its spokesperson takes his power out of the theater of the *cangaceiro*.

Thanks to the awkward configuration of his army, Coirana's challenge really seems like theater. However, this theater concentrates all the ambiguity of the style of representation in *Antônio das Mortes* because its action continues to incorporate the force of the world around it. It is on its terms that is set the great duel in the square, marked by the rhythm of the religious choir and under the protection of the *santa*, to whom Antônio bows. The duel certifies Coirana's challenge, which, in principle, is anachronistic. Moreover, he is raised from the condition of being a false *cangaceiro*—who simulates a past that is over—to the condition of being a legitimate embodiment of Lampião's legacy. Gradually endowed with evangelical pathos, he seems to acquire a mission beyond his forces, and despite his wrecked sword he dares to defy Antônio and accomplishes the full rite. Then in his agony, surrounded by devotees, he starts talking as if invested with an authority about himself, about the journey in a world full of poverty, and about the "*cangaceiros* killer," whom he accuses of being an agent of the "dragon of wealth." Dead, he has a decisive influence upon Antônio and upon the teacher; he acquires spiritual power through death, which consecrates him. His last image, crucified in the middle of the *sertão*, attests to the achievement of the desired aura: the scene of the contemplation of Christ-Coirana brings the decisive dramatic turn before the final movement of the film.

At the moment of the massacre of the people, Antônio, who was embracing Coirana's corpse, leaves it in the *sertão* without finishing the task of burying it; the sound of gunshots draws his attention. The priest and the teacher also rush back to the village and in their turn leave unfinished Matos's funeral. The priest locks himself inside the church, but the teacher goes to the place of the massacre, arriving at the hillside at almost the same time as Antônio. The latter is talking to the *santa*, admitting his sins and placing at her feet his rifle and his hat. His retirement now seems definite, although the *santa*'s gesture—holding the sword horizontally in front of his eyes—and the bloodstains on the stone at the side of the screen compose an image that calls up war. The teacher discharges his fury upon Antão's figure, beating him while uttering words of despair that evoke the national dimension of this morbid scene on the hill. This despair leads him to the roadside, to the taverns in the village, while Antônio wanders about haunted by repentance and by the image of the *santa*, with her sword and her prediction: "Then, the endless war will break out." In the city, Antônio looks for the teacher and finds him drunk. After this journey through hell they go back to the hill to receive the inspiring image. Antônio guides a weary teacher going up the hill until the image of Coirana comes into sight, and they suffer the impact of what seems to be a revelation.

The image of Coirana is introduced by a point-of-view shot in which the zoom in dramatizes the scene of the crucified: Coirana's corpse, with open arms, remains standing, hooked into a tree, showing all the emblems of the *cangaço*. One could doubt if this is a hero worthy of such solemnity. Here, however, he is more than Coirana. A symbolic figure, he updates the tradition of the avengers' call for justice, warriors with a conscience haunted by a salvationist mystique. He is the new body apt to remake the promise of the "endless war." Antônio and the teacher, after facing Christ-Coirana, go down the hill to the battle. The teacher leans over the dead *cangaceiro*, taking from him the revolver and the sword; Antônio is blessed by the *santa*, who gives him back his gun and his hat.

When the image of the dead *cangaceiro* is shown, the voice over of a folksinger starts the famous "Chegada de Lampião ao inferno" (The Arrival of Lampião in Hell). This folksong narration punctuates the whole segment, including the scene of the final battle. The song reasserts the subversive vocation of the king of the *cangaço*. Over Coirana's image, the singer endorses, on behalf of tradition, the gesture of this small hero who eventually embodies all the "insane" who, in the conservative words of the colonel, "went mad trying to transform this *sertão* created by God, which nobody can change."

Contesting the colonel, a whole system of speeches suggest the effectiveness of Coirana's sacrifice in the higher order that define people's fates. In the sequence of Coirana's agony, the scenes involving himself, Antônio, Antão, and the *santa* acquire a composition and a color treatment that reproduce certain features of Renaissance and baroque iconography: The images of the *santa* strive for the classic poise, the building of the glance that involves the peasant woman in a halo of serenity and balance; the images of Coirana, more baroque, bring drama, the expression of pain, in a process that reaches its paroxism with the use of the *cangaço* as a Passion (Figures 6.10–6.12; page 180).

Within the characterization carried out so far, the film's language and iconography endorse the authentication of Coirana's mask, the consecration of the force coming from the legend. In other words, it asserts that myth is necessary to make history, to change society, to turn things upside down. That is the reason for the typology of Christ, the evocation of the archetypical battle of Saint George. However, this view attesting to the effectiveness of myth is not alone; it exists side by side with opposing forces that scramble the meaning of the representation. There are oscillations of tone, impure actions that dishonor the homogeneity of the ritual. In order to assess the real status of Coirana within the narrative, we must examine the perspective that the film draws, in the end, for those who suffered the impact of his sacrifice.

Antônio das Mortes in the Curvature of Time

With the colonel dead, the biblical words "an eye for an eye" are fulfilled in Jardim das Piranhas. However, it would be an illusion to see the victory of the avengers as the basis for a new cohesion within the sphere of the oppressed. Once the final rehearsal is over, the "endless war" remains on the horizon, but it is not toward such a goal that the main agents of the rebellion are moving. Again, Rocha's mise-en-scène makes the calling to militancy and its problems live together: He affirms the axiom of revolution but presents a configuration of things in which we can perceive its narrow viability.

The teacher's behavior ends up reinforcing the transitory and capricious character of his commitment. Once the battle is over, his movement is regressive, fixed on the figure of Laura, whom he kisses and carries to the middle of the square even though she is already dead. The energy of the fight is channeled to the expression of this desire, previously announced in Matos's funeral. The last image of the teacher consists of a static figure, twisted, in the corner of the frame at the side of the colonel's and Mata Vaca's corpses, worn-out from the fight (Figure 6.13; page 180).

The survivors of Coirana's procession—Antão and the *santa*—leave Jardim das Piranhas to a new pilgrimage, now led by the priest wearing a white garment. In this small group one can see signs of an inclination to political struggle, and the trio of Antão, the *santa*, and the priest asserts a new unity among the oppressed race, popular religion, and the Catholic church. But the group's specific composition and confinement are far from promising effective action in any near future. The priest, as if bewitched by the charisma of the popular figures, takes upon himself the idea of fighting, in contrast to his ineffectual interference in the conflicts in the village. The *santa* in white is the syncretic figure who consolidates the group: the carrier of the African deities' power and the prophet of Christ-Coirana. However, her function is to protect by means of her hypnotic eyes, not to use weapons. Antão acts as a Saint George in the end, passing to insubordination; but his aesthetic affirmation in the paradigmatic gesture is not immediately transferred to his image as hero. Plunging the spear into the colonel, he wins approval from the audience in a cathartic moment; however, his image as a warrior is still haunted by his contemplative pose throughout the film. His time is a not-very-near future. Therefore, although inspired for a privileged moment, Antão is unable to assert himself as a leader who opens new paths. This role, claimed by Coirana, is effectively performed by Antônio das Mortes, who makes way for the "punishment" of the blind colonel.

Antônio steps out of the scene as a lonely hero, and his accomplishment in Jardim das Piranhas does not produce any significant historical change. He dispenses justice and departs, suggesting in the end a cyclic movement that points toward a fresh beginning in another place (or another film) in the same terms. Repentant, he is converted but does not seal a pact of destinies either with the oppressed or with any other social group. The battle is barely over, and the old song that identifies him as a damned fellow returns to celebrate his mythic identity, exactly when we see his static figure composing a picture in which the *santa*, Antão, and the priest start moving—no victory succeeded in dragging out from Antônio his typical look. The refrain "*cangaceiro killer*" will be repeated over his last image when we note his melancholy move, back to the camera, on the roadside.

Once the separation of the winners is defined, the narration stays with Antônio, the center of the argument. And the disparity of visual treatment between his first and last images reaffirms his displacement from a full-fledged hero, pure allegory, to a human hero, subject to hesitations and small dramas. By "gaining consciousness" he refuses his former image as a merciless killer, a personification of forces. He acquires a better definition as an individual able to suffer changes. The very first sequence launches him into the flow of time, marks him as vulnerable to natural decadence, as an old man who needs retirement. At the same time, the film preserves him as a special character, whose infallible action seals the destiny of those around him. Although emotionally vulnerable, he has an excellence that the others lack.

In this oscillation between myth and character, his major role is, again, the embodiment of contradictions. The terms of the equation change, but Antônio cannot avoid the stratagems that have defined him since his presentation in *Black God, White Devil*. There he said: "I'm gonna kill Corisco and then die because we are all the same." Because he was identified with the mission, killing the last of the *cangaceiros* would also mean his death. This is how he understood his making way for the great war, according to what was stated in the teleology of the liberation of the oppressed. A figure of the necessary violence, Antônio could only be seen as the realization of the logic of history. It was impossible to think of him as a retired hired killer, enjoying memories of the *sertão* while in the city, watching the school parade and hugging a stupid chief of police as an old drinking buddy. What happens in *Antônio das Mortes* reveals the person who is old enough to have a nostalgic relation to his past. The epic times are far away, and he accepts Matos's proposal in order to avoid boredom. This psychological dimension, though, does not cut off the sense of damnation in the style of the ancient mission: "If there is a *cangaceiro*, sir, I have to kill him too." The expression "have to" shows a trick rooted in Antônio's melancholy, whose lack has no remedy because his desire calls for his subject in order to suppress it. He is prone to repetition.

The real movement of society helps Antônio in his compulsion to repeat because it is the persistence of a state of things and the collapse of the teleology of *Black God, White Devil* that offer him his survival and the return of the *cangaço*. His task was the creation of the conditions for a new time from which he was excluded. Now we find him available in that same future that was not meant for him. The time has gone by without bringing the recondite novelty—the great war—and he is condemned not to die. Before, it was impossible to distinguish between good and evil—evil was a requirement for the building of good, and killing *cangaceiros* was a way of "saving them," making them perform their role in history. Now, in this displaced reenactment of the same struggle, the new film offers an opportunity for the ancient teleology, as it evangelizes Coirana. But this evangelization is surrounded by a melancholy—not exclusively Antônio's—that affects the whole story. In fact, we have a disenchanted history because the sacrifice of the *cangaceiro*, as an exemplary Passion, is unable to impose the pattern of hope into the whole film. There are undoubtedly movements of conversion: Antônio repents, the teacher is reborn from his nihilism, Antão becomes disobedient, and the priest eventually carries a rifle. In this movement, a time of redemption is announced. However, once the battle is over, such a time does not seem to be able to flourish. Now, the narration of the film does not crown its story with a refrain like "The *sertão* will become sea" over the peasant's flight and over the image of the telos (sea) in the end. Instead of a song that foresees the consummation of a new era, *Antônio das Mortes*, in the end, reasserts the melancholy tone typical of its frequent moments of immobility, in a kind of a reflux of the epic style. Suggested by the dissolution of the collective force mobilized for the final battle, this antiepic tone is confirmed by the final shot in which Antônio leaves to go back to the big city. On the roadside, the gas station points out the work of another time, foreign to Coirana's sacrifice; a time that goes by in a world that surrounds the scene of the fight and threatens to invade it, but that was absent in the chronology evoked in the beginning by the teacher—the accumulative time of the technological modernization and of the economic growth (Figures 6.14–6.15; page 180).

In the end, Antônio remains as the major support of the allegory, but his adventure is designed as a return to the past that ends up on the roadside, near a Shell gas station. This is the passageway at the frontier between two worlds, the *sertão* and the city, and it announces the rhythm of the technical being, the modern flow of goods that turns Colonel Horácio's mentality and Jardim das Piranhas's apathy into peripheral realities. Antônio on the roadside does not mean the threshold of a new era; it only means his return to the conveyor belt of a time that runs faster than his tired pace and seems to ignore his experience of a late enlightenment in this end of the world. The adventure is designed as a cycle in which, in the end, Antônio hopelessly faces the same conditions as he did in the beginning. Killing Corisco did not lead, in its turn, to the "great war." What did Coirana's death mean? It is difficult to accept this antihero as an agent who may be able to reconnect the world to the teleology of the revolution; it is difficult to accept that this time Antônio has participated in the preparation of the "great war." His final action produces a kind of "poetic justice" proper to the tradition of a didactic allegory in which punctual interventions of the hero repair the wrongs of the world but without requesting that logic of history expressed in the allegory of *Black God, White Devil*.

In *Antônio das Mortes*, the time of teleology, expressed in Coirana's sermon, does not in the end receive the confirmation that would clearly show the promise of overcoming the cyclic time of that endless repetition of the Holy Warrior's fight. When repenting under the *santa*'s tutelage, Antônio passes from the "wrong side" (where he was) to the "right side," confirming the assumption that he had "misbehaved" in the past. By doing so, he destroys the teleology that supposed his repression as a necessary act, as an impeller of history. Within this new reference, the aggression against Coirana is a sin that cannot be redeemed, even when he punishes the colonel and Mata Vaca. His is a place of eternal reparation; he does not even play the role of a civilizing agent because the effective changes come by technique and schooling. In Jardim das Piranhas, some signs of a world of motors—cars and trucks—and plastics are shown, and they can be found in the space of the colonel's house itself: in the domestic life, the can of lubricant oil is transformed into a flower pot and the urban femininity is associated with the artificial flower arrangement. The school is not an orderly and efficient world; rather, it is a constant presence from the opening sequence on; the teacher's status as a civil servant makes evident the marginal presence of the state in the village, although the order is centered in the figure of the colonel.

In *Antônio das Mortes*, the logic of the allegory does not expel the most prosaic data of the present, the signs of modernization that come to mark a cumulative linear time. Such signs testify to changes that are foreign to the messianic structure assumed by the teleology of history inspired in Christianity. Then this teleology is questioned both from "inside and outside." On the one hand, it is the invasion of the time of technical history that hinders the configuration of the *sertão* as a totality. On the other, the theater of the oppressed itself brings an "exorbitant" presence of circular time, of the paradigm of good and evil. Not by chance, in the end, we jump from the shot of Antônio on the road-side to the popular figure of Saint George that closes the cycle. The last image of the film repeats the first one and, again, is associated with the shot of Antônio. Coirana is dead and Antão departs, taking Saint George's spear with him. Because of his popular origin, because of the association of his figure with Ogun and other African deities, Antão is the heir of slaves who in the end asserts the rebellious vocation of the oppressed. Yet in terms of the structure of the film, the ultimate em-bodiment of the saint is Antônio. It is upon him that the *santa* confers the weapons and the task of extirpating the evil, once she knows that he is the one who has the strength. Such figures of mythical repetition, however, do not tell everything because here the legend emerges from its purity, contaminated by the world of technology.

The Avenging Hero: Myth, Industrial Genres, and Secular History

While characterizing the oscillations of perspective in *Antônio das Mortes*, I have pointed out three "orders of time" in its narrative: the prophetic-teleological, the archetypical, and the technical-material. Now I discuss intertextual relationships that allow for a better clarifi-cation of the allegory, given that Antônio's new condition as the pro-tector of the oppressed strengthens his connection to the hero of a spe-cific genre: the western.

At the end of the film, the stain that follows Antônio condemns him to renewed exile, reminding us of the hero's destiny in classic westerns. On the other hand, his image and his lonely journey better recall the hero of the Italian western, a tough guy who arrives looking like the landlord's hoodlum, who ends up as an ally of the oppressed, and who, once the fight is over, departs with the same enigmatic look he had on his arrival. Rocha's film makes clear his relation to the Italian genre, which had its summit exactly in the second half of the 1960s. In *Black God, White Devil*, there were some references to the U.S. west-ern. Then, by crossing influences, the transformation of the genre in Italy eventually led to an industrialization of an iconography closely akin to the profile that Antônio das Mortes had had since 1963—images of a lonely hero like Django seem to be inspired by Rocha's killer. In Sergio Leone's films, for instance, a more realistic context is produced by the blatant exhibition of the material interests behind the commitments in the name of justice. Parodic, the Italian western alters the rules of the genre, and it withdraws the "good guy" look from the errant and enigmatic figures who offer their skills to honor causes to which they remain strangers. In the classic format of the American genre, the hero enabled the victory of the law against the empire of violence; it transferred to a new geography and a new historical time the Saint George of the medieval legend, fighting evil to assure progress. In this context, fighting against the local bosses meant, for the civilizing hero, preparing the grounds for a legal structure of a bourgeois society understood as an ideal of democracy already achieved (in the twentieth century). The idea of modernization had an epic dimension, identified with the advance of a new order accepted as legitimate. Conversely, the law in the Italian western is that of an advance of Social Darwinism. The western scenery becomes the locus of contradictory and professional heroes, rebel figures moved by an ideal of revenge and anarchic rebellion, like the social bandit who emerged from the oppressed Mexican peasantry. That is, we are facing a configuration of rural experience closer to the tradition of the Brazilian *cangaço* such as it was represented in *Black God, White Devil*. In *Antônio das Mortes*, Rocha goes back to that national imagery and, at the same time, quotes the Italian genre—which had industrialized the style of Antônio das Mortes—reworking the choreography of violence, the enigmatic stillness of the hero, the intensity of colors.

The difference here is that Rocha legitimizes the violence of the oppressed by inserting it in a teleology of history, a path toward justice. This fact differentiates his films from the Italian western, in which evil results from a social machinery that involves everybody, including the hero. Rocha wants to keep in sight the idea of a struggle full of meaning for the community. Against the ironic evidence that "everyone is out for himself," he wants to keep the idea of revolution as a collective project. But this time he does not want the didactic allegory to be that symbolic recapitulation of the historical process and its sufferings that was performed in *Black God, White Devil*; its purpose is to assume the mythical action as the "good example" to be followed, to materialize the dream of victory of the oppressed.[2] Saint George's legend requires the staging of a moment in which justice is made and the forces of good win because tradition, since the Crusades, has established him as a victorious saint, not as a martyr. It was in these terms that the legend struck roots in the popular culture, collecting projections of a sense of justice that Rocha tries to transform into a revolutionary drive. His project is to affirm a victorious destiny against evil—the same that typifies the hero in the classic western—in a political film in which, unlike in the classic western, that victory does not create the illusion that true historical justice has already been accomplished. His problem is to reconcile such an idea with that of the mythical hero shaped both by the industrial genres and by the oral popular tradition. So he tries to mark his difference from the two versions of the western, embodying the Holy Warrior in a figure distant both from the "good guy" and from the cynical professional.

To balance its demands, *Antônio das Mortes* produces a relative instability, a constant displacement in the figure of the avenging hero. That is why the avatars of the saint are multiple: Lampião, Corisco, Coirana, Antão, and Antônio das Mortes. Antão brings with him the blessing of the *santa*; he rides his white horse and takes hold of Saint George's spear, now covered with a green-and-yellow ribbon (national emblems) in order to make clear the nationalization of the mythology and the survival of the saint among the people. Redemption will come through the action of the oppressed since they reach insubordination by "correctly" reading the religious tradition—African rite, peasant Catholicism. This correct reading will come from the national experience of pain and death, just as Paulo Martins in *Land in Anguish* hoped would happen. The passages from Lampião to Coirana and from the latter to Antão must be confirmed as essential links in a revolutionary chain. The rebellion represented in *Antônio das Mortes* claims that continuity through the words of the *santa*, but its practical fulfillment requires an unfailing Antônio, who, now serving the people, becomes the endorser of the *cangaceiros'* dignity and legacy. In the "reenactment of Saint George," it is he who suffers the contamination by the present time and becomes that figure of impurity that constitutes the bridge between myth and history.

The film insists on the "identity of nature" between Antônio and the *cangaço*—expressed in his memories of him and Lampião as equals, although enemies, respecting each other. He is designed as an emanation of the local universe, and his "manners" have not been changed by his recent life in the city. His insertion in the culture of the *sertão* is recognized by everyone, including the colonel, who considers him an enemy but does not accuse him of invading the space of tradition as he does the teacher, a city man. Therefore, he belongs to the collection of dignified heroes, associated with the local tradition, opposed to the secular characters placed under suspicion.

The border line between the "dignified heroes" and the "secular characters" is notorious. There is the register of the reenactment of the myth and there is a more prosaic register of the small dramas in Jardim das Piranhas, within a peculiar dovetail between the atemporal paradigm of the unfailing hero and the specific circumstances of his arena of action. In truth, Antônio's condition as a midpoint between a legendary killer, retired professional, and embodiment of Saint George is reflected in the mise-en-scène itself, generating a mixture of genres typical of Rocha's cinema.

This "typical mixture" is the expression of the conflict between the orders of time that rule over *Antônio das Mortes*: Coirana's rural world expresses an evangelical time that demands a type of imagery that comes from the Christian iconography; Antônio's aura is constructed from the opening refrain and other compositions that underline the image of a lonely hero, whose reference may be to the *cordel* literature or to the western; in contrast, the colonel's world opens as the space of a decaying domesticity, plagued by corrupt figures, a stage of *kitschy* melodramas that sometimes even invade the more dignified space of the oppressed. Significantly, the colonel himself takes on the figure of a dignified character, composed in its wholeness despite the crisis, whereas the notions of kitsch and corruption are associated with the more urban figures, those who came with modernization: Chief of Police Matos, the teacher, and Laura; that is, those who, from their first appearance on, embodied this linear time of material and prosaic history in their costumes, attitudes, and speech.

Typical characters of a postmythical time, Matos, Laura, and the teacher are at the center of the colonel's domestic drama, emerging from the life that was flowing in Jardim das Piranhas, with their desires, ambitions, and gossip. They belong to a world where the traditional figure of power—Colonel Horácio—has already declined (his age, his blindness), although without losing his charisma. Unable to force change to favor them, they have been immersed in a little world of sameness only threatened by Laura's impatience with Matos's cowardice—the obsequious chief of police is afraid to stab the blind old man. Coirana's arrival finds them in a situation of unstable balance and offers the dramatic trigger to the explosion of conflicts.

The decisive sequence of the colonel's domestic drama well summarizes the profile of these three urban figures. When Mata Vaca arrives in the village, Batista, the landlord's faithful servant and guide, reveals the love affair between Laura and Matos to the old man. Once the lovers are captured, the colonel is adamant that the revenge be publicly exposed, showing the lovers and generating complete hysteria in the square in front of the tavern. At a given moment, taking advantage of the pandemonium, Matos gets hold of a hoodlum's gun and kills Batista as the teacher flings his drink at Mata Vaca's face, making it possible for he, Matos, and Laura to flee into the bar. The three of them, in a tight spot, live a moment of truth marked by Laura's complaining about Matos's promises of going back to the city and by the teacher's sarcasm at the trembling chief of police. Amid silence and expectation, Laura takes the initiative, leaving the bar and saying: "Leave it to me, Horácio, I will kill this crook myself." Thrown into the scene by chance, the teacher is able to slowly leave the tavern, taking advantage of the impact of Laura's action. Matos, although carrying a gun, proves his cowardice. Mata Vaca opens the creaking door and vanishes into the tavern's darkness; silently, he returns holding the chief of police. Laura obsessively stabs her former lover, whereas Horácio repeats, "We are avenged, Batista."

Long shots and strong colors set the tone for the sequence and comment on the drama, especially in the final moments when Laura's blond hair and purple dress clash with the red on the wall of the bar and with the orange of the colonel's outfit. In the entire sequence, the sound track alternates hysterical noise and silence, characteristic of Rocha's cinema in its moments of rupture. The ingredients of the drama are worked in excess in order to make from the apparent naturalism something ostensibly "designed" and, for this very reason, symbolic in the qualification of the characters. The critics and Rocha himself have pointed out a certain Shakespearean inspiration in the composition of this family affair, with its cruel events, lived by characters deranged by power. The association is not totally wrong, but it tends to annul the mediation of a long journey of bourgeois dramas whose characters have more ordinary proportions and are more akin to what we see in *Antônio das Mortes*. In truth, it is this petit bourgeois dimension that marks Laura, Matos, and the teacher. The two men, especially, are too abased and timid in their provincial drama to remind us of great tragic characters.

From her first appearance on, Laura constitutes the stereotype of the femme fatale: smoking, with a long cigarette holder, and wearing a purple dress. Among the three characters of transition between *sertão* and city, she is the strongest—center of the intrigue that sets the mechanism of revenge. Within the stereotype, she lines up with the collection of women associated with power, courtesans in Rocha's films, figures of seduction opposed to the incarnation of a motherly, strong, virtuous, and unselfish spirit that corrects the course of men, here embodied in the *santa*, bearer of the charisma of the popular religions. The opposition saint–prostitute is enacted here so as to figure, in the sphere of men, the separation of territories between the sublime (popular-peasant) and the grotesque (petit bourgeois). Matos, the teacher, Coirana, Antão, and Antônio define their rank—sublime or grotesque—according to their relationship to the women. Laura, although granted dignity in her corrosive function, is the figure of desire that makes men plunge into the realm of the grotesque, in opposition to the *santa*, whose spiritual force makes them ascend to a higher level.

The demoralization of the chief of police is prepared for from his first conversation with the teacher, just after Antônio das Mortes's arrival. They talk about women, and the teacher drops a hint about Matos's affair with Laura, the advantages that he gets from this relationship: Everything is said with an air of debauchery regarding the chief of police's ambitions to become mayor, congressman, or senator. Matos talks about drawing capital from the south, transplanting industries, carrying out agrarian reform; he vaguely mentions a new cycle of economic growth in the northeast. Despite his vulgar appearance, he intends to be a modernizing leader. The blind colonel is declining, and it is important to be patient to inherit Laura and the advantages brought by opportunism. We can see a weak, second-rate man who takes himself seriously, unlike the teacher, who has no illusions about himself. In the tavern, the teacher mocks Matos under the eyes of an impassive Antônio das Mortes, humiliating the police authority in a scene that provokes Antônio's formal declaration about the side he chooses: the world of the colonel has lost its dignity.

As a commentator or supporter of the narrative agency in some episodes, the teacher does not really compose the figure of knowledge; his irony results from his resentment of those who drown in alcohol and live in this end of the world, the last step of an apparently irrevocable fall. His routine is the chat in the tavern, a tedious life, impotence. In the crisis, he oscillates between his usual sarcasm and a true concern for other people's problems: He helps the wounded Coirana in the square, then he helps Antônio carry the *cangaceiro* toward the hills. In these oscillations, the most vivid expressions of his desire are associated with death—for example, the macabre sex on top of Matos's corpse and the possession of Laura's dying body amid the final turmoil, a regressive fixation within the constellation of discharges that mark the killing at the end of the film. His last image is one of fixity, a return to the inertia that preceded his spasm of militancy.

The city man, in truth, did not need to get into the armed struggle to contribute to the fall of Colonel Horácio's world. The latter clearly sees the menace that the teacher represents and names him the Plague Angel. Although the presence of schooling in the rural world signals changes, the teacher himself shows much more the stagnation, the early deterioration that is installed even before progress is effective, in a half-effective process that corrodes the past but is not strong enough to build a future. Why, then, does he enlist in the battle, being foreign to the *sertão*'s heroic past?

Beyond the Pedagogical Framework—The Other Allegory

Among the secular characters of this small world in focus, the teacher is the major figure of contradiction, a symptom of the film's oscillation itself. In the grotesque dimension of his experience, he brings the intellectual into the allegory, eventually participating, in the end, in the exemplary battle.

It is not difficult to accept his sudden conversion within the rules of the film. The same magical force acts on the teacher as rules over all the conversions. The action performed in the square is a picture that, as other scenes in this film, has a certain autonomy of composition that does not need to be strongly connected to the others. This autonomy is enhanced by the use of long shots and frontal tableaulike images. This is the case of the first stage of the battle, when the colonel, Laura, and Mata Vaca's hoodlums, before taking action, keep still, facing the camera as symbolic figures, with the *sertão* in the background (Figure 6.16; page 180). This type of composition underlines the reading of the situation as the reenactment of a paradigm that can come from different contexts: from myth, from popular religious theater, from painting, from the genres of industrial cinema, from the bourgeois melodrama. Here the choice depends on which sphere the film wants to enroll each character in, and the tone of the narration can change while following a single action. When Antônio strolls through the city carrying the drunken teacher, there is an irony addressed to the characters' gloom, an irony that burdens Antônio with the mark of a time that corrodes, heedless of his glorious past. However, the following movement is of raising, of a return to the time of legend, when we jump from the little town to the hills and Antônio enters his dominion again. The narrative stance is inverted, creating with the *cordel* song and the landscape the context for a serious reading of the teacher's redemption.

Odd comrades, Antônio and the teacher, on the verge of the fight, start a dialogue that suggests their fight as a "reconciliation of culture and the army." Amid imprecations, the shouting at the enemy is suddenly cut by this dialogue, a kind of "thesis exposition" in which Antônio shows his respect for the value of ideas and offers his services. Since the beginning, Antônio has treated the teacher with reverence. But here it sounds awkward that he sets up *ideas*—associated with politics and posited as foreign to religion—as the highest value. In *Antônio das Mortes*, reason has already been put aside as a basis for historical actions, and it has been roughly represented by the inept figure of the teacher himself. Antônio declares that his commitment belongs to the sacred level, where the intuition of right and wrong is what counts: "I settle my business straight with God." Then he defines the sphere of the teacher as that of political combat and affirmation of ideologies on a human scale. When he says, "Fight with the power of your ideas because they are worthier than me," he yields to the secular level, that of historical ideologies, but his words are addressed to someone who had not expressed any ideology. The armed man delegates the authority to the one whom he has just dragged out of the bottom of the well, in a context in which there are no political ideas apart from religion that could guide him, in which the figure of the revolutionary is that of the mystic praised by tradition. His reverence is, in this context, forced, an imposed message, because in the film the feeling for justice is always framed in biblical terms. The teacher could not and does not have the "classic" function of the intellectual.

In truth, what is reenacted in this theater is that promise of a guerrilla warfare that was in fact not carried out by Paulo Martins within the universe of *Land in Anguish*. In Eldorado, weapons were put alongside myth to perpetrate the coup d'état in a cathartic instant carrying a very clear meaning: the defeat of the popular forces. When the coup happened, the antagonism between culture and the army was evident: Paulo was killed. In *Antônio das Mortes* the teacher's marginal condition, his eccentricity, leads him to war without a clear commitment. His engagement could have been understood as an example of the *geste gratuit* ("rhetorical gesture"), if the context of his intervention had been completely secular. The mythical frame introduces the inspiration of the sacred and places the avenging fighters together, reconciling culture and the army in the defense of the oppressed. In the programmatic affirmation of the revolutionary dream, Antônio switches from one cause to the other as if suggesting himself as an example to the forces of repression; the teacher becomes a militant, as if suggesting a road to redemption for those in Brazil whose reasoning has not saved them from a recent past of frustrations.

For the good of pedagogy, Antônio is enlightened; near the final battle, the teacher, the most corrosive character, opens his eyes and is born again from the ashes. However, his militancy is not strong enough to settle down. The theater in the square may reconcile the force of the army, the prestige of culture, the charisma of religion, and the spear of the oppressed. But the minute the battle is finished, this collective is dissolved along with the pedagogical allegory and its exemplary heroes. The epic-didactic effect confronts the melancholy atmosphere of retreats. Undermining the pedagogical allegory supported by the myth of Saint George is the contamination of the scene by the current historical data, which question the myth of revolution. The film calls for the force of myth as an organizing principle but reckons the effectiveness of other spheres in the production of the events. The legend needs "updating" to show its force; it has to plunge into the present and remain as a paradigm able to dominate the other influxes of time. However, the way the film reenacts the myth in the current situation does not grant it any hegemonic role, and the conflict between the orders of time permeates the entire film. The attention to the historical moment, the need to picture it, leads to an ambivalent diagnosis of the present (that is, 1969). This ambivalence defines the operation of another allegory in *Antônio das Mortes*, one having to do with the gloomy context that surrounds the film. A response to the historical juncture, this other allegory suggests a peculiar recognition of the strength of the modern and, at the same time, its condemnation.

On the one hand, the plot enhances the strength of the linear time of technology—a pole of changes that decenter the revolutionary teleology. Such an order of time has been announced since the beginning, when the rebels are clearly depicted as an invasion of the past into a present context whose signs surround the space of the pedagogical theater made of "survivals" from an ancient world. And this same order is underlined in the final shots, "competing" with the future projection of Saint George's myth: Antônio walks with his back to the camera on the roadside, close to the Shell gas station, while the energy of cars and trucks crossing the frame define another rhythm and another link to a larger world. When Rocha ends his film with the signs that integrate this small world into a global network of economic exchange, he does not help the effect of hope that he tried to express in Antão's departure on horseback. The contrast is evident, and the images of the technical world incorporate actual facts that the film wants to recognize and include in its game. Otherwise, why should its past–present opposition be so ostensibly shown from the beginning?

On the other hand, the texture of the present world built in *Antônio das Mortes* reinforces an idea of decadence that drains out any expectation of redemption. In other words, it stigmatizes modernization, whose figures are funereal: Matos, Laura, and the teacher. They carry a corrosive force from which only those who go back to the rural tradition are freed. Given this logic, it is natural that the rebellion should be impelled by the force of the past summoning the present to make history. To engender the future, one must call back the universe previous to the current decadence: the *sertão* of national heroes full of dignity. In brief, ancient Brazil is the moral reserve of revolution.

This idea of the archaic as the source of rebellion suggests a kind of peasant radicalism, in which religion and popular myth would replace Guevarism—the theory of "revolutionary focus" that inspired guerrilla movements in Latin American countries. However, although it dignifies the *sertão* and sees it as a supplier of myths that could feed the revolutionary action, the film recognizes—this is said in the other allegory—that the grounds for the action of mythical figures is polluted by progress, by technical and economic modernity. That is, the reference to the center—this source of the machinery that invades the *sertão* and makes the theater of the seekers after justice obsolete—is inevitable: The road that crosses the provincial world shows a more general structure that minimizes the battle in the square. The *sertão* here is not "the world," a closed microcosm taken as the allegory of the nation, as was the case in *Black God, White Devil*. No longer a totality, the *sertão* is the uncertain open space involved in contradictory relationships with the rest of the country.

Although sometimes schematic, *Antônio das Mortes* nevertheless makes its allegory more complex when it incorporates in its very structure the recognition of the material force of technology against the myth of nationalist revolution, achieving a kind of perception of present dilemmas that surpasses any simple return to the national-popular ideologies typical of the early 1960s. The film undoubtedly fears modernization, and it is clear in its moral condemnation of the present. But at the same time it recognizes the effectiveness of conservative modernization, knowing quite well how this came to deny the old teleology of the prophetic allegory. In this sense, Rocha has a peculiar way of dealing with the archaic–modern opposition: He turns the *tropicalist* collage upside down. In the latter, the modern exposes the absurdity of the archaic, generating a parodic incorporation of the clichés of the traditional culture. In *Antônio das Mortes*, it is the dignity of the archaic that invalidates the "spurious modernity," this new world that has resulted from a technical advance full of mistakes, effective but vicious. Rocha's allegory expresses the discord between the desired teleology of history and the logic embedded in the process that took place. The more effective forces are illegitimate; the past is a symbolic source of the revolution, but its effectiveness is jeopardized because it cannot act without being contaminated by the present, this machinery that reduces all that is sacred to a simulacrum. The best expression of this dialectic is the ambiguity of the final sequence of the film: Given the difficulty of reconciling the revolutionary utopia and the real dynamics of the actual country, Rocha juxtaposes the hope of the theater in the square and the melancholy on the roadside.

Figure 6.1

Figure 6.2

Figure 6.3

Figure 6.4

Figure 6.5

Figure 6.6

Figure 6.7

Figure 6.8

Figure 6.9

Figure 6.13

Figure 6.10

Figure 6.14

Figure 6.11

Figure 6.15

Figure 6.12

Figure 6.16

Part IV

Allegory and Deconstruction

7

The Angel Is Born: The Song of Exile

The Disjunctive Style and the Orders of Time

Bressane's peripheral world is antithetical to Sganzerla's comical province. It displays quasi-deserted sites crossed by two bandits who escape from their hideout in a shantytown to the outskirts of the big city. Society is exiled from the screen and is only represented by the bandits' victims, who pay the price of being present on their route.

The insulation of the two bandits has a graphic dimension: Emptiness dominates the visual composition. Secondary actions and confrontations with the police or with the press are absent. The bandits do not trade. Violence is their only mode of interaction with the world, and their cold-blooded crimes transcend all practicality. Santa Maria and Urtiga do not call for justice, unlike Rocha's social bandits, nor do they use the suffering past as an excuse for their present actions. Nothing is said about the reasons for their radical violence; there is only a close observation of their style as men sought by the police, alone against all. Nothing can be seen in the newspaper that one of them browses looking for news about their crime of the day before; nor is there anything on the TV, which covers the arrival of man on the moon.

From beginning to end, we follow a steady succession of the protagonists' actions, disrupted only by inserts commenting on the action but not mixed up with it. Man on the moon, for instance, is a central piece of allegory in *The Angel Is Born* because of the opposition that it creates between the two journeys: that of the astronauts and that of the marginals. Although shown in connection to an experience of the bandits—they are the ones watching TV—the image of the astronauts functions like other nondiegetic inserts that frame the main story: The engravings of fishes repeated throughout the film and, especially, the ironic sequence of a wedding in the woods.

Shrinking from answers and reducing the mise-en-scène to its minimal terms, the film installs uneasiness. Violence is isolated as if in an aquarium ready for the painful exam not attenuated by any sense of a banalizing adventure. Once again, the focus is on an experience of agony, organized in terms different from that of Paulo Martins, without all the political intrigue. One proceeds with the experience of failure, of impotence; but this is worked out on a laconic register, in opposition to *Land in Anguish* and *Red Light Bandit*. Santa Maria is wounded at the beginning of the film, and the measure of time will be set by the evolution of his wound. The subject of the allegory is the bandits' total war against society, a condition that Santa Maria tries to live as a quest, the search for the angel, a figure that he creates and Urtiga rejects throughout their journey. In its laconic observation, the film creates an original relationship between the glance and the scene, making it evident that the time of the discourse (the film) and the time of the action (fiction) do not converge. We follow the bandits very closely, we become intimate with them, but we do not identify with them. By means of clear signs of the camera's independence from the evolution of the scene, the disjunctive style is affirmed, separating narrative devices and diegesis—frequently, our look dwells on what "does not belong" in the story.

This disjunctive style characterizes *The Angel Is Born* up to the end, when the film reaches its most radical moment. At a certain point in the bandits' journey, the narrative breaks off and we abandon them exactly when we seemed to be closer. As their escape continues (and it is coextensive with the film's narrative), their condition becomes critical. The black bandit (Urtiga) drives the stolen car as the white bandit (Santa Maria) is overwhelmed by the pain of his wound. The camera, placed on the back seat, observes them, playing the role of a third party within the group (Figures 7.1–7.4; page 201). From behind, then, we follow the white bandit's suffering, and a long cry of agony introduces what will be the film's final shot. The close-up shots from inside the car are replaced by a view from a static camera observing the escape from outside. The camera suddenly abandons its companions and moves ever further away from the car as it disappears along the straight, endless line of the road, framing a fixed and symmetrical image of the highway toward the horizon. On the sound track, the cry heard is the last of a series uttered at regular intervals as if in echo of other sounds: Regular pulsations, abrupt jumps from sound to silence are characteristic of the entire film. On the image track, the stable view of the road is held for a long time. The impassive contemplation of a mute symmetry suggests a destiny beyond the horizon unacknowledged by camera or narration. The account of the bandits' experience is interrupted by the imposition of silence and immobility; for eight minutes our gaze is focused on this point in the middle of the road where nothing happens except for the incidental passing of a car. This immobilization is disturbing because of the uncomfortable duration of the still and empty shot, which signifies the endlessness of the plot. This absence of diegetic action, this flow of time that nevertheless encompasses "events" of a different order, is but a starting point. Through this interruption, the narrator reveals himself as mediator; his actions, conspicuously arbitrary rather than diegetically motivated, are the explicit and enigmatic source of all that is seen and heard. The abandonment of the characters and of their destiny is not especially disturbing because it is sudden, deserving no explanation. It is upsetting because it is highlighted by the narrator's eight-minute commentary. This extreme gesture epitomizes the disjunctive strategies that characterize the entire film. This is not the first instance of mediation made evident through difference, through distance from the experience of the characters.

The narrator's intervention is in some cases marked by a clearly detectable automatism in the development of the sound track: The presence–absence opposition concerning local sound and music is self-revealing in its regular pace and arbitrariness. A good example of this disjunctive strategy is the scene in which the black bandit arrives at a summerhouse and inspects it with a view to its possible use as a hiding place. He looks relaxed and acts naturally while, on the sound track, arbitrary interventions stimulate our involvement not with the scene as projected but, rather, with its shooting and its editing. Near the beginning of the film, in a sequence that effectively initiates the storytelling process, dramatic music, disturbing in its deep dissonance, plays restlessly for a long time while the camera, having already arrived at the meeting place, lingers, waiting for the bandits. We look for a long time at a stone wall through an unbalanced framing that produces an empty frame effect; it solicits a filling by human agents, produced only at the end of the shot when one of the bandits arrives with a wounded leg, indicating an action that has taken place offscreen while the spectator was kept looking at the wall. Arbitrary mediation is also apparent in the composition of fixed tableaux (such as the final shot of the road). Characters are sometimes observed within a strictly frontal composition; suddenly, without any motion or sound on the part of the characters, a zoom out will make an "unjustified" correction, as if asserting its freedom to focus on the scene.

In the long take of the wall, then, the main action is located off-screen, and we are confronted with inert matter. Other moments are marked by this same type of inversion, in which what would usually be outtakes become the center of attention. Residues are incorporated, and things crucial to diegetic action are discarded. This incorporation differs from that of *Red Light Bandit*, in which the standard disposable fragment was inserted within a dynamic editing so as to construct a representative picture of the whole; every brief image functioned as part of an aggregation of fragments juxtaposed so as to suggest that they actually did form a collection and that their totality could be proposed as the piling up of simultaneous events. In *The Angel Is Born*, the residual element is individually foregrounded; it is not an element in a series of flashes. It retains its specific density as residue, as an inert element whose lengthy, monotonous presence withholds the expected flow of information. The residue is retained so that it can attest to non-identification, to the separation of narrator and diegesis, and in order to display a void or excess created by the "misplaced ellipsis."

In the film's final sequence, contrasting with the plot's inconclusiveness, the long take of the road gives way to the playing of music, lending a special connotation to the irony involved in the lengthening of the shot itself. Once action and cry have faded away, silence provides the background to the squeaky sound of a record playing an old recording of a well-known popular song—"Peguei um ita no norte e vim pro Rio morar [I took a boat in the North and came to live in Rio]"—that suggests the innocent lament of the emigrant arrived in a large city. It is a song of exile that evokes the irretrievable past within family and community, and it seems in its nostalgia hardly related to the characters or to the general composition of the narrative, which is characterized by the total annulment of any reference to the past. However, it promptly evokes the beginning of the film, when another old recording of a popular song alludes to the past; its lyrics speak of painful parting, longing for the loved one, for lost happiness: "*Agora é cinzas, tudo acabado e nada mais . . .* [now everything is ashes, it's all over and nothing is left]."

The images appearing during this first song constitute a kind of preview of the film; their fragments anticipate the future, although in an entangled and achronological way. These images introduce a new stage of organization within the prologue to the narrative and set out the film's repertory of scenes. Before this previewlike montage, the dark screen and the dissonant music—sounding like an orchestra tuning its instruments—had staged an entropic origin for the emergence of the organized images. Prints of sea creatures—a shark devouring a small fish—are the first manifestation of a leit-motiv that, throughout the film will suggest the Social Darwinism articulated by the narrative situations.

The "birth of cinema" first brings the dark screen, then the pictorial image prior to the cinematographic technique. The moving image comes only after the inscription "cinematographo" a turn-of-the-century denomination of cinema in Brazil, announcing the hasty montage of preview images. From this point on, the pace of the narrative is dominated by the effect of the duration of the shots, a sense of presentness that at the end turns into a melancholy gaze—the song heard over the image of the empty road brings a notion of mourning that permeates the whole of the last shot, marked by the pain of separation and distance from the past.

In the opening sequence, after the dark screen and the montage sequence of clips from *The Angel Is Born*, the stable element is a long low-angle shot of the shantytown on the hill as seen from the paved road. The long lifeless take of this emblem of poverty is held while the samba "Agora é Cinzas" (Now Everything Is Ashes) is played to the very end. This motionless long take precedes the establishment of the regular progressive chronology that marks the film until the end. In the shantytown, the next shot shows the bandits talking in front of a shack, conjecturing about the police siege and planning their escape. They succeed in their attempt, but in an offscreen action that takes place while we look at the stone wall, Santa Maria is wounded in the leg. From this point on, the narrative follows the characters in a regular temporal flow strictly parallel to Santa Maria's bleeding. On its borders, the narrative is framed by a specific set of symmetries that relate the prologue to the final shot. Our meeting with and our separation from the protagonists are both punctuated by the complete hearing of an old record nostalgically evoking innocence. Moreover, as at the beginning of the film, dissonance is again used to close the sound track at the very end, while the "arbitrariness" of camera movements is, for the last time, reasserted in the abrupt zoom toward the horizon, the vanishing point of road and film. In a final gesture, this zooming toward sky and asphalt seals the experience of time as loss, as a plunge into emptiness (Figure 7.5; page 201). The play on this cinematic device precedes the beginning (which is not really the beginning) and outlasts the end (which is not really the end). The disjunctive strategies permeate the entire film and make clear that the condition of apartness contaminates *The Angel Is Born* on all its levels.

So far, I have addressed the frame of the story and its style. When we shift our attention to the course of the story, what we see is the experience of aggression and death, time running in a linear succession of scenes that leave aside any explanatory recollection. Let us now consider the "bleeding" of the narrative in Bressane's film.

Parataxis: The Natural Flow of Time

The journey of Santa Maria and Urtiga is a paratactic succession: first this and then that, an implied chain that refuses explanation. The narrative sticks to the characters' "here and now" in a close view that nevertheless does not facilitate the identification between our perspective and the bandits' point of view. Tracking the bandits in their escape, we only know their actions and dialogues. Except for the white bandit's wound, there is no sign of police action and nothing is said about society's reaction to their crimes. Restricted to the limited perspective of the characters, we have to decode laconic gestures and subtle exchanges of glances in order to understand any further step in the story; the succession of episodes lacks any differentiation between ordinary and decisive instants, between the irrelevant act and the scandalous crime.

The dialogue in the first scene in the shantytown is tense and understated, the long take breaking off before the bandits' decision is made clear. The next shot shows the enigmatic and enduring stone wall alone on the screen; the already wounded bandit appears only at the very end of the shot, passing in front of the camera as he escapes. We meet the bandits again in an isolated shack on the outskirts of town; the calm setting, surrounded by mountains and next to a creek, contrasts with the urgency of their situation. Again, the camera's movements establish the opposition between the time of the protagonists—dramatic time in which death is on the watch—and the quasi eternity of these forms carved by time, recalling that there is another temporal scale in this geography that does not "answer" to their drama although it is their ground. Within this calm setting, Urtiga assists Santa Maria, confirming the presence of a clear hierarchy: Santa Maria—the white—commands. Urtiga—the black—executes, providing support to his partner. The nature of their relationship is made explicit in the central episode of their escape in the bourgeois summerhouse on a hillside by the sea.

We first see this house when Urtiga looks for a quiet hiding place and checks what seems to be a good site. Camera and bandit, in a rather unconcerned way, walk about the house while the sound track evolves within the disjunctive strategy already referred to. Everything seems to be fine. The bandits occupy the empty house. A night scene suggests a sexual relationship between them. They are seen staring at one another inside a room, in another long, static take—Santa Maria stands facing Urtiga, who, his back to the camera, places his hands on the hips of his wounded companion.

Ellipsis, waiting time. Urtiga watches the entrance of the house. They read on the veranda. Time goes by. Breaking the daily routine, the lady of the house arrives with a maid and a male servant. There is a brief moment of interrogation and suspense. Once again, a single long take will suffice for the entire sequence. The camera is inside the house with the bandits, lying in ambush for the women, observing the scene as usual from the bandits' viewpoint, with no counter shots of the victims' experience. As the three enter, violence explodes: The bandits kill the male servant; they scream and beat the women while the camera tries, as it were, to accompany the process of intimidation, maintaining its vantage point, separated from the scene (Figure 7.6; page 201).

After this account of subjection, a new sequence shot takes us to the new order established in the house: Near the camera, in profile, the bandits have a meal seated at the table as the owners of the space, behaving like clumsy bourgeois, while the women in the background act like servants. Having seized power, the bandits establish a new order. During the period of confinement, the succession of long takes does not deal with causal relationships in enchained steps. Each moment has its own thickness, its own specific immobility: It is the scene at the table, it is relaxing in the veranda cradled by hammocks, it is watching TV and chatting. Everything seems like a calm weekend by the sea except for those moments in which Santa Maria gets exasperated with the obedient women. His aggression, though, does not extend to carrying out his threat of rape: In the bedroom, under the impassive regard of Urtiga, he grabs his victim on the bed, but his manifestation of power is spanking the bourgeois lady with his belt. At a certain point, in the living room, Carlos Gardel's tango leads to the dance that epitomizes the situation: It places the bodies together, heightening the women's distress and the bandits' exhibition of power. The sequence shot overloads the uncomfortable pattern of domination: Urtiga keeps a chilvaric posture, but Santa Maria insists on sexual harassment. He grabs the bourgeois lady, forces a kiss, and seems to be going for more; however, his movements show the wounded leg and the limits that figure his ambivalence of power and castration.

Suddenly, without explanation, it is time to leave. The bandits are seen preparing their supply of provisions, as if they are leaving after a holiday. They take the owner's car, and, swiftly, as if locking a door, they kill the two women. The camera records from a distance, and the architecture, in opposition to the coastal hills, frames the action and underlines the externality of an overall order of things with respect to those deaths quietly observed, diluted, and solitary in the landscape (Figures 7.7–7.9; pages 201–202).

The summerhouse, where most of the story develops, offers a synthesis of distancing strategies, as well as clear evidence that despite their proximity the camera and the characters are in fact separated. The hypothesis has hitherto been advanced that the camera, as a narrative agent, behaves like a third bandit, staying close to the others, never seeking additional information from the surroundings. This suggests solidarity, a choice to remain close to the bandits in an effort to understand the action from their viewpoint rather than through the mediation of society or through the eyes of its legal agents. And this indicates a refusal of the alternation typical of the thriller, in which the play between pursuer and pursued tends to concentrate the spectator's attention on the convolutions of the plot. The term "solidarity" is not, however, applicable in this case; a new concept is required to express the narration's near–far stance in relation to the characters. For while the film does not side with society, neither does it support the bandits. No consideration is given to the characters' motivations or presumed past privation. This presentness, characteristic of the film's style, implies a radical refusal to judge, to provide any kind of justification, either social or psychological. Lest we be tempted to understand this refusal to judge in André Bazin's terms, we must remember that *The Angel Is Born* opposes itself to neorealism and other forms of realistic discourse. This entire film develops according to a principle of compositional regularity whereby the maintenance of rigorous camera movement (stressed by the use of disjunctive sound) assures the camera's autonomy as it confronts the inner structure of each action, be it the grotesque tango, the murder of the women, or the sadistic elimination of a homosexual who happens to cross the bandits' path. The adoption of the impassive style of detached observation and the use of the inexpressive camera are not intended to achieve an effect of objectivity. Bressane's camera is by no means tranquil; his images betray an uneasiness that rules out the epithet "cold" for his distance and immobility. This lack of involvement is controversial; it expresses an explicit, historically grounded refusal of a style that Cinema Novo had turned into dogma. Bressane's immobility is dialogic and intertextual, and it refers to things from which detachment is seen as necessary. We have thus far considered the notion of detachment within the sphere of the narrator's nonidentification with the characters. This nonidentification is fundamental insofar as it is mediated by a metalinguistic consideration that opposes this film to concepts of participation and engagement characteristic of the 1960s.[1] The expressive camera of that time tended to embrace the characters, sharing their emotions, their values, their indignation. From Bressane's position, there is no yearning for identity, no desire to fuse all consciousnesses (those of the characters, the author, and the audience) into a single historical perspective.

The bandits' experience is enacted, not shared; they are irremediably isolated in a journey through transgression from which there is no return; it must be pursued to an end (which the film deliberately ignores). The narrator observes, taking care to establish his alterity, governed by the consciousness that his task is the construction of a language rather than a world and by his commitment to expose the separations that illusionism—in both escapist and in socially engaged cinema—tried to conceal: between camera and characters, between the rhythm of action and that of nature.

I have been working with a set of ideas that underline the presence in the film of a radical antiteleology, but more precision is required. The title of the film suggests an event outside the natural order, and Santa Maria's journey includes references to an angel, a reference that calls for a transcendental meaning. Ultimately, Santa Maria supposes a teleology that might take him to Heaven. On the other hand, Richard Nixon, on the TV broadcast about the moon landing, affirms another teleology, one that involves the celestial sphere, a cosmic destiny for humankind. Supported by the size of the achievement he is celebrating, he does not see any aberration in his attitude of universal leader in this raising to the sublime, to the integration of rational beings in an astronomic time that seems, thanks to technological advances, achievable for humanity. Here we hear a discourse of euphoria that denies our lived time as an instance of fall, loss, and solitude; in other words, a discourse that denies the very ideas that emanate from the songs, from the overall frame of the narrative, and from the style of looking itself. How, then, do these vectors—that of salvation and that of the unavoidable fall implicit in the natural course of time—relate in *The Angel Is Born*?

The Family, the Cinema, the Angel: Lost Innocences

In addition to the insertion of the engraved representations of the struggle for life among fish, the film's paratactic succession is interrupted by an extradiegetic divertissement that solicits the comparison of film styles. In radical contrast to the tension inside the summerhouse, a short home movie presents a merry wedding scene in the woods. The film crew appears to be totally preoccupied with the event; handheld camera movements contrast with the film's overall immobility. This insert introduces a caricatural representation of institutional happiness: Along with the profusion of handheld camera movements, there is a search for lighting effects typical of the amateur (like the sunshine filtered through the trees), and we follow playful children dressed in their Sunday best while the happy couple smile shyly at each other, all to the accompaniment of "I wanna girl just like the girl that married dear old Dad." The combination evokes a kind of innocence—that of the home movie celebrating marriage as the absolute telos—removed from the stylistic and fictional universe of *The Angel Is Born*. This insert follows the sequence of the bandits at the table, during which the white bandit states the legitimacy of the newly established order. And it is followed by the scene on the veranda, in which the same bandit mockingly reads the lady's diary. The entries of daily tasks, mingled with "maxims and thoughts," ends by exasperating him. Faced with the bourgeois woman's plaintive relativism, he is unable to keep his sense of humor. The themes of love and marriage are again present in the diary's "axioms," full of skepticism and disenchantment: "An optimist is someone who still expects to go to Heaven someday"; "Only marriage will turn a rose into a cabbage"; "Love is like a butterfly, it lasts only a few hours." We are far from the utopian mood evoked in the extradiegetic insert.

The bandit's seriousness in the face of the woman's kitschy formulas can be seen inscribed in the film itself, which develops situations that exclude that good-humored irony typical of *Red Light Bandit*. The atmosphere now is one of bitterness and deep distress. Instead of seducing the spectator, Bressane's cinema aggressively adopts an enigmatic attitude while displaying the bandits' brutal violence.

The invasion of the bourgeois house breaks the private order and shakes the illusions of safe shelter brought by the closed space. The interaction between the women and the bandits reveals the flaws of family affairs. Santa Maria insists on the opposition between the "theater of society" and his more impulsive posture. Any resistance on the part of the women generates a physical aggression rather than witty statements. What is essential is that the extreme violence here offers the occasion for the invaded world to let its mask fall. The concern is to explore the idea of general discomfort, to make it clear that such uneasiness, although it may find its more tragic dimension in the bandits' transgressions, has a softer version, equally pathetic, in the disappointment expressed by the song "Peguei um ita no norte e vim pro Rio morar," associated with the sad experiences of poor migrants, and in the philosophy of the bourgeois lady. In *The Angel Is Born*, discomfort endures as a consequence of a film style that removes the layers of convention that one finds in the news brought by the media in the regular dramas and stereotyped fiction, layers that protect us from the direct perception of brutal experience. The way the images are organized enhances two lost innocences.

The first is that of socially engaged realism, in which the outlaw is portrayed as victim and society as the space of corruption that leads him astray and annihilates him. This kind of engaged cinema assumes that a film begins with a preparation, an account of motivations, and that the denouement is the moment of totalization, a moment in which meaning springs forth. The ending of *The Angel Is Born* is, in contrast, not diagnostic, and the spectator is thrown into a state of discomfort. The eight-minute shot of the road is a clear assertion of inconclusiveness, of the refusal to establish a perspective from which the entire trajectory may be retrospectively examined. The arbitrary zoom in at the very end of the shot epitomizes this rejection of teleology, commenting ironically upon the expectation of ultimate revelation. The gratuitous zoom is an aggressive misapplication of that technical and aesthetic device whose function is to instantiate the movement of attention that defines a horizon, a point in the future that the eyes can reach.[2] The final zoom in runs counter to the narrative impulse and to the role played by perspective, two elements consistently used in mainstream cinema to centralize the representation and to maintain the impression that there is a meaning for the world that is represented (a meaning grasped and transmitted by the narrator). The choice of a road to express this antiteleological stance opens a very specific debate with Cinema Novo: The road (or straight line) representing the opening up to a new consciousness or the "dimension of the future" had been a favorite ending convention of Cinema Novo.

At the same time, the road that figures the plunge into emptiness crowns an abysmal experience, referring us to the drama lived in Paulo Martins's dunes of agony. It is not by chance that *The Angel Is Born* brings back, throughout, the rarefied content of the final images of Rocha's film. This rarefaction, now elaborated from beginning to end, produces an original internalization of the socal crisis: The antiteleology sets its roots on the formal level and changes the relationship between film and spectator. It does not call for adhesion; it exhibits an exile.

In opposition to the aggression addressed to the innocence ascribed to this kind of engaged film, a second, more remote innocence is addressed in sympathetic terms, despite the acknowledgment that it belongs to the past, having been condemned by social evolution. The magic screen and its age of innocence—the heroic age that witnessed the birth of cinema—is evoked within a very suggestive context.

Near the end of the film, the bandits are seen at an old-fashioned amusement park, of a kind nowadays to be found only in city suburbs or in the provinces. The theme of death is introduced, first through the voice of the wounded bandit, who asks his companion: "If I die, what are you going to do?"; and then on a billboard for one of the park's attractions: In a long shot, the two bandits are seen in the foreground and in the background at screen left is seen a poster with the slogan "Encounter with Death." To relax the tension created by the intimation of death or separation, the bandits stage a musical number, creating as they sing a moment of wholeness and relaxation, warding off the haunting ordeal of escape and their dread of the future. Their playfulness introduces the image of a poster for the *cinematographo* with its associations of magic, as if in return to the birth of cinema. The following image is clearly symbolic: The two bandits are seen in a dark room, isolated as always, staring at what is presumably a screen from which emanates the magic light. A single take shows them in profile; the room is small and a few elements of decor suggest a projection room. Here the act of going to the movies is an allegorical evocation of origin, presented not as primarily a diegetic constituent but, rather, as commentary, establishing its own context of intertextual relations. Urtiga is having fun and is ready for magic; like a child, he is swept by fantasy, unconcerned with the urgency of the situation stamped on his companion's face and posture. Santa Maria, wounded and suffering, shows concrete signs of his agony and bleeding, remaining indifferent to whatever transpires on the screen.

The sequence in the projection room synthesizes the difference between the two characters, the basis of their complementarity and of their mutual dependence. A pact has sealed their relation, making their separation inconceivable and confirming the radical opposition between themselves and the world. Their respective stances toward that opposing world are, however, different. If in their exchange of glances they establish a space for identification, a level of immediate communication, the confrontation with the exterior differentiates Urtiga's relaxed pragmatism from Santa Maria's tension. The former is usually absorbed in essential tasks, either in fulfillment of the latter's command or out of his own sense of opportunity acquired from experience.

Usually, the white bandit is anxious, full of inner conflicts that crystallize in acts of ruthless violence, betraying the impulse to retaliate for past offenses. His mystical discourse presupposes a prospective view, a concern with future salvation. He constructs a personal mythology in which his criminal career is seen as a quest, a kind of descent into hell after the Fall, the cardinal sin whose reverse side is purity. He is constantly on the watch, as if for a sign of redemption. His anguish is a synthesis of contradictory impulses: nostalgia for purity and "radical criminality."[3]

Within this opposition between Urtiga's realism and his partner's vision, the pair reenacts, in a peculiar way, the paradigm of the quixotic journey. For Santa Maria, the broader meaning of the combat stems from a faith that we can question from the outside without denying the authority of his role as impeller of the story; however, all the practical continuity of the journey is sustained by the proficiency of Urtiga, whose look never detaches itself from the here and now and from the material world around him and whose action provides whatever is necessary. In his adherence to the world, Urtiga outlines a path that is not one of purity and uplift; rather, he brings the metaphor of the angel to the grounds of immanence. On the practical level, he plays the role of this mysterious entity searched for by the white bandit. Material, quotidian, he cannot be "seen" by Santa Maria, who searches for the enlightened moment, unaware of this bodily angel who cares, watches, drives the car, and comforts.

One specific shot articulates their difference with extreme clarity. Urtiga, standing next to the car, is searching through the newspaper for police activity and for information to guide their next move. Inside the car, Santa Maria looks anxiously around; unconcerned with the persecution of the law, he looks for a sign from his angel to fulfill his expectations of salvation. He looks intently at a boy who withdrew from his group in the park to urinate near a tree, in a sequence in which decoupage and musical comment play with the metaphysical promise but suggest its ultimate emptiness (Figures 7.10–7.13; page 202). The film constantly explores this tension between the creation of an atmosphere of "imminent revelation" and its dissolution. This sequence reproduces the central rhetorical move of the narrative; there is an invitation to teleology and also its frustration.

If Santa Maria's apocalyptic vision allows no space for Urtiga, ironically, the narration takes sides, and Urtiga's role of guardian angel and as symbol of loyalty is emblematically represented in the shot succeeding the *cinematographo*. The inscription EXIT defines the walk outward from the projection room, in fact to the terminal station of *The Angel Is Born*, where we witness a radical moment of agony. Santa Maria cannot bear walking and slides with his back glued to a wall until he sits on the floor surrounded by pain; Urtiga bends down and comforts him, hugging his neck, an emphatic gesture punctuated by the dramatic repetition of a boat whistle that seems to underline the sense of urgency, almost as in a countdown. The frontal composition generates a *tableau* effect, suggesting the emblem of consolation (Figure 7.14; page 202). A religious iconography is evoked here to figure pathos, dramatizing the extreme condition of the protagonist. The singularity of the experience elicits this symbolic fulguration within the insulated, precarious, bloody, and inescapable world of the bandits. However, such a symbolic scene does not have the authority to suspend the flow of time and avert the sure fate of death. It is not a ritual that implies the cyclical movement, the discontinuities between high and low. It is an instant embedded in the horizontal chain of action and outcome that anticipates the final disjunctive gesture of the narration at the road. Like the zoom in at the end of the film, any attempt at establishing a frame of reference to the here and now of the characters remains deliberately suspended; there is a lack of responsiveness that undermines any search for perspective.

Santa Maria is the figure of the random quest, one that is never clearly stated. Urtiga's behavior is so regular and unperturbed that it produces an enigma never explored by the narration. When the camera's glance deviates from the bandits' path of action, it focuses on the landscape or on seasonal events—a passing boat, the hills cut against the sky, the city lights, the sea beating against the rocks—all suggesting a stable and indifferent order in contrast to the tense situation of the characters. Detached, the camera develops a specific regularity of composition that decenters the diegetic action and foregrounds its puzzling strategies, and the film presents a laconic narrative that marks its distance both from the sheer fantasy typical of the old, innocent cinema (the object of homage) and from the discursively realist cinema (the object of irony). In its allusions to both there is a "devitalization" through which the quoted pieces are emptied of their original force. The road at the end dissipates in a void; the long initial take of the shantytown is lifeless; the amusement park is empty; the projection room is deserted.

In this experience in a desert world, the strongest reference to the celestial sphere—the space of the angels—arises from the technological adventure: man's landing on the moon, shown on the video screen, a scene in which the spacecraft and the TV set assert a world that denies the practice of the bandits. The opposition between Santa Maria's liturgy and the conquest of the moon defines my next axis of inquiry, once it is clear that Bressane's film moves within the denial of these orders of time.

The Sky, the Earth, and the Sea of Quietness

In *The Angel Is Born* the bandits move in an insulated space, and society is reduced to its minimal conditions. Historical events, however, enter into the bandits' exiled world through the media, bringing the suggestive simultaneity between the scene in the summer-house living room and the astronauts' adventure. The bandits and their women prisoners, like a family on a holiday, watch the satellite transmission of the astronauts arriving on the moon. This transmission provides the radically contrapuntual element: science, technique, social organization, institutional power. From all the material covered by TV, Bressane chooses the moment of the political message of this power: Richard Nixon praising the astronauts. Speaking on behalf of mankind, he underlines his pride: "Because of what you have just achieved, the skies became part of man's world. . . . talking from there, from this sea of quietness, you inspire us to intensify our efforts towards peace and quietness on Earth." Nixon's speech takes the technical achievement as a promise of fulfillment of all human dreams. However, while proclaiming his idea of the *Pax Americana*, Nixon unwillingly creates the irony: the "sea of quietness" taken as a model is a desert, totally lacking life, a place where the act of conquest requires a radical isolation of man from his environment.

The opposition between the living room and the moon denies the discourse of unity, making it sound obscene. Together with this image of alterity, the transmission provides a specular image of rarefaction: The astronauts on the TV and the bandits in the room paradoxically converge in their wandering within a space of exile, the astronauts exploring an unknown territory to ratify the teleology of progress, the bandits exploring the other face of our old planet, denying and defiling this teleology.

The formal symmetry of the situations generates a singular perception: The adventure on the moon involves the use of an extreme version of security mechanisms already effective on earth, especially those used for protection not exclusively against the environment but also against human transgressors; these security mechanisms are radicalized when, in their turn, the bandits create their own safety bubble. That is, the astronauts, as an image of alterity in respect to the outlaws, by the common feature of rarefaction, provide an image of identity: They are all equal in the condition of being separated from other people in a special kind of seclusion. Excluded, the bandits must exclude, surviving through radical violence and isolation. The astronaut on the moon seems to accomplish the dream of man's redemption through the domination of nature on a planetary scale. He goes to utmost lengths through technology—the Western model—and in doing so undergoes a special experience separating him from others. Down on earth, the bandits undertake something like a descent into hell, an excursion from which there is no return to the underside of this world beneath the moon. They are equally estranged from humanity, symbolically on another planet, but they lack high technology and institutional support. Their individual gesture of trangression has its price: The paradigm of escape, not that of the conquest, defines their allegorical journey.

Santa Maria judges Nixon "a big moron," and Urtiga states that he has been "on the moon" for a long time; these ironies may have their charm as a refusal of the codes of power and its cynicism. But given the disparity of forces, they signalize the truly quixotic aspect of the journey that in practical terms finds little advantage in this self-centered pattern of reaction on the part of the bandits. Power does not show here its more prosaic agents, whether policemen or any other figure that might be placed in the protagonists' range of experience. The process of totalization—a recurrent feature in the films I analyze—is structured here in its minimal terms to enhance the scheme. Power only appears in its "major adventure" to intensify its contrast with the modest nature of the journey we follow. The bandits' experience pictures very well the tragic dimension of an aggression that has no hope for success. They are condemned to that succession of violence and cruelty that society takes as barbarism, in opposition to that kind of calculated violence that can be practiced by the winners and that is taken as a sign of civilization because it has the authority to "cleanse" itself as a legitimate convergence of militarism and science. Here aggression and bleeding define a borderline situation that, opposed to the extreme of technical asepsis in NASA's expedition, offers an emblematic representation of the contradictions of a state of things in which, to quote Walter Benjamin, "there is no document of civilization which is not, at the same time a document of barbarism."[4]

Having refused the teleology of progress, optimism, and the bourgeois sense of security, *The Angel Is Born* asserts, in its own texture, its organization of time as the Fall. As in other films here examined, the feelings of impotence and failure are again dominant, now no longer linked to political mistakes or historical illusions of intellectuals and no longer displaying the conciliatory stratagems of the trickster as seen in *Macunaíma*. Here the transgressive gesture has no doctrine. It is a radical example of people taking action that undoubtedly carries some parallel to a political radicalism that is willing to use violence in the process of struggle. Nevertheless, the representation of social violence here loses the funny dimension of parody without acquiring the noble dimension of a revolutionary stance. The paradigm of violence finds a new translation, a translation no longer anchored in the ascending movement of the oppressed or in the comic journey of the bandit as modern dandy, when it was, somehow, more gallantly shown. There is a clear presence of an economy of desire in the way the bandit deals with aggression: without mercy, brutal in his individualism, harsh in his disaster. In the end, after defeat, the protagonist's suffering admits no other translation than the elemental cry: a pain exiled from any transcendence.

The narration and the characters converge in their aggression toward the teleology of technical progress. But the disjunctive style of *The Angel Is Born* makes clear the split of stances, the difference produced by the fact that the transgression of the camera and of montage takes place on the level of language. The rupture here implies the evocation of the age of innocence—the *cinematographo*—and the acknowledgment of its impossible return; there is a double sense of proximity and separation that reveals itself to be productive for the elaboration of a poetics. In its confrontation with the present, such a poetics involves a deconstructive move addressed to the dominant cinematic codes. Refusing to accept the exclusive technical terms of modernization, the film raises again the issue of the relationship between time and cinema. The loss of innocence means a radical recognition of the transient character of experience and of the construction of temporality as sheer succession.

As an agonistic representation of structural gaps—between experience and language, look and scene, journey and origin—Bressane's film presents its allegory as the site of the nonreconciled, of characters cut off from material progress or any other promise of salvation, living an experience that reaffirms the endless work of death.

Figure 7.1

Figure 7.5

Figure 7.2

Figure 7.6

Figure 7.3

Figure 7.7

Figure 7.4

Figure 7.8

Figure 7.9

Figure 7.12

Figure 7.10

Figure 7.13

Figure 7.11

Figure 7.14

8

Killed the Family and Went to the Movies: The Ersatz Carnival

The Family Killer and the Lost Women: Mutual Inclusion

In *Killed the Family and Went to the Movies*, violence and un-easiness are again constant elements. In this film, however, the allegorical site of the unreconciled is shaped as a panel of disconnected actions, as a collection of minor episodes, unlike the rarefied world of *The Angel Is Born*. The principle of juxtaposition, characteristic of allegorical constructions, is now expressed in a series of events without a context, extreme situations of domestic criminality recorded with no concern for elaborate explanations. As in *The Angel Is Born*, laconism and disjunction mark the presentation of the episodes, but the enactment of criminal actions involves a new dramatic structure. There are more inserts, and this time they affect the continuity of the central story, creating a mosaic of encapsulated dramas. Violence does not come from the exterior into the space of the house but erupts as a result of an internal crisis. There is a game of repetitions in which the regularity of the composition is adjusted to the regularity of the theme: passionate crime.

Like *The Angel Is Born*—which was made at the same time in 1969—*Killed the Family and Went to the Movies* also presents in its title a sentence stating a "fact." In the former film, the metaphysical dimension of the fact began the riddle; here, the contrast between the common and the uncommon connected by the conjunction "and" defines a new strategy of awkwardness. Once the film begins, the immediate staging of the announced crime generates the allegory. The first episode corresponds literally to the enunciation of the film's title, which combines paratactically two orders of fact: One is extraordinary ("killed the family"), the other ordinary ("went to the movies"). The narrative, devoid of emphasis or dramatization, follows the paratactical order of the sentence. In less than ten minutes, Bressane condenses the promise of the title. A single sequence exhausts what should, as prescribed by the usual pattern, supposedly evolve during the eighty-minute projection: preparation, postponement, complication, and denouement. In *Killed the Family*, six brief shots and a single long take is all that is needed for the character to consummate the crime; one subsequent shot shows him going to the movies to watch *Lost Women in Love*.

A minimalist scheme is used to state the bizarre "family romance." First, there is a short scene in which the son, in his twenties, is sitting at the table for dinner with his parents. The camera observes them impassively from the hall. The young man, without a word, witnesses an argument between his parents about the temperature of a beverage—a minor skirmish in the conjugal war. The brevity of the scene clearly indicates that it is a pretext for releasing resentments and complaints. The next shot shows the young man in his room, lying on the bed—the posture of fantasizing—and playing silently with a razor. The static camera observes him from the hall. After a few seconds, a close-up shows his ritual in detail: He is passing the razor slowly along his own neck. There follows another brief psychodrama: In front of the TV set, his parents argue about the channel. Again, the static camera observes everything from the hall. The young man crosses the room and bids them good night. They ask, "Are you going already?" After a new ellipsis we are back to the bedroom and the mute ritual of the razor (Figure 8.1; page 217). The silence is broken by the sound of dripping water. A cut to the bathroom shows the young man placing drops in his eyes and making grimaces. He seems to take pleasure in this act, executing it slowly and with a kind of childish delight. A weird figure of regression, he is silent and discreet in front of his parents, he takes his time performing his private rituals, and he is meticulous in his personal care. His violence does not result from the classic oedipal conflict; his father is far from representing authority, repression, or obstacles; he is more adjusted to the inert condition that recalls the modest clerk whose private life consists of gossip and boredom, offering nothing that could be imitated. The family looks more like a residue, a dead load that the young man gets rid of with no further problems. In the sequence shot of his criminal act, he is pragmatic, rapid, and efficient. Using the razor, he quietly kills his father, who is totally engrossed in the TV, and in an offscreen action he kills his mother in her room (we hear only her cry). He then returns to the hall (where the camera is placed) and wipes the blood on an armchair. During this sequence shot, the camera moves for the first time. The long take starts with the image of Christ hanging on the wall—a traditional picture in Catholic lower-middle-class homes (Figure 8.2; page 217). Without leaving the hall, the camera pans around in order to catch the young man's visible displacements and waits while the killing of his mother is consummated offscreen. The slow camera movements and the absence of emphasis through editing or musical commentary set the descriptive tone of undramatized evidence.

From the dripping blood on the armchair (Figure 8.3; page 217), Bressane cuts directly to the entrance of the movie theater: The young man calmly buys his ticket and enters to see the film whose title is advertised on the marquee, *Lost Women in Love*. About the young man and his family we will hear no more. The film of his choice, *Lost Women in Love*, becomes the subject around which *Killed the Family*, the film of our choice, develops. Thenceforward, the story of the "lost young women in love" at the bourgeois mansion in Petrópolis is the reference that, after each insert, guarantees the continuity of a story provided with beginning, middle, and end. However, between *Killed the Family* and *Lost Women in Love* there is an ambiguous relationship that undermines the stability of the central plot enacted by the two young women. First of all, Bressane's film is framed by images of the actresses who play the young women in *Lost Women in Love*: *Killed the Family* opens and closes with shots of the two women. The first image of the film shows the actress Marcia Rodrigues, who plays Marcia, facing the camera, smiling, getting serious, talking to someone offscreen; the second image is similar to the first, showing Renata Sorrah, who plays Regina, in the same space. The last image of the film brings the two together smiling to the camera (Figures 8.4–8.6; page 217). Apart in the beginning, joined together in the end—these framing shots condense the course of the women's union. The composition of these shots is reminiscent of home movies; the women are in the foreground and there are trees in the background; these same trees will be seen at the Petrópolis house, the scene of their story, which indicates that *Lost Women in Love* acts as a frame for *Killed the Family*, rather than the reverse. If the protagonist of *Killed the Family* goes to see *Lost Women in Love*, which is thereby absorbed as a diegetic element among others within *Killed the Family*, then the images of the film within the film intrude beyond the moment when *Lost Women in Love* is introduced, as fiction, through the killer's choice as moviegoer.

This paradoxical play of mutual inclusion contains other elements. Late in the film, Marcia rather unconcernedly says that she had recently seen a Brazilian film. This fact is considered exotic by the two women who, obviously, do not value the cinema of their own country (this is a piece of irony directed to the Brazilian spectator). Marcia says, "It reminded me of you," alluding to a previous experience shared by both women, which coincides perfectly with the situation that they are presently staging. In other words, Marcia has been to see a film whose description identifies the film that we are presently watching, that is, *Killed the Family*. She says she did not like what she saw, mentioning the inexplicable series of "crimes in poor and messy places that have nothing to do with the two girls."

The spectator, anxious to link what is separated in the film and striving to make sense out of the mosaic of violence, sees his own possible reaction to the film childishly expressed by one of the characters. Apart from the irony directed at the spectator as judge or interpreter, this conversation plays a double role within the film's structure: It completes the circle of mutual inclusion, since it is now the character of *Lost Women in Love* who introduces *Killed the Family* into her own world. It also reinforces the predictability of the end.

The beginning is not the first term in a cause–effect relationship but, rather, an element that establishes the structural paradigm that will be valid for the rest of the film: The family killer episode provides the tone, sets the style of representation, and announces the basic pattern involving "figures of separation" whose contradiction, either mute or declared, is reconciled only in death. The violent end of *Lost Women in Love*—which is also the end of *Killed the Family*—is to be expected as a final display of cathartic violence within a film whose action has exposed its rules on different mirrors: the "crimes in poor and messy places that have nothing to do with the two girls."

Double Plotting: Mirror Effects

Some narratives develop the comparison between two individual destinies by means of an allegorical "double plotting." This strategy allows for the juxtaposition of two opposed story lines, revealing similar aspects of actions and characters socially distant from one another. *Killed the Family* uses something structurally analogous, a variation of the basic double plot pattern in which the juxtaposition does not involve two homogeneous narrative situations; rather, it confronts two social contexts: those of isolation in material comfort, characteristic of the bourgeois young women, and the mosaic of violence in five episodes involving characters in privation. On the one hand is the linear progression of a single situation; on the other, the eruption of the "messy inserts," in which the constant reference to the milieu of the poor, the homogeneous repertory of motives for the crime, and the constant use of disjunctive strategies connects the various separate segments.[1]

The mansion in Petrópolis, near Rio de Janeiro, is the meeting place of the "lost women in love," a space for a plunge into the web of personal memories and class traditions. The garden, when the story begins, is defined as the space for Marcia's husband's shooting practice, conducted under her bored look (this shooting practice is symmetrical with the one that "unites" the girls in the end of the film). After this first scene in the garden, Marcia's husband travels abroad on business. In Rio de Janeiro, her mother talks Marcia's friend Regina into keeping her company: "You must help her overcome this crisis," Regina replies: "You may count on me." In Petrópolis, Marcia dismisses all the servants. Gradually, the space of seclusion is established. Regina travels to Petrópolis. The two meet and take special pleasure in being together. The tone of the relationship is intimate in the subjects of conversation and in its spaces: bathroom, kitchen. Friends since childhood, schoolmates at a convent school, they exchange confidences: about marriage and social life. Both feel frustrated and are fed up with the tedious life of bourgeois housewives. Marcia's friend advises her to be patient, reasoning that boredom is everywhere and that "it could be worse." At first, Regina acts as though she were more worldly than her friend and teases Marcia for her good behavior ever since school. She tells her friend to learn how to play the marital game instead of going through all the trouble of switching husbands—after all, passion and mariage never match.[2] Lack of authenticity and bourgeois hypocrisy are recalled as efficient strategies that give a clean and civilized dimension to adultery, contrasting with the passionate crimes found in the sphere of the poor such as represented in the inserts. "In my way," she says, "I do as I please; I am happy." This rings false, however, and only serves to stress the similarity between the two women: their resentment of societal representation in which they feel like objects on display and their temptation toward a break, which will eventually come true. From their talk of the society of "dead people" that surrounds them—as if contaminated by extreme gestures displayed in the inserts—they begin to act out their fantasies, at first in a playful physical release through music. In a sequence that extends the allusions to home movies presented at the beginning, the women dance, mime the gestures of jazz musicians, and finally disappear behind a curtain with the farewell gestures typical of old film choreography.

In between two successive inserts, their release reaches a new stage, and in the bedroom a new intimacy will be experienced. Looking at old photographs, they exchange memories while the sound of a piano brings an innocent touch of silent cinema. As they look at the pictures, they touch each other's hands and exchange glances, tender smiles, and whispers (Figures 8.7–8.8; page 217). Marcia rises and gets the school uniform out of the wardrobe to "try it on." Regina, still lying in bed, shows her desire while staring at Marcia, who is offscreen. Once desire is figured, the camera leaves the girls and brings the image of the gun cabinet in the house, a kind of anticipation that suggests a connection between the girls' liberation and those guns eventually withdrawn from the family's aristocratic collection. As their intimate party advances, they enact a return to adolescence, parodying repressive maternal social etiquette.

The women's laughter, which intensifies as the double killing approaches, betrays the presence of a repressed melodrama, of "another scene" that has been displaced so as to open the space for this ritualistic resolution in which simulation and experience, the serious-dramatic and the playful-carnivalesque, are found. Kitchen and bathtub provide awkward settings that contrast with the gestures of impersonation from which the women derive fun.

Their game culminates in the manipulation of weapons and in the make-believe shooting that eventually results in true death—they kill each other. Everything unfolds according to an amalgamation of Eros and Thanatos, following the traditional path of fulfillment in death of absolute passion. The girls' love story condenses the classical components: unhappiness in marriage, the plunge into an experience of extramarital passion, hidden, transgressive. It triggers the expected outcome: the union through death as a confirmation of the absolute character of the relationship, a relationship incompatible with the prosaic world of everyday tasks and conciliations. However, here everything is far from reproducing the solemn tone of this kind of story. The sequence of actions has that touch of make-believe already underlined, a touch that shuns dramatic involvement and fosters the playful side of the situation. The Romanesque paradigm is very obviously called up but only to be submitted to parodic displacements. These begin in the film's title itself—*Lost Women in Love*—which alludes to kitsch products of the entertainment industry. At the same time, the film seeks a serious-dramatic effect in the final sequence when the corpses lay on the ground. In order to fulfill its purposes, the girls' theater must bring a bitter taste, a plunge into mourning that dissolves the playful atmosphere. Here, Bressane's typical irony, produced by the insistent look at the scene, acquires a special role. A sentimental song acts as a comment to the girls' blood pact—"I feel sad just by thinking of losing you," sung by Roberto Carlos, is heard over the images of the corpses on the floor (Figures 8.9–8.11; page 218). When the film introduces the last shot of the girls (Regina's feet), the record, by some disruptive factor, gets stuck at the same point, playing it over and over again. This refusal to end reminds us of the last shot in *The Angel Is Born*, and the annoying repetition of the song is now the last aggression that closes *Killed the Family*'s representation of violence, which is marked by redundancy and the reiteration of a basic narrative pattern as the film deals with juxtaposed domestic dramas.

The different episodes, exhibiting similar actions and similar strategies, end by composing a play of mirrors that foregrounds their link, although they are presented as separated realities. The most explicit mirror effect connects the pact between these bourgeois women with the brief story narrated in the third insert. Two adolescent girls swear loyalty and eternal love; the camera observes them according to Bressane's near–far scheme: A long shot shows them far from the camera in an open space of busy streets, electrical wires, and an overpass while, on the sound track, their dialogue is heard as if it were happening offscreen near the camera. A series of short scenes provides a few "explanations" for the criminal action, which, as usual in the film, happens abruptly. Emphasis is on the opposition between their forbidden love and society, and a pact strengthens their relationship in the face of the repression exerted by the mother of one of the girls and by the malicious gossip of the neighbors. As in the earlier paradigmatic episode of the family killer, the conflicts are laconically stated, and the final outburst of violence is shown in a single sequence shot. The frail, harmless, silent girls are played by the same actresses who enact the bourgeois tragedy in Petrópolis. In this episode, they have the shy and courteous behavior of simple girls from the poorer suburbs, but they are also more straightforward when it comes to violence. There is no ambiguity in their outburst, in the crime perpetrated in the small, tastelessly furnished living room. In a frontal shot, one of the girls strikes the old woman in the foreground while her friend calmly polishes her own nails in the background. The static camera observes the action and, when the old woman is dead, draws back to show the dark wall separating the kitchen from the living room; this dark wall acts as a frame for the action in the center of the picture, thus intensifying its tableaulike composition (Figure 8.12; page 218). The long duration of this shot produces an obsessive contemplation of the fait accompli and an estrangement effect underlined by the playing of an old carnival song sung by Carmen Miranda—"*Oi que terra boa pra se farrear* [Hey, what a lovely place to have fun]." The disjunction already present in the camera movement is reinforced by the music, which opposes, to the scene of crime, the elegy of the tropical land as the locus for pleasure and feast.

This is the pattern followed in the presentation of the "crimes in poor and messy places" triggered by conjugal misery, resentment, and unwanted revelations. The structure of echoes and repetitions that is typical of *Killed the Family* performs an anatomy of marriage seen through the eyes of Regina's philosophy of survival. Within the scheme "theme and variations," the narration chooses what should be shown and what should be hidden from the audience's eyes, producing systematic changes from episode to episode. The most condensed is the episode of the man who "killed for love," introduced in our first leap from the Petrópolis mansion. In this case the camera arrives at the spot of the crime after it has been committed and behaves like a reporter or a detective. The film concentrates on the representation of the moment immediately after the catharsis, without looking back, without observing the decisive gesture. The camera keeps on exploring the impoverished scenery, in a glance that reminds us of the kind of inventory typical of the documentary cinema of that time. The entire scene is presented in a single sequence shot, which, as in the crime scene of the first episode, opens on a religious picture on the wall in a poor house; the handheld camera then proceeds to circle about the scene, showing the benumbed lover, played by the same actor who enacts the role of the family killer, holding a knife and sitting by the corpse of a woman lying face downward on the ground (Figures 8.13–8.15; page 218).

Then the camera explores the scenery, describing the furniture and walls, until it spots a group of onlookers at the doorstep (onlookers to the crime or to the filming?), whereupon it returns to the center of the scene and shows the blood on the floor beside the victim. On the sound track, the offscreen sentence "I killed out of love" is repeated over and over again until it is replaced by an old carnival song of obsessive love: "I can't get you out of my mind, oh my love." Though gesture and motivation are in accord with the obsessive passion evoked by the song, the association of carnival and domestic tragedy remains enigmatic.

The last insert is another presentation of a news brief, closing upon the same combination: sequence shot, domestic crime, carnival song on the sound track. The setting is the kitchen of a poor house; the killer, a drunk and jealous husband; the victims, his wife and child. The novelty of this insert is the direct connection that is established after the killing between the space of the scene and that of the music. Initially, the music functions as an offscreen commentary, referring to the figure of Pierrot and to amorous disillusionment as the camera focuses on the killer sitting on a chair beside his wife's corpse. As though emerging from a deep stupor, the new version of the family killer—played by the same actor as in the earlier inserts—gets up and begins to dance to the song. The image of this weird dance is interrupted by an unexpected change: The camera draws back abruptly and focuses on a back window facing a dirty wall, where the broken glass and dirt provide an image of neglect and privation. This image of a precarious detail condenses in a last fragment the tableau of social erosion built through the different inserts, whose poor and tasteless settings have been ostensibly investigated by the camera.

The film's pattern is that of a disciplined voyeurism, like that of the police investigator, the news-seeking journalist, or the social anthropologist. The feature common to all episodes is the disjunction between composition and diegesis, with the camera as stranger, newcomer to the sphere of action, attracted by the details of the environment in a detached posture of description that turns naturalism into allegory.

Individual Transgression as Ersatz Carnival

At first, the burst of carnival imagery in the crime scene causes perplexity, and one could interpret such contrast in terms of the opposition between good (the energy of collective utopia and the innocence of songs) and evil (aggression and passionate violence). In fact the relation is more complex and as the last episode explains, carnival as metaphor (rather than metonymic contrast) is integrated with the scene to figure the idea of catharsis. In *Killed the Family* such a catharsis is taken as violence that resolves accumulated tensions and individual conflicts. On the other hand, considered as a symbolic transgression, a moment of rupture with normal life, it can be seen as a perverted version of that discontinuity brought by the feast as a space of unity beyond individuation. On the level of an ethics of individual responsibility, the crime is seen as an inevitable Fall, a sin that asks for punishment (Thou shalt not kill!). But, on the symbolic level, it may bring a counterpoint of liberation, a rupture from a resentful order, an affirmative ritual that, in its way, is an adultered space of fusion (love–death). That is, violence acquires here its uncommon connotation because the void created by the lack of explanation is fulfilled, as the film develops, by this formal order of repetitions that give a ritualistic dimension to the acts of transgression. The collection of gestures seems to be answering to a hidden demand and would make sense within an order of things surely apart from the Christian framework provided by the pictures hanging on the walls of the houses. Not named, this order transcends each particular scene and creates an atmosphere of agony that displaces both moral judgments and causal explanations. This aggressive choice on the part of the filmmaker is not sheer blasphemy against religion and science. It expresses the unavoidable character of people's malaise within a certain juncture, repeatedly expressed in violence and crime. There is no progression in the experience outlined in *Killed the Family*, just repetition and death. The decisive point is that the catharsis does not, and indeed could not, reach the utopian stage of the collective feast evoked by the songs; that is, it does not fully cope with the symbolic demand it seems to allude to since it implies destructive acts that become effective in the isolated sphere of private life. The juxtaposition created by the vertical montage (collective feast–private scene) suggests the crime as ersatz, as a substantive experience that remains beneath the paradigm of sacrifice that is in its horizon. Understood as a love gesture, a fusional movement, it fulfills an impossible fate of reconciliation, an impossibility that the melancholy tone of the carnival songs in the film incorporate.

The carnival songs, even when fully integrated in the collective feast itself, many times distill the feeling of the ephemeral character of happiness, a mixture of liberation and disappointment. In Bressane's film, they assume their full condition of life affirmation amid anguish, a transfiguration in which we hear echoes of the entire course of samba culture in the Carioca urban space. The camera's look at the scene of crime requires the samba framework to make its persistence meaningful, as a plunge into the dimension of rite that exorcises loss, desperation, and death.

In these terms, the representation of conflicts in *Killed the Family* tries to work the uncommon experiences without creating a point of view that condemns the bad conduct from above. Focusing on family crisis, the film stands back from the melodramas of resentment, the banal violence, and the cynical view disseminated by the media. It seeks a different effect by performing a kind of observation oriented to creating estrangement exactly when it seems to be simply reproducing banal newspaper headlines—"Killed the Family and Went to the Movies," "Madly in Love," and "I Killed for Love" could all be on a newspaper's front page. We have the cliché without the usual treatment given to crimes of passion. There is no teleology of guilt and redemption, and the evocation of Paradise is here rather ironic. On the one hand, the carnival song sung by Carmen Miranda refers to the "lovely place to have fun," parodying the romantic poem of exile "The Song of Exile" written by Gonçalves Dias in the nineteenth century. On the other hand, lost in a fragmented world, the characters in Bressane's film carry out within four walls a series of crimes that seem to confirm unredeemable violence as a structural feature of the "lovely place."

This notion of violence as a structural element is most evident in the insert at the middle of the film. There, again within four walls, the violence of power is displayed in a paradigmatic representation: torture inflicted by the repressive state apparatus. This is violence as method rather than as catharsis: the utmost expression of a diseased social tissue. The figure who throughout the film performs criminal acts—as son, lover, and father—receives his punishment in a series of torture sessions, short scenes compounded of electricity, cries, and blood (Figure 8.16; page 218). The fact that there is no attempt to identify the victim and no speculation on the circumstances reinforces the allusion to the period around 1970, at the height of the military dictatorship's repression. Since the Brazilian police also use torture on common prisoners, the specifically political connotation is made by a detail. The chief torturer threatens the prisoner, saying that things are going to get worse, adding: "You asked for it yourselves." The plural pronoun implies the existence of comrades and refers to a space whose representation is forbidden: the social and political struggle, the armed conflict then in process. This reference is reinforced by the fact that the insert follows the musical number staged by the bourgeois women, a piece of innocent entertainment preceded by a clear allusion to censorship. Marcia, reading the newspaper by the swimming pool, quotes Dom Helder Câmara: "The situation in Brazil . . . I know, you know, he knows."

The fragmented representation of social experience, tempered with scattered, although striking, allusions to repression, assumes the tenor of a political allegory. The film's structure—its principle of juxtaposition and play on noncontextualization—suggests through its voids and silences the network of interdictions that condemn social agents to isolation. In *Killed the Family* the repressive society finds an oblique representation that thematizes its fractures through the eruption of microtragedies in closed spaces, informed by bourgeois ennui or lower-class privation. The reiterated allusion to the absent "communal spirit" of carnival suggests this imaginary resolution of social contradictions as a ritual that "knows" the privation on which it feeds. The "momentary explosion" reveals its hidden face.

In *The Angel Is Born* the "song of exile" referred to the rarefied world of those who live on the margin of society, destroying privacy or wandering around open spaces without origin or destination. *Killed the Family*'s microtragedies are not produced by an invasion that destroys the equilibrium of domestic life. Rather, they are the unfolding of an internal crisis; their space is "normality" itself, a terrain already thoroughly undermined. In different ways, these two films, ostensibly inorganic in their development, are journeys into the ugly side of the empirical world, fragments of ironic pessimism suggesting the experience of underdevelopment as exile and damnation in the world, as a sequence of unredeemed catastrophes on the outskirts of history.

At this stage, the allegory expresses categorical denial of its first term. The purgatory of meaningful violence represented in *Black God, White Devil* is replaced by the hell of peripheral violence represented in Bressane's films, a realm of misery in confinement in which there is no place for redemption. And melancholy is present in the old recordings of popular songs of migration, of amorous disenchantment, and of lost happiness and through the references to a cinema that has lost its innocent magic. Bressane evokes a journey from which there is no return, a painful separation from idealized origin, a universe in which are reversed the ideal harmony of family life and communal fulfillment and the purposeful action of historical agents lucidly preparing a better future. The transgression and confinement of Bressane's films generate a bitter image of disenchantment. In them, the experience is enacted by social beings determined by alien forces beyond their understanding. They act as social beings caught in the "storm of progress," subjected to the trauma of urban experience and atomization.

We have in *Killed the Family* a sui generis dialectic of fragmentation and totalization. Each fact remains in its singular isolation, but as the film advances the mosaic of situations goes on creating an allegorical context for the transgressions, suggesting that they are different re-enactments of a common drive that crosses differences in class, gender, and circumstances. In the beginning, discomfort comes from the abrupt confrontation with the family massacre; later the repetitions make clear that the "shock experience" is not planned as a result of the un-expectedness of the facts. What is striking is the fact that the questions raised by the opening story remain unanswered and end up resonating with the entire series; the inserts do not come to explain anything but to make us feel encircled by other events of the same sort. The film is a continuous challenge because of its structural violence, which is placed on the level of language, but it does not seek the same effect created by the protocol of distance inspired by Bertolt Brecht, as that protocol oc-curred with the cinema of the 1960s and 1970s. Undoubtedly what I have called disjunctive style mobilizes procedures that had been la-beled as deconstructive tools: arbitrary camera movements, staged se-quence shots, explicit comments, discontinuity, blocking of episodes. But Bressane's film does not organize these procedures in order to call attention to an elaborate argument. Its central aim is to shock, and its aesthetic program defines film experience as a ritual that implies a deeper involvement with spectacle, outside the frivolous frame and the automatism expected from commercial cinema. When I say "deeper" I refer not only to the idea of a stronger commitment to the contents of the scenes and its relation to experience, life, and reality. I also mean the severe posture with which the film proposes a new relation to the transgressive scene, forcing the spectator to take the risk of an undesirable inward trip.

At the end of the 1960s, Brazilian cinema, by different means, brought to the scene the radical experiences of a culture of violence, including the anatomy of a patriarchal tradition and its rules on love and sex. In the urban experience, this tradition was suffering clear transformations, which were taken as a central theme by the popular music and the theater of the decade. The family issue generated an uneasiness that demanded a cinematic language before it could be expressed. Some films approached the theme in terms of conventional drama, a less interesting way of translating to screen the cultural atmosphere inflected by *tropicalism*. More advanced, *Killed the Family* was an outstanding work within that context. As an allegory of the Brazilian social crisis, it did not separate the reflection on crime from the discussion of the act of going to the movies. In these terms, it placed itself as a challenging experience, an experience in which cinema does not consider itself as a good entertainment exterior to the circle of violence that it observes but recognizes itself as part of the process, an exercise of the look that carries with it the same problematic of love and death that it focuses on.

Figure 8.1

Figure 8.5

Figure 8.2

Figure 8.6

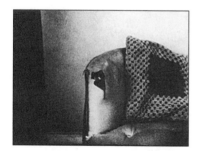

Figure 8.3

Figure 8.7

Figure 8.4

Figure 8.8

Figure 8.9

Figure 8.13

Figure 8.10

Figure 8.14

Figure 8.11

Figure 8.15

Figure 8.12

Figure 8.16

9

Bang Bang:
Passage, Not Destination

Process, Not Product

At the end of *Killed the Family and Went to the Movies*, the two actresses, side by side, smile facing the camera. This last image closes the series of portraits and dissolves the heavy atmosphere created by the scene of their death, reasserting the combination of game and violence that had permeated the entire film. The return of the dead women, relaxed and smiling, is no doubt an instance of Brechtian estrangement-effect, but the final shot is not an act of aggression addressed to the audience. A more disturbing challenge occurs in *Bang Bang*, Andrea Tonacci's version of the structural aggression that was being radicalized around 1970. Crowning a constant sabotage to the progression of a story, the film ends with the ironic image of the actor laughing at the audience.

In the evolution from the "aesthetics of hunger" to *Land in Anguish* and thence to Marginal Cinema, space is developed within Brazilian cinema for reflexivity. Glauber Rocha's films contain a number of quotations and references that, for the initiated spectator, work as subtexts in a manner similar to those of other young filmmakers in the 1960s. Bressane's films combine nostalgia and aggression to create the view that there is a film style to be built, illusions to be destroyed, and educators to be displaced in his bitter, lacerated critical approach to social and cinematic development. Situated midway between Rocha and Bressane, *Red Light Bandit* stands as the clearest point of inflection on the path to metacinema. In Sganzerla's film, the consideration of cinema is an explicit element, part of the audiovisual texture itself, part of the network of references that provide a structural foundation for his parodic approach. Sganzerla uses plagiarism as a way of life, as a style. Andrea Tonacci's *Bang Bang* defines more sharply the reflection on the vehicle (cinema) and its language. It is, in this sense,

219

the final term of my detailed textual analysis, the point at which the allegory of underdevelopment, as outlined here, reaches dissolution. Tonacci rejects the approach that aspires to encompass social totality. He deliberately establishes his own limits and invites the spectator to reflect on the film experience itself. He is not committed to the establishment of a diegetic universe as an allegorical site of hunger and rebellion, of garbage and corruption, of human violence and exile. His cinema, rather, tends toward a deconstruction in which a diegetic dissolution rejects interpretation as irrelevant. He favors neither country nor town. Nor does he propose a diagnosis of the diseases afflicting Brazilian society. Unconcerned with the "national question," his entire work refers back to the cinema.

His characters—if they can so be called—are fragments of a fictional world generated by a century of cinematic experience, figures out of old genre movies, presented as caricatures and summoned for the staging of the narrative cinema's paradigmatic game: the chase. Their action is intrinsically linked with the play on language. Despite what its title promises, Tonacci's film frustrates all narrative and genre expectations. On the one hand, its concern is that constellation of shotguns, speed, and disaster that form the urban experience that found in film noir its popular mythical transfiguration. On the other hand, only the fragments of that tradition are present here, mainly as raw material for strange juxtapositions, a game of repetitions in which there is no continuity of action. Tonacci's antiteleology is radical. Diegesis is mere pretext, and the film's aim is to challenge our modes of perception.

Although refusing a serious discussion of social types, *Bang Bang* deals with the same issues of violence and disaster that permeate all the films I have examined. The grotesque, the gap between pretense and performance, and emblematic objects like the automobile play a central role in the film. Its pop dimension reminds us of the *tropicalist* context, but one cannot find here that same concern for national culture. We see a lot of wandering, but we are far from the social themes of migration, cultural conflicts, and marginalization typical of Cinema Novo. What comes to the foreground is the more universal aspects of the journey. As to the paradigmatic action (the chase), Tonacci is only concerned with the presentation of the characters' gestures, not with any sign related to the idea of motive or purpose. What matters is the performance of a noncontextualized game.

The opening sequence shot of *Bang Bang*, which constitutes a central metaphor for the film's structure, is a good example of Tonacci's deconstructive turn (Figure 9.1; page 232). From the back seat of a taxicab the static camera observes the driver, the passenger, and the street through a wide-angle lens, maintaining the same composition for nearly ten minutes—the duration of this long take. As it begins the driver, alone, must make a swift turn to avoid running over the protagonist, who steps in front of his car. The protagonist gets into the car, angry with the driver: "Are you nuts, do you want to knock me down?" He tells him, however, to "get going." The nonsense continues throughout the ride; they keep going around, neither of them knowing which way to head. The passenger never stops nagging the driver but never tells him where he wants to go. They argue about nothing at all and eventually start a fight; finally the passenger is thrown out of the car. The shot fades out; the punctuation is slow and conspicuous.

An identical scene will occur in the middle of the film, shot in the same way, and the second version of a similar long take inside the car divides the film in two parts. In one, the urban space prevails; in the other, it is the open space of the highways that provides the setting for the wandering. The cab ride reproduces in detail the film structure as a whole. The experience of watching *Bang Bang* is comparable to a ride whose destination and route are never defined; the ride is a pretext for an argument. As announced by the cab scene, Tonacci's nonpurposiveness sets a paradox insofar as it feeds on the discourse on purpose—a discourse in which the characters perform contrary to their intent. In his outraged complaint about the taxi's lack of direction, the passenger feigns an intention of destination that he should, after all, indicate himself.

Like the passenger and the cab driver, the gangsters in *Bang Bang* reveal their awkward behavior from their first appearance on. The three men and their old car all come out of the same warehouse, the site of the credit sequence of *Bang Bang*, the second sequence shot of the film. In a garage, packed with auto parts and other industrial scrap, the camera encounters the three motionless gangsterlike figures. As the camera moves toward them, they begin to act like stage properties in a huge storehouse, human types awaiting rental for performance in a genre movie. Suddenly, for no apparent reason, one of these figures, who happens to be blind, starts firing a gun at random. This is the first instance of a gesture to be repeated throughout the film. The camera, as if in fright, starts withdrawing as the credit letters move toward it (Figure 9.2; page 232). In its movement of withdrawal the gangsters are revealed as suspended on a platform above ground. They must descend to start their performance. They do so, getting into a big, old American car from the early 1950s, another reminiscence of countless old movies (Figure 9.3; page 232). The movement of withdrawal continues, and the high-angle shot now discloses the ample space of the warehouse in a composition that is reminiscent of the tracking shot in the opening sequence of Eisenstein's *Strike*. In that shot the factory was revealed as the stage on which the class struggle was enacted, the space of work and the dynamic social experience that was the theme of the film. Here, however, a slower tracking shot discloses a universe of immobility, filled with junk and industrial scrap—raw material for the *bricoleur*. Tonacci reassembles the fragments of a classical diegetic cinema whose scraps, in *Bang Bang*, play a different role since the game in which they now participate is a categorical refusal of telos. The film plays throughout upon the spectator's compelling impulse to relate sequences chronologically, spatiotemporally, or causally. In Tonacci's metacinema, every bit of action leads nowhere.

The episode that opens the second half of the film, placed just after the second version of the car ride, instantiates the same logic, now in terms of sound and dialogue: The fluency of the narrative is suspended while the characters make "fluency" the very topic of conversation. The setting is a bar—a paradigm of the encounter point in shoot-'em-ups (in Portuguese, *filmes de bang bang*). But this is a bar without a bartender. An enormous mirror behind the counter reflects everything present, even the camera. The bar scene has two stages. In the first, the protagonist (the passenger, now in the role of "pursued") enters. A drunk insistently offers him a beer, which he refuses. Annoyed, he stands by the counter where a telephone keeps ringing, but it remains silent whenever he picks up the receiver. In the second stage, a woman enters (the dancer from a previous scene) and they sit at a table by the glass window overlooking the street. We start to believe that something is finally going to happen, but as the camera moves back and forth between the man and the woman, they merely keep initiating a dialogue over and over. To the sound of different background noises, they try different ways of greeting each other. Unable to reach a consensus, the discussion about the greeting formula becomes the subject of conversation. They end by agreeing that the world "Hi!" should substitute for expressions such as "How are you?" and "Good Morning." The desirability of using as few words as possible is contradicted by the articulation of the discourse, which is prolix and redundant. In this metadialogue, an explicit reference is made to the phatic function of language, stressing that the contact between the interlocutors is more relevant than the message itself.

As a metaphor of the cinematographic experience, this sequence in the bar represents what happens in *Bang Bang*. The fundamental issue is that of procedures maintaining contact between film and spectator rather than the implementation of scenes produced toward a specific narrative goal. In *Bang Bang* the process of film conversation is more important than its result. This can be generalized as follows: For Tonacci, it is a question of process, not product; of passage, not destination.

Serial Composition and Metamorphosis: The Magician, the Dancer, and the Automobile

Bang Bang is an accumulation of sequences that function as pretext for structural variations on a single theme. The play on the chase takes place within the closed space of a hotel (the lobby, the elevator, the guest room), along the automobile's movement on a highway, on the ground floor, on top of a building, on a city street, on a prairie, on a side road. The gangsters, the passenger (the supposed victim), the dancer, the old car, the bar, the hotel, the highway, and the magician who stands for cinema itself provide the material necessary to the endless game made of the renewed encounters between pursuer and pursued. The rule in the film is the display of inconsistent actions performed by weird agents, including an ape (one of the protagonist's masks).

The protagonist, so far called the "passenger," has no past and in the succession of misadventures he seems to be always beginning again. Impassive, he faces the chase with good humor, without any anxiety, only engaged in the exterior and pragmatic side of his action, without expressing any commitment. He is the opposite of Cinema Novo's typical hero. Not by accident, everything in *Bang Bang* takes place in transient, impersonal, anonymous spaces—the hotel, the bar, the road. Everything points to an unrooted figure without specific bonds that could stitch together an identity. The taxi passenger, the hotel guest, and the ape facing the mirror correspond to different masks that cannot be taken surely as belonging to the same character, although they are played by the same actor. Discontinuity is the mark of this central figure, and we can say the same of the female counterpart, so far referred as the passenger's partner in the bar dialogue.

Immediately following the presentation of the basic elements of the chase, the space of the hotel becomes the site of a series of episodes. First, the passenger, wearing the ape mask, has sexual intercourse with the female figure, who, in this sequence, acts the stereotypical delicate and passive victim. Her presence in *Bang Bang* is intermittent—she appears and disappears when the game warrants. When the passenger, unmasked, meets the gangsters in the hotel lobby, she is no longer there; but she will reappear later on as the Spanish dancer on top of a building. Meanwhile, the film explores the effects of the editing process, which is associated with the performance of a magician.

A set of brief shots and the music typical of the suspense film prepare for the first lobby scene, building up expectation. The passenger steps out of the elevator and his frontal position in relation to the camera (now standing for the pursuers) allows for a play with depth of field in exploration of the symmetry of the lobby's architecture. From a close-up next to the elevator, the film cuts to a long shot of the lobby along the same axis. The elevator ride shows everyone smeared with blood, an implausible element since the victim does not look hurt or even worried at being in the hands of his captors. In the hotel room, the lack of coherence in the actions persists. The passenger is now shown alone in the bathroom. The room is empty. As the audio logo of Twentieth Century Fox is heard, a magician appears and claps his hands: We hear music and, out of nowhere, there appear a dove, a cigarette, and some playing cards, which fall on the floor. Curiously, in this evocation of the film industry, the magician seems to be as surprised as we are. Gaining in self-assurance, he once again claps his hands, and a gangster appears in drag directly in the foreground, eating a sandwich. He claps twice again, and the blind gangster appears— gun in hand and ready to shoot—followed by the dandy gangster, concerned, as always, about his looks. Then another clap, and the passenger appears, summoned by the magic wand of montage. Each clap brings about alterations in the decor; when the entire group is assembled, the floor is a real mess, with paper scattered all about, as if there had been a fight. One gangster cries out: "The suitcase, where's the suitcase?" Upon a clap of the magician's hands, the suitcase falls on the group from above. The blind man, hearing the noise, shoots. The transvestite is totally aloof from the criminal plot; all he wants is food and drink. Upon another clap of the hands, the passenger disappears, the dandy becomes a woman watching herself in a mirror, and the gluttonous transvestite becomes a man sitting at a table covered with packages and bottles in the foreground; he is eating. Inside the room, a bizarre jukebox starts playing a carnival song. The combination is grotesque: At the sound coming from the jukebox, the dandy, now a woman, shakes his body; the fat glutton, now a man, belches; and the blind gangster shoots at random. Upon a new clap of hands, the room is emptied. The passenger enters the room, picks up a gun and the suitcase, and calmly leaves. We hear the magic clap of hands and see the passenger inside the elevator face-to-face with the magician himself, who now seems disposed to direct participation in the action; he points a threatening gun at the victim (Figure 9.4; page 232). Contrary to all expectations, the scene dissolves.

An arbitrary jump takes us to the top of a building for a new stage of the game: that of the long takes. The Spanish dancer is performing; her figure, all in black, stands out in contrast to the clear sky and the buildings low in the background, and she moves as if stepping on the screen's bottom edge (Figure 9.5; page 232). The dance remains, for quite a while, the focal point of our attention. The usual pattern, whereby the cabaret dance is a mere backdrop, an exotic punctuation of the central narrative action, is inverted. Here the gunfight episode and the chase form brief interruptions of the Spanish dance and music, which are dominant and autonomous elements. Long takes and camera movements contravene the editing principle at work in the scene inside the hotel; the magician is gone, and his handclaps are replaced by the continuous development of the dance. The dancer's figure and her swaying movements, dominating the skyline of buildings, call for horizontal pans. Her figure imposes itself before the camera, dominating the scene against a background of gray sky and the tops of buildings. Her power and control contrast with the awkward chase within the hotel, in which clumsy gangsters have their action manipulated by the editing process. The dancer's performance imposes its own rhythm and evokes the fascination typical of the early cinema of attractions[1] or the avant-garde tradition that reworked that primacy of the long take.

In *Bang Bang* we begin with the reference to genre films, but the dancer's sequence makes us think of cinema as conceived by Germaine Dulac. This avant-garde filmmaker searched for cinema as music, as art in which gesture and composition should integrate without any exterior purpose. This experience of harmony and autonomy created by a dance performance would be, in Dulac's view, in opposition to the mechanical and ugly agitation typical of action films made of fragmented pieces joined by montage. Tonacci juxtaposes both harmony and "agitation," but he does not contrast the value of the body and the supposed nonvalue of technology. His cinematic construction makes clear that the recuperation of harmony—or the leap to a superior stage of dialogue with the world and the human body—does not result from a move back to artisanal creation, against montage. Rather, it requires an impulse to work the basic film technologies in a way surely incompatible with mainstream cinema. In *Bang Bang* formal relations define the level of coherence. These involve the play on paradigmatic oppositions as manifested in a series of changes and contrasts produced by movements, both of camera and within the frame: changes from close-up to long shot or from horizontal to vertical, contrasts of scale in the relation between human figure and object, alternating predominance of noise and dialogue. What should be diegetic action is no more than a support for the exercise of compositional procedures. The rigorous quality of camera movement and montage contrasts with the awkwardness and grotesque aspect of the action-film characters. Order and competence are on the side of the specifically cinematic strategies; disorder is on the side of the pro-filmic.[2]

Here the emphasis given to nonprogression, to discontinuity, is clearly connected to the political discussion of 1968–70, when deconstructive moves tried to destabilize a certain order of representation. Tonacci wants to de-automatize perception and, in its endless starting over again, the film reminds us of the surrealist juxtapositions and their attack on teleology. In the 1970 juncture, this dialogue with surrealism is mediated by Godard's *Weekend* (1968), a film in which the aesthetics of black humor offered an apocalyptic view of consumer society and of its ritual of mobility supported by its major fetish, the automobile. Godard depicts the obsession with speed typical of modern capitalist society as a kind of perverse lack of harmony: that which finds its emblems in the images of car accidents explored by the filmmaker since *Pierrot le fou*. Godard's constellation—technology, automobile, regressive behavior—finds its rarefied, minimalist version in Tonacci's film.

And *Bang Bang* reminds us of Luis Buñuel's films when the bandits are not able to find satisfaction because their *déjeuner sur l'herbe* ("picnic lunch") is endlessly delayed and never really accomplished.

After variations on urban architecture, the film develops the car's displacements. A night tracking shot of the city streets reasserts the rules of the game: One gangster holds a flashlight, which allows us glimpses of the fight inside the car; the blind gangster shoots at random. The image fades and the black screen provides an interval for the introduction of the first (daylight) shot in the countryside, the space for the horizontal expansion of the chase. The camera, placed at the back of the car, reproduces, with a wide-angle lens, the composition of the cabride sequence. All the elements for action are again present: the gangsters, the supposed victim, the car, the suitcase, the guns. The group inside the car wakes up, behaving as if on their way to a picnic (the back of the car is stuffed with baskets and bottles). The car begins to move. Action-film music dramatizes the ride, but nothing really happens.

Whereas in the bandits' regressive posture eating is the typical obsession, the passenger is linked to the realm of bathrooms—not kitchens— and an entire sequence is organized to make possible his act of defecation as part of the landscape. A long shot focuses on plain and mountains; the image appears out of the darkness, and music begins a crescendo; movement is reinstated. In a five-minute chase, the camera pursues a jeep over a landscape that resembles Monument Valley, and the music slowly accelerates, maintaining an excitement that never reaches its climax. At the top of the mountains the passenger stops his car and, seen from a distance, sits on his feet, supposedly finding relief from the pressure created by a medicine he took in the hotel bathroom. Again the chase is dispersed as it had started, but the promise is renewed: the montage, under the music's command, creates another full-fledged chase, with the participation of all the elements: the jeep, the big old car, the gangsters, the woman, the protagonist in his ape mask. The action, as if asserting once and for all the impotence of its agents, is a mere pretext for a disaster scene.

Again the dark screen and leap to another space take us to the surprising image that finally shows an outstanding event. In a long shot, a high-angle view of the road—the camera on a crane—shows the aftermath of disaster. A carefully framed image shows the car already burning on one side of the road, after the fact (Figure 9.6; page 232). The spectacular view and melancholy piano music give an allegorical dimension to this image of disaster in that particular landscape—the wind, the road, and the mountains in the background last for minutes on the screen until the passenger's jeep arrives to help the victims.

This time the road, although again metaphorical, is not the site of a suggestive ending, as occurred in many Cinema Novo films and in *The Angel Is Born*. *Bang Bang* goes on with its game of repetitions, even after the destruction of its major relic, the American car from the 1950s. As I suggested, this emblematic object evokes the design of an entire epoch in which the *streamlined* car embodied in its forms the fantasies of speed typical of an affluent society and its promises of consumption and mobility. Here the disaster takes part in the series of odd behaviors that permeate the all scenes, behaviors that remind us of *The Red Light Bandit*'s world. The difference is that the way the burning car is shown on the screen brings a sense of a solemn estrangement created by the awkward image of destruction that acquires a connotation of fate that, although ephemeral like everything else in the film, dramatically asserts death as a discontinuous eruption, as the inescapable limit of any game.

Once the streamlined car is abandoned, there is a leap to another location along the road. There are the passenger, the blind man, the dandy, and the putative fat mother. This bandit in drag does not join the others in the jeep. He stays closer to the camera, facing the audience and eating bananas, as in the beginning of the film. Surrounded by what seems to be the provisions for the delayed picnic, he gives us his last message, beginning to offer a distorted synopsis of the film: "Once upon a time there were three bad bandits. They say that one was the mother, but no one knows for sure. They robbed, killed . . . " The plot summary is cut short by a cream pie, thrown from behind the camera, in the storyteller's face—an emphatic gesture expressing the filmmaker's scorn of conventional plot.

The examination of the last sequence of Tonacci's film takes us back to the hotel bathroom, a location already marked by the ape-mirror-camera set of the first part of *Bang Bang* that has been its most uncanny scene.

Estrangement Effects: Film and Spectator

At the end of the film, the camera meets Paulo Cesar Pereio (who plays the passenger) in the hotel bathroom and observes him fixedly, as it did at the film's beginning. Unmasked, no longer a taxi passenger or a victim to the gangsters, Pereio is just an actor, dressing after a shower. As he puts his clothes on, he looks directly into the camera and smiles a cynical, good-humored smile, singing the same waltz he had sung in his ape mask before he had intercourse with the woman in one of the first sequences of the film. We have heard excerpts from this song, always inappropriately timed: "I dreamed you were looking so lovely at a ball of rare splendor." We now hear the entire song, in an emphatic interpretation that stresses the ironical connotation of its final words: "It was all but a dream, I woke up." Like the actor, the film ends in an explicitly aggressive address to the daydreamers sitting in the projection room. A continuous and irritating laughter evokes the record playing in Godard's *Une Femme mariée*. The image of the actor fades; in the center of the dark screen there appears the optical mask of this laughter, as if emerging from the filmstrip's border. The spectator is held at a distance, observing the visual rhythm of a final sonorous attack by the deconstructive discourse.

The movements of this optical sound track placed in the center of the screen are synchronized with—and in fact correspond to—the provocative laugh we hear at the film's end. The spectator is taken from a promised shoot-'em-up to a piece of *underground* cinema that evokes structural films in the exposure of materials. The serial game made of film parameters reaches its closure here, in this moving geometry, pure surface.

In the entire film, the only completed action, the bizarre and isolated sex sequence at the beginning of *Bang Bang*, provides no relief in this respect. The female figure, like the heroine of a silent movie (her face is emphasized by an iris-in), lies in bed waiting for the ape-man. In the bathroom, a camera, reflected in a mirror, encounters Pereio donning the ape mask and a pair of eyeglasses. He acts like a man getting ready for bed; he takes medicine, smokes, shaves (with an electric razor) and, as though drunk, sings the nostalgic waltz, looking into the camera so as to highlight the bizarre quality of the scene (Figure 9.7; page 232). Inside the bedroom, he jumps around and makes sounds like an ape. He hastily possesses the silent woman under the sheets and withdraws, without forgetting to put his eyeglasses on. This sequence develops unobstructedly, providing an isolated moment of fulfillment, a single experience of orgasm that the film in general represses. Ironically, the subject of this experience is an ignoble double, a grotesque mediator of spectatorial identification. The mask, as a source of estrangement, has its effect amplified by the ape's insistent stare to the audience while singing in a loud voice to compensate for the annoying noise produced by the camera in the bathroom. Depending on the position of the cabinet mirror or of the ape's glasses, we can see the reflection of the camera on both surfaces. That reflection reveals only the camera, alone in front of the ape, continuously shooting—there is no film crew, no person seen except this narcissistic figure that nostalgically sings a sentimental song. This awkward set composed of ape, mirror, and an autonomous camera creates a sense of radical alterity, given the fact that the scene remains self-enclosed and excludes us and any other human figure. Who shoots?

The mask was taken from *The Planet of the Apes* (1968), the Hollywood science fiction film whose theme is World War III as apocalypse. Its presence in Tonacci's film evokes again the idea of a doomed civilization that was already suggested in the image of the car accident. The passenger is there alone, moving within a kind of labyrinth that he takes as a comic site that deserves only his cool, ironic response. At every step he is at ease facing the absurd, a fact that makes him an accomplice of the constant dissolution of the world performed on the screen. At the end, his aggressive smile makes clear his distance from the spectator's discomfort. If comedy requires the presence of a specific target, here the "victim" is the spectator; this time the cinematic apparatus does not provide for the audience the island of security that people usually seek in the dark room. The "other scene" alluded to in the passenger's allegorical journey is that involving the interaction between film and spectator. The terms of their dialogue—the rules of the game—have reached a critical point and now demand a new learning process within which the audience must find its way without much help from the established codes.

In these terms, the real "passenger" is the spectator, facing a film that presents itself as a "bad object." *Bang Bang* addresses the audience directly, but through a technique of estrangement, reserving for itself both pleasure and smile. Discomfort is generated by the relation established between film and spectator, as the world is suspended. Everything in the film returns us to the nature of cinematic experience, eliminating any residue of a "message," depriving both daydreamer and spectator in search of meaning. Image and sound develop a game of another sort, producing nonidentification and dispossession as strategies implementing the consciousness of language as a play on difference.

When the image of the actor's smile is replaced by the optical sound track made visible on the screen, the whole body of the film is there displaying its materiality. The vertical strip made of those little bright dots in constant change does not "say"anything, but it makes it clear that, in cinema, it is always the lightened celluloid that enunciates (Figure 9.8; page 232).

Figure 9.1

Figure 9.5

Figure 9.2

Figure 9.6

Figure 9.3

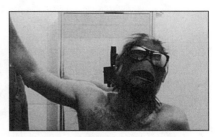

Figure 9.7

Figure 9.4

Figure 9.8

Part V

Further Developments

10

Trends of Allegory
in the 1970s

Migration, Character's Journey, Allegory

In the trajectory I have focused on, Brazilian modern cinema moved from the messianic hope, exemplified by the teleology of *Black God, White Devil*, to a radical disenchantment. This disenchantment was translated into films that saw recent history as a fatal disaster and that sometimes saw the crisis of representation itself as an essential part of the contemporary agenda. The deconstructive moment—1969–70— foregrounded the question of cinema, discussing the status of the image in contemporary society, refusing the usual forms of contract between the critical film and the audience. Tonacci's antiteleology, in particular, sets up a game that asserts the radical autonomy of the filmic structure. Nevertheless, a residual trace of representation remains, and one can talk, as I did, about its protagonist—profile and action—as an allegorical figure of noncommitment, a lonely and lost wanderer who has gone astray in a labyrinth who reminds us of a Kafka character but who is presented with a clearly detached good humor. Unlike Manuel, Paulo Martins, Jorginho, Macunaíma, Coirana, Santa Maria, Urtiga, and the family killer, the passenger is a target for no apparent reason except for the sake of the game, and his journey is not shaped to make him stand for any segment of society. Understood as a kind of trickster or dandy who epitomizes different kinds of parody, he belongs to a collection that includes Macunaíma and the Red Light Bandit, among other ironic characters in Brazilian cinema. However, while Macunaíma is presented as the personification of the national character and the Red Light Bandit metaphorizes an identity crisis lived in a clearly defined peripheral urban environment, the passenger is a totally "deterritorialized" figure. Unlike the other two, his experience has no national dimension. His identity plunges into a more radical void than Macunaíma's, "the hero without a character," and ends up more un-

235

stable than Jorginho's, the bandit conceived as a media construct. He has neither roots nor home, and we cannot even say that his space is the flaneur's city, the journey in the streets that would place him as a voyeur. The passenger has a constitutive indetermination, but his status as a lonely piece in constant movement does not stop him from asserting the prominent place that the journey has in Brazilian cinema, this cinema full of migrating characters involved in different life stories or different games. As seen in my analysis, both the desire to produce global interpretations of the nation and the desire to play on the signifier in reflexive films take territorial displacement as a major trope—a choice that establishes a privileged ground for allegory.

Migration is one of the significant tropes in the allegorical period that started with *Black God, White Devil* and lasted for two decades. Allegories foster the symbolic use of places; they suggest displacements as spatial metaphors for time; they provide visible outlines for social processes, as is evident in *Black God, White Devil* as well as in *Macunaíma*, films in which the migrating character mediates a totalization.

Migration was the key social experience in the great Cinema Novo trilogy of 1963–64. On the brink of the 1964 coup, *Barren Lives* (Pereira dos Santos), *The Guns* (Ruy Guerra), and *Black God, White Devil* dealt with this trope in different terms: Their scenery was the drought-stricken *sertão* and their social problem was the property structure of rural land. That is, they identified the social problem with the point of departure of the migration movement: the *sertão*, described as hell in opposition to the open spaces of migration that meant the way to salvation. Manuel thirsts for justice and symbolically runs toward the sea. Fabiano, grazed by the colonel, leaves in search of the city. The deprived people of *The Guns* come from the *sertão* to crowd around the village warehouse, generating a movement opposite to that of the soldiers from the larger town, who come to control the religious crowd. In the three films, movement is a positive gesture against a background of stagnation; there is a promise of change in the spatial displacement, taken as an instance of crossing, realistic in *Barren Lives*, visionary in *Black God, White Devil*, and causing estrangement in the urban–rural conflict in *The Guns*.

After 1964, the major issue is the migrant's experience in his new place, as in *The Big City* (Carlos Diegues, 1966). The big city is the strong pole that means change but in a direction very opposed to Paradise. The journey to leave the *sertão* does not reach the heralded sea but, rather, the poor urban world, without any sense of hope, already announced in Graciliano Ramos's novel of the 1930s. In 1974 Pereira dos Santos filmed *The Amulet of Ogun* in the periphery of Rio de Janeiro. In a popular narrative woven by an urban singer, this film reworks the topics discussed in several Cinema Novo films based on migrating characters. It can be taken as a sequel to *Barren Lives*, with the young son of Fabiano's family as the protagonist who arrives in Rio and gets involved with gangsters. Pereira dos Santos's version of violence and poverty occurring in the periphery of the city embodies a new "popular cinema" striving to communicate with large audiences and with the assertion of popular values: Afro-Brazilian religions and the cultural codes of the city poor. In opposition to the bitter allegories examined here, Pereira dos Santos's narrative incorporates the popular magical view of things in order to voice resistance, hope, and optimism against violence and misery. His film has an epic tone that is against the grain in 1974, when Brazilian political cinema tended to stress the tragic face of the national condition and the illusions brought by the so-called economic miracle (1967–73).

Between 1964 and 1974, Brazilian cinema, no longer motivated by the certainty and epic spirit of *Black God, White Devil*, assumed tropicality as an experience of continual pain, and it privileged a somber figuration of its specific geography. Rocha himself started the process in the baroque drama of *Land in Anguish* and its anti-utopian version of the European "discovery." Marginal Cinema, for its part, around 1970 took migration as a paradigm for allegorical constructions that sometimes involved ironic references to colonial times. In *Orgy* (*Orgia*, 1970), made by João Silvério Trevisan, the journey becomes a senseless gathering of drifters who move toward defeat. The space of violence against the natives becomes the space of the disintegration of the conqueror. In an ironical allusion to the pilgrims' myth of the redemptive New World, this tropical space of damnation is, in more than one film, associated with the idea of the Garden of Eden. Luiz Rosemberg makes *The Garden of Foam* (*O jardim das espumas*, 1970), in which extraterrestrial beings land in an allegorical space to find only social injustice, guerrilla warfare, torture, and suffering. In Neville D'Almeida's *Garden of War* (*Jardim de guerra*, 1970), we find the same Kafkaesque space found in *Bang Bang. Brazil Year 2000* (*Brasil ano 2000*, 1969), made by Walter Lima, Jr., uses a postnuclear parable to discuss the relationship between national identity and modernization: The developed nations destroyed themselves and have left the planet to the under-developed, and the country's failure within this new state of world affairs resurrects the idea of a congenital technological incompetence. Lima's film focuses on the attack on racial prejudice against Native Brazilians to allude to the official ideology of modernization. In its opposition to the country of the "economic miracle," cinema underlines the theme of the culture that was exterminated by foreign powers, emphasizing the destructive side of technical and economic advances. Such identification with the defeated Natives did not aim at assuming specific values of the indigenous culture; it basically took indigenous culture as a signifier of the predatory nature of capital expansion, a symbol of the *difference* of the oppressed.

The melancholy of the defeated is represented in Gustavo Dahl's *Uirá: An Indian in Search of God* (*Uirá: Um índio à procura de Deus*, 1974). Here, the Indian's pilgrimage in search of Heaven is turned into a wish for death after he suffers defeat and disenchantment in his encounter with white men. The clash of cultures is represented in a parodic reworking of European discovery narratives in *How Tasty Was My Little Frenchman* (*Como era gostoso o meu francês*, 1971), made by Pereira dos Santos. This film plays on the idea of the natural "savage, sinless life" in order to destroy idyllic expectations of a harmonic encounter between cultures, making the audience confront the inevitable violence implicit in territorial expansion. The Frenchman is well treated as he is integrated into the tribe and is slowly prepared to undergo the cannibalism rite in which his flesh will be consumed. When the time of his death comes, he utters a threat that sounds like a prophecy to the 1971 viewer: "Soon my people will arrive in ever-increasing numbers to avenge my death and destroy you all."

Iracema and Sad Tropics

Pereira dos Santos reworked the travel literature in a parodic reading of Hans Staden's account of his encounter with the Native Brazilians in the sixteenth century. Jorge Bodansky and Orlando Senna take as a reference José de Alencar's *Iracema*, written in 1865. This novel belongs in the body of nationalist works that Alencar wrote to inaugurate a genuine account of the nation and its history (Figure 10.1).

Within his romantic framework, Alencar transfigured the encounter of colonizer and colonized as a love story between a virginal Indian

Figure 10.1. *Iracema* (1974–75), by Jorge Bodansky and Orlando Senna

maiden and a noble Portuguese soldier. They meet when the Portuguese, lost in the woods, enters Iracema's view as an unknown, threatening figure and is hurt by the arrow that she, in a quick move, shot at him. Repentant and in love, she looks after him and makes her tribe accept the European as a friend. They become lovers, and she breaks the law that linked her virginity to her role within the religious system of the tribe. From their romance a child is born, but the entire experience ends tragically with her death. There is no coercion and no exploitation in Alencar's allegory of national formation. In contrast, something much crueler and with a strong dose of grotesque naturalism occurs in the 1974 movie, in which Iracema—the name is an anagram of America—is the young indigenous Brazilian from the Amazon who gets to know a cynical lover on the occasion of the construction of the Trans-Amazonian Highway. The filmmakers restage the encounter between the Native and the white man as a new tragedy, shorn of the idealized feelings and romantic contours that marked Alencar's book. The Amazon is the promised land, chosen to carry the connotation of "virginity," of untamed nature to be "discovered" and conquered; and the story has a blatantly perverse content that prevents the spectator from seeing a love affair. Iracema migrates through the Amazon, traveling from her little village to a state capital—Belém—only to be swallowed by the city, to become a prostitute, and to hit the road, unleashing a vertiginous process of personal destruction that leaves her destitute in a distant outpost, lost in the jungle.

To shoot *Iracema*, the film crew traveled along the highway and its side roads, covering an extension of frontier land and producing a collection of images that evidence the predatory dimension of progress. Ecological disaster, labor exploitation, slavery, and women's prostitution define an administered hell whose end product is just a detour leading nowhere through the core of the jungle. The overall circulation of goods and human beings includes the two protagonists, Iracema and Tião Great Brazil, the truck driver who exploits her naïveté and ends up abandoning her in a far-away spot among other decayed women in a pathetic ending. Their relationship is at the center of the journey and is an original combination of role-playing and interviews conducted by the leading actor, Paulo Cesar Pereio, who addresses different people from the region. The interaction between fiction and documentary produces a strong dramatic effect, and the cinema verité tradition is made strange by the blatant theatrical contamination produced by the way the film approaches "real people" who are constantly provoked by Pereio. This leading actor is the agent provocateur, the very center of the process, here reworking his "detached" performance as the passenger in *Bang Bang*—again cynical, outspoken, and good-humored within a context of human misery and violence, now enhanced by its "authenticity" as part of the real Amazonian experience captured by the film crew. Through Pereio's provocation, the film reveals the domination that its making implies, and the entire social process of invasion reveals itself as not only being the theme of the film but also the organizing principle of the mise-en-scène.[2]

Because of her path from innocence to decay, Iracema becomes a symbol of the nation and its problems, caught within a predatory developmental model that produces battered forests, contraband lumber, the burning of the jungle, and the prostitution of uprooted young girls. The "open veins" of the Amazon, now the target of a national project (Greater Brazil), are here the result of a late process of technical and economic invasion, a kind of new frontier, where rape and women's destruction is taken as the central metaphor to refer to the ecological disaster and the social effects of a certain pattern of capitalist development in Brazil. Iracema's image at the end of the film—defenseless, decadent, ailing, and abandoned in the middle of the road—suggests that the detours, corrosion, alienation, and destruction of Brazilian life are directly linked to the idea of the arrival of "civilization."

Coinciding with the heights of the Brazilian "economic miracle," the film takes Iracema's journey as a perfect symbol for the state of the nation. Since 1970 the military government had taken the country's natural abundance as a sign of a grandeur supposedly acquired through the ongoing economic process, and the official propaganda had turned every geographic site into material evidence of the country's potential as a world power. In this sense, the construction of the Trans-Amazonian Highway, which crossed the enormous expanse of "untouched" jungle, was a powerful symbol. In 1974, to document the actual process of the region's brutal transformation on film provided an invaluable counterweight to the rhetoric put forth by the regime. For this reason, the film was banned in 1974 and was not seen by Brazilian audiences until 1980.

Bodansky and Senna went beyond reportage to compose a multileveled masterpiece that provided a powerful image of conservative modernization. *Iracema* builds the national allegory in terms of Galeano's formula—the "open veins of Latin America"—focusing its attention on the economic enterprise of exploitation. Iracema's identity is developed in those aspects that define her vulnerability: poverty, loneliness, lack of experience, ethnic background evidenced by her features, and fascination with the "big world" represented by the driver. Her values and worldview are relevant not in their own right but only to the extent that they help us understand why she is available and must concede to Tião's command. Other films take the conflicts and the domination engendered by migrations as a historical process in which the politics of identity can be discussed in different terms. More emphasis can be given to systems of representation and their specific forms of shaping historical experiences, engendering human pilgrimage and cultural clashes.

Migration—the protagonist's allegorical journey—can be taken, for example, to deconstruct the very idea of national identity. Bressane's *Caraiba Monster* (*O monstro caraíba*, 1973) organizes the hero's peregrination in a peculiar way: Here the search for origins, instead of any specific encounter with the oppressor, is the very cause of the loss of identity. We follow the melancholic Caraiba Monster in an endless track through different times and places, which suggests the lack of any stable historical referent for the development of the national identity. Oswald de Andrade's critique of notions like national roots and purity inspires the decentered representation of national history as an infinite regressive move to an always-irretrievable beginning. This deconstruction of national identity gives continuity to the project of the Marginal Cinema in 1970. Unlike Macunaíma, for instance, the Caraiba Monster cannot even find a geographic site to define his origin, turning the nation into a kind of unstable intersection point, a historical passage with no real demarcation for start and end, an element with no substance.

Arthur Omar's *Sad Tropics* (*Triste trópico*, 1974) stands like a perfect synthesis of the question of national allegory as related to migrations and cultural conflicts. Omar's movie was filmed the same year as *Iracema* and *Uirá*. Like Dahl's film, it takes the Native Brazilian messianic pilgrimage as a central object, but melancholy is now worked within another key, linked to the very formation of the national imagery. Like *Caraiba Monster*, it takes Brazil as a privileged place where migratory flows converge. However, like no other film made in Brazil, it articulates a whole constellation of issues related to human displacements: the European crossing of the Atlantic Ocean, the slavery system and the African diaspora, the messianic movements in Brazilian territory, the urban ritual of carnival, the connection between avant-garde movements from the 1920s and medical transgressions, petit bourgeois voyeuristic tours around the world, and filmmaking (Figure 10.2).

Sad Tropics condenses all these issues around the idea of "displacement" in order to set an original play on symmetries involving rural and urban Brazil; city and country are taken as stages for religious experiences that, although seemingly opposed, reveal secret identities and point to a tragic destiny shared by different strata of the population—in the tropical country, sadness and irresolution are everywhere.

An experimental film, *Sad Tropics* is placed as an antidocumentary that simulates newsreel film strategies to tell a fake historical biography like those told by Borges in his *Universal History of Infamy* (1935). On the sound track a conventional voice-over tells the story of the Brazilian Doctor Arthur, and his journey, first in Europe as a student and man of letters and then in the Brazilian countryside as a doctor, magician, and messianic leader. We do not see a single image of his journey, although different clips of old documentary films and still photographs simulate the presentation of episodes of his life. The main strategy of the film is a vertical montage that produces enigmatic com-

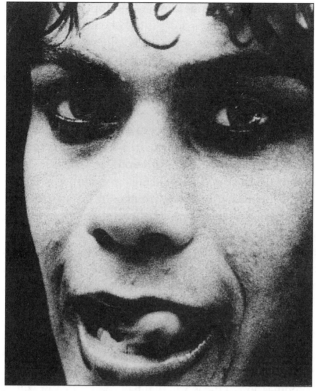

Figure 10.2. Carnival mask from Arthur Omar's series "Anthropology of the Glorious Face," which derives from the image of carnival as developed in Omar's *Sad Tropics*

binations of voice-over commentary—centered on Doctor Arthur's biography—and documentary footage taken in a variety of places, with the dominant presence of images from Rio de Janeiro's carnival. Joining together a bulky collection of images taken from different sources, the film organizes its visual material like a mosaic composed of repetitions and regular alternations placed in opposition to the linear development of the story in the sound track. The scenes from Rio de Janeiro streets, where a pageant of masks enacts the traditional popular theater of carnival, are now presented on the screen in an original way and acquire a tragic dimension never captured in Brazilian cinema, which is usually more concerned with the cheerful aspects of the popular feast.

Doctor Arthur's biography becomes stranger as he plunges into a magic world in the countryside after his cosmopolitan European experiences. The second half of his story is full of witchcraft, miracle cures, and messianic pilgrimages in which he is followed by a sect of Native Brazilians who carry out pre-Columbian traditions. This narrative is woven together with intriguing images, either from carnival or from different engravings that represent heretical activities and the violent repression of the Inquisition in the sixteenth and seventeenth centuries. These images, although not extracted from the aural biography, have a close thematic connection with it. Symbolic suggestions, historical references, anthropological illustrations, and esoteric rituals mark the continuity of Doctor Arthur's imaginary journey, which was invented by the filmmaker not merely to initially play a trick on the audience, but mainly to discuss essential topics linked to Brazilian history: millenarism, the cultural status of carnival as a collective ritual, the role of heresy in the national formation since colonial times.

Discussing the status of religion in Brazilian history, *Sad Tropics* has as a major focus the problem of the brutal repression of difference in the Western tradition, the parade of torture and violence in which the "discovery" of the New World was one of the more typical episodes. The conflict, in Omar's film, is placed in terms of a paradigm reenacted many times in Brazilian history, a paradigm that opposes a repressive dominant reason to alternative, "heretical" experiences and forms of codification of the world that have permeated Brazilian social life since colonial times. Within this view, *Sad Tropics* presents carnival as a Dionysian expression of a tragic feeling associated with the historical disasters evoked by the film in its visual collage. The images of repression through the centuries culminate with an allusion to Prussian militarism, which, ironically, takes us back to Euclides da Cunha's book *Os Sertões*, in which he describes the Brazilian army as Prussian, evoking broader and less immediate references to the displacement of the troops from the coast to the hinterland that resulted in the Canudos War. In Omar's collage, along with the inventory of pictures displaying torture and repression, the film maintains a regular parallel between Doctor Arthur's metamorphosis in Brazil's rural area and Rio de Janeiro's carnival, suggesting unexpected similarities. Carnival is shot in such a way as to suggest its awkwardness, bringing to the surface the uncanny face of metamorphosis. It is designed like an expiatory ritual. Its masks end up revealing themselves as having the same content as the mourning expressions printed in other images of the film, such as the final image in which we "see" the scream of a woman who is watching a military parade with a small national flag and a child at her side. *Sertão* and sea are made equals, the sadness of the tropics is everywhere, and the formula of the passage from the *sertão* to the sea is a materialization of a dream losing its power. What is configured is a wandering in time with no telos, no redemption: the history of the continent as the history of the repetition of violence.

Deconstructive in its own way, *Sad Tropics* offers a language game that forces us to redefine our relationship with cinematic sound and image, to test our way of "assembling" reality based on materials given to sight. As to the question of the messianic quest, the film closes a cycle that began in *Black God, White Devil*. Omar gives a new sense to pilgrimage, now connected to the more general trope of travel, whatever its purpose may be. Such a trope is introduced by the title—which allude to the Brazilian memoirs written by Claude Lévi-Strauss—and develops in Doctor Arthur's biography, in the collage of pictures taken during the filmmaker's own trip around the world, in the reference to the melancholy of the Native frustrated in his search for Paradise, and in the itinerancy of the carnival parade through the city. In relation to *Black God, White Devil*, *Sad Tropics*, although addressing the same questions, produces a radical reversal in its treatment of the messianic hope. The search for Paradise now acquires a tragic sense: The theory of history that used to orient the epic representation of messianism is now dissolved. Because of his daring medical knowledge and experiences, Doctor Arthur is regarded as a person with magical powers, but the destiny of his visionary message is far from that lived by the pilgrim who inaugurates a new era and saves his followers. Again, like Kurtz in Joseph Conrad's *Heart of Darkness*, his movement is toward the grotesque, as expressed in his awkward death amid nature and his anomalous decomposition. The examination of his corpse, under the eyes of the positivistic and ethnocentric medical science in fashion in 1900, leads to the diagnosis of madness. In *Sad Tropics* this diagnosis is read in the same terms used during the examination of Antônio Conselheiro's corpse after his defeat in Canudos at the end of the century. Omar quotes *Os Sertões*, reworking a reference also used by Rocha. However, this is done in the tragic tone of da Cunha's book: Antônio Conselheiro is evoked as an aberrant corpse, exposed to the conqueror's dissection. He is no longer the vigorous source of the prophecy incorporated in *Black God, White Devil* to command history.

Once the path of Brazilian cinema is observed in its relation with the imagery of the messianic salvation, it is possible to configure, between *Black God, White Devil* and *Sad Tropics*, a movement that, in the particular relation with this theme, repeats the passage from hope to despair that characterized the shift from Cinema Novo to Marginal Cinema in the late 1960s. In the beginning we are sure of salvation, and the allegory of hope that represents the plunge into delirious experience is a kind of stratagem on the way to freedom. In the end, after several expressions of disillusionment, we get to the allegory in which the journey of the visionary hero leads to an abyss, and history, seen through the eyes of the oppressed, becomes not the realm of reason but the realm of disaster.

Melodrama and Allegory:
Family as a Microcosm of Nation

In the 1970s, alongside the allegories built on migrating characters, we find the concise allegory set within four walls, dramas in which the question of the family as a microcosm of society comes to the foreground. Here the tensions arise from moral issues and the axis of the drama opposes tradition and modernity.

The ironic trial of the family started in Brazilian cinema in the late 1960s, when *tropicalismo* set the tone and patriarchy became a basic target because of its central role in the legitimization of censorship and other repressive measures taken by the military. The demoralization of characters linked to family traditions represented the demoralization of values embodied by the successive father figures in power. The authoritarian regime accelerated the economic growth of the country, but on a symbolic level it undertook the strong defense of archaic values— such as the rigid moral codes and the traditional family structure— threatened by the same capitalist development that was fostered by the government. Aware of this process, the artists, in their debate with the new ways of consumer society, looked for new strategies to express their ironic stance vis-à-vis the contradictions of Brazilian conservative modernization.

Beginning in 1969–70 there is a significant displacement toward the "family drama" as a focus for the interest of cinema. Generation gaps mark *Copacabana Fools Me* (*Copacabana me engana*, Antônio Carlos Fontoura, 1969) and *Brazil Year 2000*; familial aggression propels the episodes in *Killed the Family and Went to the Movies*. The fall of traditional families receives attention in films as a sign of crisis and change, as in *The Heirs* (*Os herdeiros*, Carlos Diegues, 1969), *The Murdered House* (*A casa assassinada*, Paulo Cesar Saraceni, 1971), *The Gods and the Dead* (*Os deuses e os mortos*, Ruy Guerra, 1970), and *The Monsters of Babaloo* (*Os monstros do Babaloo*, Elyseu Visconti, 1970). There is a displacement of emphasis in the approach to society, a sharper presence of psychoanalysis as reference, since the first pulsations of Marginal Cinema.

Through the 1970s, the experience of the new generations with the media and sexual freedom fostered this cinema that was concerned with the question of private life as mediation for the discussion of society. Within this framework, I can name two different trends that can be traced back to modern Brazilian theater. One recovers the traditions of *Teatro de Arena* and playwrights like Gianfrancesco Guarnieri, Oduvaldo Vianna Filho, and Ferreira Gullar: *In the Family* (*Em família*, Paulo Porto, 1971) and *They Do Not Wear Black-Tie* (*Eles não usam black-tie*, Leon Hirszman, 1980) highlight the relation of the familial drama to class conditions and to economic life. The other trend underlines the universe of passions, desire, and sexuality, fostering the dialogue with the work of Nelson Rodrigues, a playwright who offered an array of characters and situations to a cinema concerned with the anatomy of the family within the climate caused by the frustration of political hopes.

In this process, Arnaldo Jabor becomes a key filmmaker. In adapting Rodrigues's work, he found a certain tone of speech adequate to discuss the country, such as in *All Nudity Shall Be Punished* (1972) and *The Marriage* (1975). His style shows a rare skill in incorporating some traces of culture—bad taste, hysteria, roughness, provincialism—that had been a target for *tropicalismo*. In these two films, he introduced new forms of mise-en-scène to disclose the intimate link between political alienation and the features of a genre—melodrama—that he appropriated to underline the contradictions embedded in Brazilian modernization.

Jabor's interrogation of the family reached its most comprehensive version in *It's All Right* (*Tudo bem*, 1978), an overt national allegory that was, in fact, rehearsed in *All Nudity Shall Be Punished* and *The Marriage*. These two films depict a patriarchal authority under siege, a kind of "middleman" unable to fulfill the tasks that tradition dictates to him. His destiny in modern society is to live a misadventure in which he is the first to violate the codes that should determine his behavior. Both films recognize a certain liveliness in the way the observed father figures struggle with their contradictions, but they are clear in their ironic look at the poor man attached to old moral demands that hinder his deepest desires, hidden no more. Herculano, from *All Nudity Shall Be Punished*, is a melancholy widower who falls in love with a prostitute and confronts the moral constraints placed by his own conservative mind and by his morbid and traditional family; he gets involved in a passionate struggle that leads him to a sad humiliation and drives Geni, the prostitute, to suicide. Sabino, from *The Marriage*, is a rich businessman who, on the eve of his daughter's marriage, has a nervous fit and becomes a torn father who goes beyond all limits to let his incestuous drive conquer all moral resistance in a daring and clumsy assault that results in a grotesque failure, blame, humiliation, and religious delirium. Both Herculano and Sabino have masochistic and sentimental tendencies that make it clear that they belong to an obsolete world whose dramas could only be represented as tragicomedy. Confronting modernization, the father figure is not up to the challenges; rather, he loses the battle because of the corrosive power of time, which defines the passage of generations as fall and decadence. If the father falls and fails, the victorious youngsters, in their turn, display only a mean-spirited individualism that deprives them of the value of their liberation. Both films observe the dramas without endorsing any of the agents' points of view, in a general ironic posture that displays a total lack of hope.

To expose the father to humiliation is a straight dialogue with Rocha's baroque allegory. Jabor relates the family drama to the political critique of a military regime that assumed the moral codes of patriarchy as one of its major ideological values. Presenting Herculano and Sabino as mediocre embodiments of the traditional moral codes, the films undermine the official ideology, here represented by two impotent father figures who display their contrast with Porfirio Diaz, from *Land in Anguish*, the cinematic symbol of the victorious tradition in 1964.

For their part, the youngsters in these two Jabor films belong, in fact, to a series of figures with which, since 1968, Cinema Novo filmmakers had had a difficult relationship. They are young rebels, but they are mixed up in leading their own lives. Closely observed as a symptom of bad times, they are unable to overcome the family order in crisis, joining the collection of wrecked figures that, from film to film, defined a diagnosis of general unhappiness. As suggested here, the passage from the concern with the public sphere—the representation of the struggle for political power—to the anatomy of private life provides another way of reaching the "diagnosis of the nation," typical of Cinema Novo's practice. The process of general disqualification found, for instance, in Jabor clearly expresses the disenchantment with Brazilian modernization as it took place within the framework set by the 1964 coup d'état. This disenchantment marks the point where the political cinema of the young filmmakers encounters the work of the conservative playwright (for example, Nelson Rodrigues). Both get together in the search for the "unpleasant" work, in the aggressive character of their intervention in culture. Jabor conducts a kind of anatomy of decadence engaged in denouncing a certain style of domination rooted in the Brazilian social formation and a set of symbols of national identity cherished since colonial times.

There is undoubtedly a broader framework for this trial of the family in Brazilian cinema. The "family crisis" and the generation gap were central themes on the agenda of the social sciences in several countries, in the 1960s and 1970s because the changes in the social status of youth and the economic progress of the postwar period generated experiences of sexual freedom and the replacement of family authority by other forms of institutional control. The set of issues around such a crisis and around the new articulations of the family is much broader; here I want only to underline the meaning of this process in a Brazil undergoing modernization but officially claiming to mobilize "Christian values" against a supposed expansion of communism, a major obsession of a doctrine of national security coined by the Cold War.

Aware of this moral content in the process, cinema showed a willingness to perform psychological investigation, an effort to understand the unconscious drives that take part in the shaping of the social order. The disappointment with political reality had already shown that political behavior was determined not only by rationality and the expression of material interests but also by contradictory psychological propensities that the filmmakers wanted to better understand. In this movement there was a certain retaliation against the image of their audiences, who were generally treated aggressively. On the other

Figure 10.3. Arnaldo Jabor's *It's All Right*

hand, there was the dimension of self-analysis, which, once included in the debate about society, was a decisive gesture for Cinema Novo, defining its strength and risks during the 1970s, since the tradeoff with tradition did not happen without a residual compromise with the symbolic world under examination. This fact establishes clear limits to the view that Brazilian cinema had of modernization. The best example of the force and the limits of that view is *It's All Right*, the film that synthesizes the development of the national allegory as social psychology derived from melodrama (Figure 10.3).

Different inspirations flow into *It's All Right*: on the one hand, Nelson Rodrigues and his marital tragicomedy; on the other, Glauber Rocha and his totalizing posture. The middle-class family apartment becomes a microcosm of the nation, a theater of populism, carnival euphoria, messianism, migrations, and violence. Jabor juxtaposes archaic and modern in *tropicalist* terms. Market culture and rural folklore, indigenous rites and tropical nature, TV and patriotic symbols define the kitschy world of the family. Present since the film's overture, the articulation of familial life and national imagery proceeds throughout the film. Juarez, the retired head of the family, reminiscent of Herculano and Sabino, is the central mediator point. He brings to the middle-class Rio de Janeiro apartment the mythical universe of the "original" elements of the nation, and he sees himself as its guardian. Conservative, he spends most of his time evoking his youthful experiences, the good old days of political struggle, his old nationalist pride in fascist colors, memories that strongly contrast with his ordinary current life. A weak man, with no family authority, he constitutes the folkloric Right, a perfect target for comedy, like a Fellini-style fascist on the Italian scene. His course will be one of increasing bitterness as he recognizes his sexual, social, and familial impotence. His children are associated with decadence, now expressed in radical terms.

In this ordinary and unsurprising world, the catalyzing element is Alzira, the housewife, for whom progress means building a nice setting to make everything seem "all right" in order to please the guest (a rich American). Alzira fills in the space left by her husband's decline and engages herself in remodeling the apartment, an enterprise that forms the axis of the allegory because it generates a steady invasion of family space by the working figures belonging to the lower social classes, therefore transforming the apartment into a microsociety. The workers' task is to prepare the setting for the final party, a homage to the American, her daughter's fiancé. In this process, the traditional imbrication of intimacies between bosses and servants comes to the foreground, everything within an informal economy, that of low wages compensated by courtesies that uphold the family's pride as "generous" people. There are minor conflicts that serve to identify stable comic types and to compose the desired social panel. The poor tell stories of their neighborhood and compose the sphere of the "popular grotesque"; the housewife acts motherly. But the invasion becomes more acute and reaches its peak with the arrival of the homeless family of one of the masons. He explains to Alzira that his father was one of the masons who built Brasilia; he shows pictures, creating a kind of "the dream is over" feeling, to talk about his father's disillusionment and migration after that major engagement. Thus the film defines the analogy between the small contractor's business in the apartment in the 1970s and the construction of the capital of the country in the late 1950s. The national monument–city, as well as this small remodeling of the apartment, is denounced in its position of preparing the ground to receive foreign investments, of testifying to the "all right" side of modernization. This effort to transform the facade, keeping the structures, involves the renewed exercise of the exclusion principle: Require the people to perform the building work, and then reject it or circumscribe it so that it leaves no traces or stains.

The tensions in the apartment, comical in the beginning, change in tone when the "popular excesses" create a disorder that the family order cannot restrain. The first collective excess is the carnival drumming at lunch break, which transforms the apartment into a *samba* hall, driving the head of the family crazy. Later on, the maid has a nervous fit and leaves her room with wide-open eyes exhibiting two open wounds on the palms of her hands. She crosses the apartment, wanders through the streets in a trance, and ends up provoking a pilgrimage to her room, which has become a holy shrine. A crowd enters the scene and squeezes through the corridors until Juarez, exasperated, takes courage and banishes them all, thus reestablishing order. These two episodes mark the presence of two traditional forms of "popular excess" that threaten the world of orderly religion and work. Toward the end of the film, a third form of such excess creates the worst nightmare, endangering the party. During the last working day, a conflict between two masons over a stolen banana leads to a crime: There is a corpse in the middle of the room that is soon to be filled with guests. When we start wondering how the corpse and the blood will be removed from the floor in time, the answer comes through a fast cut that introduces a smooth camera movement that places us among the guests—the party is already at its peak. Everything seems normal, but we know the reasons for Alzira's peculiar positions while stepping on certain points not covered by the newly installed carpet. In the service area, the maid guards the mason's corpse. The juxtaposition living room–maid's room acquires a symbolic dimension, since the alternation of the two opposite spaces on the screen is repeated many times until our attention shifts to the American guest. Surrounded by Alzira's family and the other guests, he talks about the global village, and communication via satellite, and he draws the attention of the audience of dazed Brazilians, who follow him singing "Around the World" as an ode to technology. To end the discourse, the aerial image of Foz do Iguaçu erupts, and the waterfall offers the terms of the catharsis—a luxuriant but free fall.

While bringing the whole country into the family world, *It's All*

Right incorporates in its structure a tradition of Brazilian sociology founded by Gilberto Freyre, presenting a new version of the classic dichotomy—*Casa Grande* (master's house) versus *Senzala* (slave quarters)—established in Freyre's book *The Masters and the Slaves*.[3] It introduces a new dichotomy, "living room–maid's room," which updates the encompassing social diagnosis based on the family nucleus and its spatial hierarchy. At the same time, Jabor's allegory is sarcastic in its attack on traditional Brazilian boasting—the eulogy to the exuberant nature as a suggestion of the glorious future of the country; the repetition of the formula "It's all right," which covers social iniquity; the idealization/annulment of the people taken as a part of nature to be tamed. However, the show of popular lack of discipline—carnival, *cordel*, beatitude—retains a residue of the stereotypical vision of the people. The film mocks the home owners' distress, but the comedy underlines, perhaps too much, hysteria and violence as traces of the dominated classes. Of course there is the hidden stain of the patrons, but above all there is the grotesque mask of the servants. Jabor enacts here his penchant for a generalized belittling, asserting an overall Brazilian misery and the absence of positive historical subjects in any class of society: a pessimistic view that finds ironic expression in the final image of the waterfall with its apocalyptic overtones.

Although in the 1970s Brazilian society was more complex, Jabor insists on the matrix of colonial times, placing the family as the center of his reflection on the country. Making this choice, he condenses Cinema Novo's answer to the bureaucratic-authoritarian regime, denying the "economic miracle" as the productive force of a new sociability, a new quality of life. The issue is to mark the conservative side of the Brazilian model, to denounce modernization as a change of skin that conceals the persistence of a colonial mentality, the repetition of archaic forms of domination, and the submission to external powers.

Begun in the late 1960s, the "trial of the family" led by Cinema Novo found different ways of marking the private space as the root of political apathy that favored the military regime. Such apathy was taken as a steady national trace by films that excluded from their fictional world the more organized segments of society, as was common in Cinema Novo since the 1960s. Even when more comprehensive in its allegory, as in *Land in Anguish*, Cinema Novo insisted on the political weight of a historical tradition that created the conservative, delirious, and authoritarian mentality. In this sense, although the allegory in *It's All Right* does not take into account the country of the time, it draws attention to aspects of Brazilian sociability that are often disregarded in the political debate but that are essential for understanding the schemes of power. That is, we have here again that effort to capture peculiarities of social life that Cinema Novo reiterated in its observation of the country, always more sensitive to the residues of archaic mentality, of patriarchal style, and of populism. A central feature in Cinema Novo was its ability to recognize the political effects of that typical intersection of temporalities present in a divided society in which tradition and modernity clash and accommodate each other.

Rocha's Testament—
The Crisis of the Overt National Allegory

Glauber Rocha is the filmmaker who best represents the allegorical impulse that had a central role in Brazilian culture in the 1960s and that found significant developments in the 1970s. Curiously enough, it is *The Age of the Earth* (*A idade da Terra*), made by Rocha himself between 1978 and 1980, that closes the high allegorical season of Brazilian cinema (Figure 10.4). In the 1980s, and even in recent Brazilian cinema, one still finds allegorical journeys of migrating characters and family dramas with national overtones. For example, *Bye Bye Brazil* (1980), by Carlos Diegues, reworks that displacement from the Amazon forest to the highway already presented in *Iracema*, now leading an entire family to Brasília, the country's capital, where they find a kind of successful, although melancholy, ending to their journey. *The Roses of the Highway* (*A opção*, 1980), made by Ozualdo Candeias, turns the network of highways built during the Brazilian "miracle" into a fan belt conceived for the circulation of women as commodities. Eduardo Coutinho's *Twenty Years After* (*Cabra marcado para morrer*, 1984)—the last great Cinema Novo film—summarizes twenty years of Brazilian political life under dictatorship while documenting its own research and analyzing the process of a family diaspora caused by political repression between the early 1960s and the early 1980s. These films, among others, show the continuation of an impulse toward totalization, the diagnosis of the nation, in narratives that invite the audience to perform allegorical readings. Nowadays the recovery of film production in Brazil, after the acute crisis lived

Figure 10.4. Glauber Rocha's *The Age of the Earth*

between 1990 and 1993, brings us new examples of allegorical strategies, such as *Savage Capitalism* (*Capitalismo selvagem*, 1993), made by André Klotzel, and *Saturday* (*Sábado*, 1994), made by Hugo Georgetti, both concerned with the connection between their particular plot and national features related to underdevelopment.

These examples from the 1980s and 1990s, although a sign of new developments in the question of allegory, correspond to a more episodic occurrence of this mode of representation. Moreover, they constitute a kind of allegory less radical in their totalizing impulses than one can find in Rocha's cinema. Rocha has always attempted comprehensive views of history observed on a large scale. The scope of his reflection demanded the alternate strategies of modern cinema as they took place in the 1960s and early 1970s, fostering that mode of representation defined by a play on discontinuities and an aggressive refusal of "normal" plots. As we have seen, in Brazil political engagement and modernist concerns favored national allegories—or their aggressive deconstruction. Rocha's *The Age of the Earth* is the ultimate example of the peculiar combination of both impulses. As an overt national allegory, this film is an ambitious attempt to present a synthetic view of contemporary experience from a Third World perspective; as an experimental film, it dialogues with the main strategies developed by Marginal Cinema and its deconstructive drive.

After the first heroic stage of Cinema Novo in the 1960s, Rocha has been the only Brazilian filmmaker to continue to refer his films to a utopian Third World illumination supposedly in progress. From *Der Leone Has Sept Cabeças* (1970), made in Africa, and *Cabeças Cortadas* (1971), made in Spain, to *Claro* (1975), made in Italy, he enacted the rituals of dominant-class moral decadence and that grotesque violence and corruption that makes declining colonial powers obscene. In contrast, he has always underlined different forms of lively popular mobilization against the death principle embodied in the oppressors. In *Der Leone*, the actual process of struggle provided the historical background for the allegory concentrated in the representation of the anticolonial war in Africa. In Spain and, after 1976, in Brazil, life principle and hope found their representation in a variety of syncretic popular rituals understood as signs of a religious revival with revolutionary overtones. Those collective rituals were seen as promising visions of the overcoming of misery and hunger, the elimination of an oppressive and ethnocentric power strucure. In this direction, *The Age of the Earth*, although not the first, represented his major effort to resume his allegorical account of contemporary history after his years abroad, taking his own country's nature, social space, and architecture as the stage for his "cosmic theater."

In 1980 this theater did not present the same homogeneous space that provided a solid ground for the rich variety of historical experiences condensed in his allegories. In the 1960s he invented his own outstanding style combining a ritualized dramatic space—place of the political schemes—with the profusion of handheld camera movements and the discontinuous montage that created the specific tension of his mise-en-scène. Blatantly theatrical performances were observed by documentary-style camera work, provoking in his audience the sense of being surpassed by the events, of having a limited point of view while facing an ongoing reality not yet mastered by the narrative agency. And those formal tensions could be seen as an expressive translation of his contradictory impulses: the move toward abstraction and conceptualized images, as implied in his allegorical schematization of history, and his plunge into the realm of the senses, his desire to include all the relevant aspects of the bodily experience on the screen, to be in touch with the contemporary empirical world without missing details. This baroque contradiction found in *Land in Anguish* an extraordinary resolution, but between 1970 and 1980 Rocha's cinema showed how difficult it was to achieve the same aesthetic result in his subsequent works. His last film, in particular, suffers from the uncontrolled interaction between abstraction and sensuality. As a visual experience, *The Age of the Earth* is an extraordinary example of a radicalized use of the handheld camera very close to its objects, exploring bodies and tissues as never before in Rocha's career. As an allegorical scheme, the film is too general in its scope, as the title suggests, and the baroque pedagogical theater, fragmented as it is, does not support the "planetary" diagnosis. Nevertheless, as a problematic work, the film formally acknowledges its own aesthetic drama—it is the filmmaker himself who lucidly points out the unfinished nature of his work. There are open signs of incompleteness: the absence of credits, the filmmaker's refusal to sign the film, and the final discrete effacing of the images without the conventional words "The End." Together with these more obvious marks, there are structural signs that evidence the filmmaker's choice not to create symmetries that might suggest an anxiety for a formal closure of the discourse.

The opening image of *The Age of the Earth* is a long take of the Alvorada Palace, the presidential house, in Brasília. The sun rises behind the palace, literalizing the idea of dawning (*alvorada*) as if suggesting that site as a center for the entire collective action shown later in the film. There is a mythical level clearly implied in this first long take. But although many of the sequences take place in the Brazilian capital, there is no formal return to this kind of ceremonial shot, and the ending simply dismisses all chances given by the rich visual material available to build any connection with the beginning. The film "melts" as if its movement from the center could not but result in a sheer dispersion only compensated by Rocha's voice-over. This imposes itself in a long speech near the end of the film. The filmmaker takes the platform and explains the origin of the film and how the concern with the Third World's Christ was triggered by Pasolini's death. He talks about human history, violence, the world's power systems, transformations, speed, despair, vertigo. But hope comes through the allusion to a philosophy of love rooted in Third World religion—Christian, African, syncretic, ecumenical, and above all, popular. Rocha knows that his images and sounds can only illustrate that idea, as fragments of a chain only grasped by the believers. Aware of the fragmentary nature of his plot, he knows that this time he depends heavily on the force of specific images of people involved in rituals, and more than ever before his sense of the world needs the body engagement of an experimental film. As a result, *The Age of the Earth* synthesizes the history of Brazilian alternate cinema since the 1960s.

Structured as a heterogeneous mosaic, from its first to its last sequence, the film displays a radically discontinuous series of visual essays on specific topics of Brazilian life. In opposition to his other Brazilian films, Rocha's theater now takes place in various regions of the country, a choice that enforces the idea of a national mythopoesis, also suggested by the use of the three major symbolic cities as locations: Salvador, Rio de Janeiro, and Brasília, the successive capitals of Brazil from the colonial times to the present. Through its multiple locations, the film explores the opposition *sertão* (Brasília)–sea (Salvador and Rio) to visualize ethnic and cultural diversity, clearly shown by the enormous number of people who populate the screen throughout the film. Popular Afro-Brazilian festivals in Bahia, carnival in Rio, evangelical preaching in Brasília, Umbanda ritual, the feast of Iemanjá (the Sea Goddess, in Afro-Brazilian religion), dance in the streets, open air experiences of many kinds—all these events enable Rocha to build the notion of a collective quest, religious in nature, that contrasts with the isolation of the film's main character, Brahms. Brahms is presented as the decadent imperialist whose trip to Brazil, although successful in economic terms, is the occasion for his display of family decadence, neurotic sex, cynical demagogy, and personal sadness. Brahms, an American with a Viking-like body, showing off his kitschy fake blond hair, remains at the center of the pedagogical theater enacted by half a dozen figures designed to convey dominant-class decadence: the Brazilian conservative leader who stands for the traditional elite, unable to confront Brahms in his search for power, the ambitious woman who fits the paradigm of the tyrant's mistress attracted to power, and the rebel son of the imperialist who can only display his awkwardness and impotence.

Because of the moral nature of Rocha's allegorical scheme, the film's fragmentary structure presents a residual narrative dimension that, together with the operatic farce enacted by Brahms and his partners, brings to the foreground a collection of biblical references that provide the framework for many of the episodes involving the religious figures. These two sides of *The Age of the Earth*—its experimental play with discontinuity and reflexive strategies and its narrative paradigms—do not profit from their juxtaposition. In other words, the vigorous dialectic of fragmentation and totalization typical of Rocha's cinema does not find here the same meaningful resolution as before.

Through its geographic diversity and free mixture of genres—drama, interviews, documentary footage—Rocha's film combines the two major allegorical patterns of the 1970s: (1) migration, here deployed as the pilgrimage of an ecumenical Christ—white, African, indigenous—who crosses the big cities with his message of love; and (2) the family drama, which again leads to a total denigration of its main characters, here enacting the oedipal scenario as an illustration of a grotesque imperial decadence. Political struggle and social reform are seen as part of a cosmic theater featuring life against death, a theater that takes big cities, especially Brasília, as the locus of death drives figured in the urban design itself and in monuments shown as funeral pieces. The National Theater in Brasília becomes a pharaonic pyramid built by slaves. This esoteric geometric figure is taken as the major reference to describe the world division of power—a pyramid with the First World countries at the top and the Third World at the base. Apart from all the biblical citations, the model for the representation of decadence and the source of the major and problematic analogy in *The Age of the Earth* is the Roman Empire. There is a view of contemporary life as a corrupted realm whose last hope comes from the emergence of a new slave religion on the outskirts of the world order, as in the dawning of Christianity.

In his attempt at reinvigorating the messianic hope in a cultural context more inclined to pessimism and atomization, Rocha produced the last example of an overt and totalizing national allegory involved with some sort of sacred level of reality. The central role played by myth and the messianic hope in his last film reminds us again of *Black God, White Devil*, but only to suggest that the new historical juncture hardly provides the material able to sustain a figural representation of historical teleology. In the 1964 film the teleology resulted from the staged recapitulation of the past, not from this inventory of the present that suffers from a dramatic dispersion only compensated by the filmmaker's open voice. Rocha does not try to disguise his own crisis, and the assertion of teleology is made in the context of a rather emotional and improvised speech that also acknowledges the lack of measure in history.

The allegory that tried to escape from the dissolution of the nation inspired by that consciousness of disaster typical of Marginal Cinema, *Iracema* and *Sad Tropics*, ends up exploding its own system. Unable to account for the profusion of elements brought into the audience's view, *The Age of the Earth* asserts the positive force of Brazilian syncretism against the violence embedded in history. Nevertheless, Rocha's own difficulty in connecting all his pieces shows that redemption now is a sheer matter of faith, far from being at hand. As time goes by and the present kind of modernization consolidates its achievements, it becomes more difficult to see the present juncture as *Black God, White Devil* did—as a manifestation of the Hegelian "astuteness" of reason.

Conclusion

Before 1964 it only seemed natural that economic transformation and technical progress would bring effective social change, a democratization of power and the affirmation of popular culture. The early 1960s promised the redemption of the oppressed. The coup of 1964 inverted the game of power, or rather, revealed the foregoing illusions, generating a new juncture where Brazilian modernization did not fulfill the expectations of the leftist nationalism. In this work, I have tried to characterize different responses by the filmmakers when Brazilian cinema was trampled by a process that showed the power of an international economic juncture and defined the fantastic growth of mass culture in Brazil. Against what was predicted by Brazilian orthodox leftist social theory, history showed that economic growth, associated with political conservatism and with the maintenance of all the existing inequalities, was still possible. It showed also that in combating such modernization, which excluded and still excludes most of the population, moral justice was not enough. The modern Brazilian *cinéma d'auteur*, apart from the aesthetic disputes, found its common ground in the critique addressed to the idea of an ongoing great historical accomplishment set by patriotic euphoria and promoted by official propaganda.

There was a need to say that this was not the desired modernizing change, a task that was fulfilled in several ways, in a more or less directed language. It was not by chance that my analysis turned up no attempt to make heroes out of the agents of economic growth and purely technical transformations. The characters who integrate themselves into the process of modernization are seen as corrupt opportunists: Tião Great Brazil, *Iracema*'s driver; Venceslau Pietro Pietra, the industrialist from *Macunaíma*; the bourgeois Fuentes and detective Matos, the developmentists, and the grotesque, unreliable characters in Rocha's films; J. B. da Silva, the chief of the gang, who has international connections in *Red Light Bandit*. In *The Angel Is Born*, the figure who manages the political dividends of the technical development is Richard Nixon; in *Killed the Family and Went to the Movies*, the daily TV ritual dissolves the conservative world of the family but, on the other hand, brings with it an invitation to atomization, to the experience of the "lonely crowd."

Against atomization, modern Brazilian cinema was made by young people who engaged in politics and expressed a singular concern for citizenship and participation, responsible for what can be observed a posteriori as a huge appetite for history, a typical haste that caused difficult experiences, sometimes exile or death. Within the cultural sphere, such voluntary action triggered a cycle of rich aesthetic proposals, passionate debates, and the tendency, on the part of filmmakers and artists, to see their choices as dramatic, historically crucial. This is very blatant in all the films commented on here, from Rocha's baroque dramas to the deconstructive aggressions in the cinema made between 1968 and 1970.

I have examined a course in which cinema had to work out its own political crisis, thematizing the paradigm of failure as lived by characters belonging to different social spheres, all shaken by a process that surpassed them, in which they acted as sovereign subjects neither in the public sphere of political struggle nor in the private sphere disturbed by the conflicts between morals and desire. In its observation of the several fronts on which the effects of the economic development were clear, cinema had to find its balance between two different and difficult-to-reconcile drives: on the one hand, to defend modernization in principle as a force able to dissolve the traditional patriarchy and certain forms of extreme class exploitation found in Brazil; and on the other, to criticize actual modernization as a limitless force able to barbarically destroy humanist values linked to the elevation of consciousness and the quality of people's lives. The tensions present in this difficult task, which has afflicted scholars worldwide, become more acute under conditions in Latin America, where technical and economic modernization is largely a byproduct of mechanisms of economic dependence that are very hard to discuss on the cultural level. For more than twenty years, Brazilian modern cinema has confronted this ever renewed dilemma in handling the tensions between modernization and cultural identity, up to the moment when the national question lost its power in the early 1980s.

This dissolution of the national question took place gradually in Brazilian cinema. The rupture with Cinema Novo's nationalism started with Marginal Cinema. Sganzerla, Bressane, and Tonacci showed a kind of step-by-step displacement in which the reference to the opposition between national and foreign lost its relevance. In its allegory addressed to the urban experience of underdevelopment, Marginal Cinema did not pinpoint the problem of the threat to national identity—it exposed experiential hell, internalizing the social crisis in the form of the films. It had a very different notion of its task and did not incorporate, as Cinema Novo had done, the sense of being the spokesman for the "imagined community" of the nation. The sense of mission did not disappear in 1970—as the continuity of Rocha's and other filmmakers' work attests—but it started losing ground from that moment on in a process that became clearer some years later when the rise of a new generation of filmmakers in the 1980s changed the dominant trends in Brazilian film production. Since Marginal Cinema, there has been a clear adoption of U.S. film noir imagery as a major reference, and this dialogue, with its specific approach to urban violence and marginalized heroes, only increased in the 1980s. The thriller, the detective film, and films showing nightlife in big cities are a significant presence among recent Brazilian films, evidencing the filmmakers' interest in more globalized themes and subjects. This change in production parallels the change in the shape of young audiences, now composed of people for whom political engagement, the national question, and the avant-garde experiences do not have the same meaning that they had for the 1960s generation. Simplifying, one can say that the modern cinema of the kind studied here was gradually displaced from its hegemonic position in Brazilian film production in a two-stage process. In the 1970s, the Cinema Novo generation itself moved toward a more decisive incorporation of market values, keeping the national question on the agenda and continuing its debate with the remnants of Marginal Cinema, who were excluded from the new state-based system of production; in the 1980s, a new generation made its own proposals and took Cinema Novo's "aesthetics of hunger" and national style as the tradition to be denied.

After the sheer confrontation with the Brazilian government in the late 1960s, Cinema Novo became the major partner of the federal government in its official film policy from the mid-1970s on. Within a more conventional aesthetic framework, part of the nationalist concern was incorporated in a film production that, in works like *Dona Flor and Her Two Husbands* (*Dona Flor e seus dois maridos*, Bruno Barreto, 1976), *Lady on the Bus* (*Dama do lotação*, Neville D'Almeida, 1978), and *Bye Bye Brazil*, was quite successful in the market, together with thrillers like Hector Babenco's *Lucio Flavio: The Passenger of Agony* (*Lúcio Flávio: O passageiro da agonia*, 1978), and the comic genre derived from children's TV programs. Around 1979–80, Brazilian cinema reached its best position ever in the internal market, at the moment when the nationalist ideas of the Left, conveniently adapted, found their place on the Globo TV network. Both in the market cinema financed by Embrafilme—the state agency for films—and in the *telenovelas*, there was a production of fiction based on literary classics and the representation of episodes of Brazilian history. This kind of official nationalism—derived from state policies in film and private investment in television—presented a more conventional version of Cinema Novo's cultural concerns, adjusted to the needs of light entertainment. "Adjusted" here means the construction of a fictional world more engaged in the celebration of the national as commodity than in its discussion in relation to social questions and the economic setbacks of the country. What had previously been a problematization of the national imaginary became a rite of identity in which the *telenovela* or the film celebrated what was recognized as the peculiarities, including eroticism, that generated the charm of the country. As time went by, while cinema entered its period of acute crisis in the 1980s, Brazilian television confirmed its efficiency in the use of the formula, ironically updating the "exportation culture" demanded by the modernist Oswald de Andrade in the 1920s. Although favored by the kind of unwritten pact that in the mid-1970s, conciliated Cinema Novo's nationalism and the conservative state apparatus, Brazilian cinema did not, and in fact could not, take steady advantage of the strategies of modernization set by the government. Those in power were very careful and competent in their media policies, giving decisive support to the electronic consciousness industry, which became the major ordering force of the conservative symbolic realm in Brazil. Official support for the arts (films included), undoubtedly effective from 1975 to the early 1980s, was a compensation that, in the new republic installed in 1985, was not able to repeat the successes of the previous period. Identified with the state financing agencies, cinema shared the crisis of the developmentalist state as the neoliberal era took gradual control of the country. Brazilian cinema was accused of "lack of efficiency," as if the presence of the state in film production were a kind of anomaly only found in Brazil.

The source of successive frustrations, national culture as a social value lost its prestige, while the culture of the media, advertisement, and conservative politics created the pathetic illusion of a "country in tune with the new international trends"—an impulse of imaginary identification with the First World with tragic consequences, as President Fernando Collor's period (1990–92) has demonstrated. Within the new atmosphere shaped by pragmatism and the hegemony of market values, the cultural products linked to different kinds of utopian impulses found very little space; hence the decline of the modern, problematic, national allegory—which refused the recent postmodern wedding of myth and commodity—and of the radical deconstructivism that was its counterpart. As I have observed, allegory is still part of Brazilian film culture; however, once conceived as a mode of representation with political implications, in recent years allegory has been far from performing the same key role it had in the period I have examined. It had too much to do with political engagement, totalizations, historical hopes, or moral indignation to keep its strength in the new stage of Brazil's timid but steady insertion into the process of economic globalization, a process that so far has favored capital concentration and high-tech audiovisual production for the international market.

The modern Brazilian *cinéma d'auteur* was linked to a set of cultural proposals that required quite a different development in the country's political life. Such proposals collapsed as the hegemonic mass culture shaped the country's mind. Although in the new wave as lived in Brazil the national question has been dropped out of the agenda and aesthetic experimentalism seems to be something archaic, one must be careful in assessing this overall process. I believe it would be reductive to interpret such eclipses of the topics that I have discussed here as advance or regression without a more accurate examination of the culture produced from 1980 on, a period outside of the scope of this book. As a suggestion, though, I would like to end by referring to the feeling of discomfort that derives from the fact that, when one comments on the aging of the cultural world studied here, which is now a chapter in Brazilian history, one has to recognize that such aging cannot be associated with a sense that the questions addressed by the films have been overcome. Brazil still lives with the social problems taken by the allegories as central issues for debate, and the cultural process has not provided the grounds for any evolutionist proclamation about the obsolete nature of the modes of representation discussed here. Everything has changed, and old solutions were made irrelevant by technical and economic developments, by the movement of society. On the other hand, everything remains, because Brazilian modernization still proceeds, at least up to now, as a repetition of the same blunders and inequalities on another level.

Notes

Introduction

1. I refer here to Rocha's manifesto "For an Aesthetics of Hunger," written after he made *Black God, White Devil* (1963–64) and read in Europe in 1965. For the English version, see *Brazilian Cinema*, ed. Randal Johnson and Robert Stam (New York: Columbia University Press, 1995).

2. See Julianne Burton, *Cinema and Social Change in Latin America: Conversations with Filmmakers* (Austin: University of Texas Press, 1986); Zuzana Pick, *Latin American Cinema: A Continental Project* (Austin: University of Texas Press, 1993).

3. "Towards a Third Cinema" is included in Bill Nichols's anthology *Movies and Methods* (Berkeley: University of California Press, 1976).

4. For a detailed account of the notion of Third Cinema in its various senses, see Teshome Gabriel's *Third Cinema in the Third World: The Aesthetics of Liberation* (Ann Arbor, Mich.: UMI, 1982) and the book edited by Paul Willemen and Jim Pines, *Questions of Third Cinema* (London: BFI, 1989). See also Ana López, "Toward a 'Third' and 'Imperfect' Cinema: A Theoretical and Historical Study of Filmmaking in Latin America" (Ph.D. diss., University of Iowa, 1986).

5. Written in 1969, Julio Garcia Espinosa's "For an Imperfect Cinema" was first published in English in *Afterimage* 3 (Summer 1971): 54–67; in a new translation by Julianne Burton, it was included in *Jump/Cut* 20, Special Section on Twenty Years of Revolutionary Cinema (May 1979): 24–26.

6. For a panoramic view of the Brazilian cinema, see Johnson and Stam, *Brazilian Cinema*. For Cinema Novo, see Randal Johnson's *Cinema Novo × 5: Masters of Contemporary Brazilian Cinema* (Austin: University of Texas Press, 1984).

7. See Fredric Jameson, "Third World Literature in the Era of Multinational Capitalism," *Social Text* 15 (Fall 1986): 65–88; and Aijaz Ahmad, "Jameson's Rhetoric of Otherness and the 'National Allegory'" *Social Text*, 17 (Summer 1987): 3–25.

8. See Hayden White, *The Content of the Form: Narrative Discourse and Historical Representation* (Baltimore, Md.: Johns Hopkins University Press, 1987) and *Tropics of Discourse: Essays in Cultural Criticism* (Baltimore, Md.: Johns Hopkins University Press, 1978); Timothy Brennan, "The National Long-

ing for Form," in *Nation and Narration*, ed. Homi K. Bhabha (London: Routledge, 1990), 44–70; Alex Callinicos, *Theories and Narratives: Reflections on
the Philosophy of History* (Durham, N.C.: Duke University Press, 1995); Doris
Sommer, *Foundational Fictions: The National Romances of Latin America*
(Berkeley: University of California Press, 1993).

9. This text appears in a collection of Schwarz's essays translated into
English; see Roberto Schwarz, *Misplaced Ideas: Essays on Brazilian Culture*
(London: Verso, 1992).

10. See Antonio Candido, "Literatura e subdesenvolvimento," *Argumento* 1
(1973); this essay is included in the anthology of his work *On Literature and
Society*, trans. and ed. Howard Becker (Princeton: Princeton University Press,
1995).

11. In his speech in one sequence of Jean-Luc Godard's *Vent d'Est*, Rocha
expresses this concern with national cinema and its specific demands as opposed to purely avant-garde projects.

12. E. J. Hobsbawm, in his *Nations and Nationalism since 1780: Programme, Myth, Reality* (Cambridge, Eng.: Cambridge University Press, 1990),
provides the historical data that places this Brazilian postwar nationalism in
an international context.

13. The ISEB (1955–1964) (Instituto Superior de Estudos Brasileiros—
Higher Institute for Brazilian Studies) was an interdisciplinary center created
by the Brazilian government to foster the consolidation of a "national
thought" on economic, political, and social development. In 1964 the military
government closed it, accusing its members of subversive activities. See Caio
Navarro de Toledo, *ISEB: Fábrica de ideologias* (São Paulo: Editora Atica,
1977).

14. Some readings of Benedict Anderson's excellent *Imagined Communities: Reflections on the Origin and Spread of Nationalism* (London: Verso,
1983) have explored his ideas on aspects related to nation as a discursive category, an exploration that has clarified many questions while discussing identity politics. But such exploration is sometimes done in a way that forgets the
other side of the question: the practical reality of the nation-state as a territory,
as a crystallization of political powers, economic boundaries, barriers to migration, population control, and life conditions. It is essential to remember
this while discussing Brazilian cinema since much of what is described in the
practical conditions of this cinema is linked to the practical reality of the
nation-state and its history.

15. The English translation of Euclides da Cunha's *Os Sertões* is *Rebellion
in the Backlands* (Chicago: University of Chicago Press, 1944).

16. For the "Cannibal's Manifesto," first published in 1928, see Oswald de
Andrade, *Do pau-Brasil à antropofagia e às utopias* (Rio de Janeiro: Civiliza-
ção Brasileira/INL, 1972). On anthropophagy as metaphor, see Robert Stam,
"On Cannibals and Carnivals," in *Subversive Pleasures: Bakhtin, Cultural
Criticism, and Film* (Baltimore, Md.: Johns Hopkins University Press, 1989).

17. I take "figural realism" in Erich Auerbach's sense as explained in *Mimesis: The Representation of Reality in Western Literature* (Princeton: Princeton

University Press, 1974), in which the allegorical process is understood as a vertical connection between two historical events separated in time. Another form to refer to this allegorical process is "typology," the set of operations performed by Christian thought to connect the events narrated in the Old Testament to Christ's life as depicted in the New Testament, the latter being a fulfillment of the prophecies stated in the former.

18. The two landmark dates are 1964 and 1968, the year of the coup and the year of the Institutional Act Number 5, a repressive law enacted on 13 December 1968 to stop demonstrations organized by the opposition and attacks on the military regime occurring in Congress.

19. Angus Fletcher, *Allegory: The Theory of a Symbolic Mode* (Ithaca, N.Y.: Cornell University Press, 1970).

20. In Júlio Bressane's work, the bitter irony leads to a disjunctive style that can be taken as an instance of Paul de Man's notion of allegory as "rhetoric of temporality," separation, and exile. See Paul de Man, "The Rhetoric of Temporality," in *Interpretation: Theory and Practice*, ed. C. S. Singleton (Baltimore, Md.: Johns Hopkins University Press, 1969). In Tonacci's *Bang Bang*, the notion of quest is a constant false promise and the decentered play of language instantiates the deconstructive axiom "The depth is the surface."

21. *Chanchada* is a popular comedy genre, almost always featuring songs related to Brazilian carnival. Its peak occurred between 1948 and 1960. The *chanchada* was a typical instance of representing on the screen the figure of the *malandro*—a kind of national trickster that since the nineteenth century has marked Brazilian imagery and celebrated an individualistic behavior against the rules as a trademark of a representative character of the nation.

22. For more details on the Companhia Vera Cruz, see Maria Rita Galvão, "Vera Cruz: A Brazilian Hollywood," in Johnson and Stam, *Brazilian Cinema*.

23. On this question of reflexivity in the cinema of the 1960s, see Robert Stam's *Reflexivity in Film and Literature: From Don Quixote to Jean-Luc Godard* (New York: Columbia University Press, 1992).

24. For this political turn of pop effects in Europe, see Andreas Huyssen, "The Cultural Politics of Pop," in *After the Great Divide: Modernism, Mass Culture, Postmodernism* (Bloomington: Indiana University Press, 1986), 141–159; for the Brazilian case, see Otília Arantes, *"Depois das vanguardas,"* *Arte em Revista* 7 (1983): 5–20.

25. On U.S. underground cinema and politics, see Annette Michelson, "Film and the Radical Aspiration," in *The Film Culture Reader*, ed. P. Adams Sitney (New York: Praeger, 1970), and David James, *Allegories of Cinema: American Film in the Sixties* (Princeton: Princeton University Press, 1989).

26. On the post-1968 cultural atmosphere and the crisis of the subject, see Vinicius Dantas and Iumna Maria Simon, *"Poesia ruim, sociedade pior,"* *Novos Estudos—CEBRAP* 12 (June 1985); English version, "Bad Poetry, Worse Society," in *On Edge: The Crisis of Contemporary Latin American Culture*, ed. George Yúdice, Jean Franco, and Juan Flores (Minneapolis: University of Minnesota Press, 1992), 141–160.

1. *Black God, White Devil*: Allegory and Prophecy

1. The *cangaceiro* is the rural social bandit—of the "avenger" type, according to Hobsbawm's terminology—that up to the 1940s inhabited the arid backlands of the Brazilian northeast. The *cangaceiros* usually formed nomad groups concentrated in criminal activities necessary for survival, sometimes having connections with political disputes among landowners. See E. J. Hobsbawm, *Bandits* (New York: Laurel Editions, 1969).

2. The word *sertão* refers to a culturally unified area of the Brazilian countryside extending from the central part of the country to its northeast. It corresponds in geographic terms to a specific site—the backlands—and in social terms to an enduring semifeudal structure in which power was based on land ownership; its legends deal with gunfights resulting from land disputes, family feuds, and social banditry.

3. Corisco, the character in the film, is based on Corisco, the real *cangaceiro* who died in the early 1940s. This name (which in Portuguese means "ignis fatuus" or "will-o'-the-wisp") is derived from popular legends about the incredible speed of his jumps. To have a "closed body" means to be invulnerable to any attack by human agents. According to a popular belief, this condition is attained by means of secret magic prayers taught or even directly performed by religious men.

4. *Cordel* literature refers to a folk narrative, written in rhymed verses, from the northeastern part of Brazil. The printed poem used to be hung in ropes—*cordas*, in Portuguese—while being read aloud by the seller or poet.

5. The expression "civilization of leather" derives from the peculiar historical formation of the *sertão*, which allowed for the establishment of an almost self-enclosed social system based on cattle raising.

6. The formula *sertão*-sea, Rocha's central metaphor, is inspired by one of Antônio Conselheiro's speeches to his followers. This major messianic leader of Brazilian peasants collected thousands of people in Canudos in the 1890s, forming a religious community that was finally destroyed by the Brazilian army after many expeditions organized to exterminate the "heretics."

7. The original title of Rocha's film—*Deus e o Diabo na Terra do Sol*—does not present the opposition Black (God)–White (Devil) with racial connotations; therefore, it does not suggest a reading of Sebastião and Corisco as representatives of ethnic groups or their cultures. In the allegory, they condense historical figures that were involved in religious experiences inserted in what is called "rustic Catholicism." Sebastião, in particular, evokes the *beatos* imbedded in that tradition, by no means representing African religion.

8. Corisco was killed by a military police officer in the early 1940s, not in the way the film represents his death. Sebastião epitomizes many *beatos*, although the major reference remains Antônio Conselheiro, who died in 1897. Antônio das Mortes is an allegorical figure that merges many repressive agents who, in fact, did not act by themselves.

9. See Walter Benjamin, *Illuminations*, ed. Hannah Arendt (New York: Schocken Books, 1976), pp. 83–110.

10. The dialogue of *Black God, White Devil* was all dubbed in a sound studio, and Rocha had Othon Bastos, the actor who plays Corisco, dub all the lines spoken by Sebastião. Throughout the film, we hear one single voice for the words uttered by both characters.

2. *Land in Anguish*: Allegory and Agony

1. Mario Faustino was a Brazilian poet who died in 1962 at the age of thirty-two. As a literary critic, he wrote for the *Jornal do Brasil* in Rio de Janeiro; he published *O Homem e sua hora* in 1955. Rocha knew Mario Faustino personally and was stricken by his death. The verses quoted in *Land in Anguish* were taken from Faustino's posthumous book *Poesia de Mario Faustino*, ed. Benedito Nunes (Rio de Janeiro: Civilização Brasileira, 1966).

2. S. M. Eisenstein, "A Course in Treatment," in *Film Form*, ed. and trans. Jay Leyda (New York: Harcourt, Brace & World, 1949), 104.

3. Pier Paolo Pasolini, "Le Cinéma de poésie," in *L'Experiénce hérétique: Langue et cinéma* (Paris: Payot, 1976), 150.

4. In the film's original title, *Terra em transe*, the word *transe* refers to a state of being possessed by hidden forces, suggested by Rocha as a state that pervades the entire country at that specific historical juncture.

3. *Red Light Bandit*: Allegory and Irony

1. The expression "red light" (translation of *luz vermelha*) in the title comes not from "red-light district" (in Portuguese, "Boca do Lixo") but from a kind of flashlight used in robberies by the actual bandit, who was active in São Paulo in the 1960s and who inspired the film. The red light became his trademark, and the papers named him "the Red Light Bandit."

2. The expression "Boca do Lixo" is literally translatable as "mouth of garbage" and refers to the São Paulo red-light district; it is differentially contrasted with its bourgeois counterpart, the so-called Boca do Luxo ("mouth of luxury"), the section of the city devoted to the sophisticated nightlife of the middle class.

3. *Red Light Bandit* is replete with references to the works of Orson Welles, from his radio broadcasts of the 1930s to *Touch of Evil* (1958). Welles has long been one of Sganzerla's preferred directors, which is evident in his work as a film critic during the early 1960s.

4. One detail makes this reference to prophecy more ironic: The first time we hear the sentence repeated by Jorginho, the words come from the figure of a dwarf lost in the city and arrested by Cabeção, who says, "Arrest that idiot dwarf" while he is seen jumping as Corisco does at the end of Rocha's film.

5. The actress who plays Janet Jane, Helena Ignes, was married to Rocha

in the early 1960s. In 1968 she was no longer personally or professionally associated with Rocha but had worked in many Cinema Novo films and could be taken as representative of this movement.

6. A kind of domestic game played with special buttons on a table's surface, reproducing the structure and the rules of soccer.

7. In these last sentences, Sganzerla quotes Oswald de Andrade's preface for his modernist book *Serafim Ponte Grande*, written in 1928–29 but only published in 1932. What Oswald states about his character, Serafim, is here attributed to the bandit's character. The latter moves around in a precarious world, and his little robberies are far from the transatlantic nimbleness of Oswald de Andrade's petit bourgeois. But besides the affinity of the anarchic gesture of the characters, there is no doubt the same taste for discontinuity and nonsense in the composition of the commentators' speech.

8. Dom Helder Câmara was, at that time, the most famous archbishop in Brazil, well known for his progressive militancy in the early 1960s and his conflicts with the military government after 1964. Mineirinho was a famous outlaw killed by the Rio de Janeiro police.

9. The order of things in the film recalls, in its humor, the enumeration of Jorge Luis Borges's Chinese encyclopedia, the same one that generated Michel Foucault's fit of laughter and fed the project of his book *The Order of Things: An Archaeology of Human Sciences* (New York: Vintage Books, 1973), as he himself notes in the preface.

5. *Macunaíma*: The Delusions of Eternal Childhood

1. For a detailed analysis of *Macunaíma*'s narrator, see Randal Johnson's *Literatura e cinema: Macunaíma. Do modernismo ao Cinema Novo* (São Paulo: T. A. Queiroz, 1982). On *Macunaíma*, see Johnson's text in Johnson and Stam, *Brazilian Cinema*, and Stam's "On Cannibals and Carnivals," in Stam, *Subversive Pleasures*.

2. See Randal Johnson's analysis, and also Heloísa Buarque de Hollanda's *Macunaíma: Da literatura ao cinema* (Rio de Janeiro: José Olympio Ed./ Embrafilme, 1978). In both of these works, the change in the narrative genre is understood to be toward this "more critical attitude." This hypothesis, to be better evaluated, would require a deeper discussion of what is implied in the narrative genre and levels of mimesis carried out in the book. The film displaces the motives of the journey, changing aspects of the legend that are at the core of the literary argument; the difference between the two principles of internal coherence is clear. Here, only the film is at stake.

3. Monteiro Lobato was a leading Brazilian intellectual in the first decades of this century. Storyteller, essayist, publisher, art critic, and a passionate advocate of progress, he created the allegorical figure Jeca Tatu to express his exasperated critical view of the inertia of Brazilian rural life. Jeca Tatu personifies many bourgeois prejudices against the southeastern peasants, who are

blamed by this allegory for an economic backwardness that had structural causes and required more than goodwill for its solution.

6. *Antonio das Mortes*: Myth and the Simulacrum in the Crisis of Revolution

1. The synthetic character of this first sequence, which announces the confrontation of myth and history, allows Marie-Claire Ropars to place the first ten shots of the film as the key for her interpretation. See Marie-Claire Ropars, "*Le Film comme texte*," *Le Français aujourd'hui* 32 (January 1976): 27–46.

2. Rocha justifies his treatment of the dream of the oppressed and his affirmation of the mythical conscience as a source of the Revolution in "The Aesthetic of the Dream," written in 1971, partly as an answer to a review published in *Film Quarterly*. See Rocha's text in *A revolução do Cinema Novo* (Rio de Janeiro: Alhambra/Embrafilme, 1981).

7. *The Angel Is Born*: The Song of Exile

1. Rocha's style is the best example of the engaged camera. This Cinema Novo feature made the photographer Dib Lufti famous, especially for his work with the handheld camera in many films.

2. See Annette Michelson, "Toward Snow," *Artforum* 10 (June 1971): 30–37.

3. I borrow this expression from the Brazilian critic Fernando Mesquita. See Fernando Mesquita, "A solidão lunar," *Cine-Olho* 5/6 (June 1979): 71–75.

4. Walter Benjamin, "Notes on the Philosophy of History," in *Illuminations*, ed. Hannah Arendt (New York: Schocken Books, 1969), 256.

8. *Killed the Family and Went to the Movies*: The Ersatz Carnival

1. Six inserts interrupt the story of the bourgeois women. Three of them display the domestic violence discussed in my text; another thematizes official torture. The remaining two present isolated, out of context gestures that comment on aspects of the film.

2. The conversation on marital life and Regina's remarks that "it could be worse" are commented on by an insert (the second one), which offers another lower-middle-class counterpart. A housewife finds a suspicious message in her husband's drawer just after he leaves. The next shot shows her entering a house, looking for something. The camera follows her through the corridors, but when she opens a door to watch a scene that disturbs her, we are not shown what she sees: The episode is interrupted before our question is answered.

9. *Bang Bang*: Passage, Not Destination

1. I use the expression "cinema of attractions" in the sense given by Tom Gunning in "The Cinema of Attractions: The Early Film, Its Spectator, and the Avant-Garde," in *Early Cinema: Space, Frame, Narrative*, ed. Thomas Alsaesser (London: BFI, 1990), 56–62.

2. I use "pro-filmic" in Christian Metz's sense, meaning everything that is placed or every action that takes place in front of the camera.

10. Trends of Allegory in the 1970s

1. On Alencar's novel, see Sommer, *Foundational Fictions*, 138–171.

2. For a more detailed account of this process, see Ismail Xavier, "*Iracema*: Transcending *Cinéma-vérité*," in *The Social Documentary in Latin America*, ed. Julianne Burton (Pittsburgh, Pa.: University of Pittsburgh Press, 1990), 361–372.

3. See Gilberto Freyre, *The Masters and the Slaves (Casa Grande e Senzala): A Study in the Development of Brazilian Civilization*, trans. Samuel Putnam (New York: Knopf, 1946).

Select Bibliography

Ahmad, Aijaz. "Jameson's Rhetoric of Otherness and the 'National Allegory.'" *Social Text* 17 (Summer 1987): 3–25.

Anderson, Benedict. *Imagined Communities: Reflections on the Origin and Spread of Nationalism.* London: Verso, 1983.

Andrade, Mário de. *Macunaíma o herói sem nenhum caráter.* São Paulo: Martins, 1970; first published 1928. English translation, *Macunaíma: The Hero without Any Character.* Translated by E. A. Goodland. New York: Random House, 1984.

Andrade, Oswald de. *Do pau-Brasil à antropofagia e às utopias.* Rio de Janeiro, Civilização Brasileira/INL, 1972.

Arantes, Otília. "Depois das vanguardas." *Arte em Revista* 7 (1983): 5–20.

Auerbach, Erich. *Mimesis: The Representation of Reality in Western Literature.* Princeton: Princeton University Press, 1974.

Avellar, José Carlos. *A ponte clandestina: Teorias de cinema na América Latina.* Rio de Janeiro: Editora 34/EDUSP, 1995.

——. *O cinema dilacerado.* Rio de Janeiro: Alhambra, 1978.

Baudry, Jean-Louis. *L'Effet-cinéma.* Paris: Editions Albatros, 1978.

Benjamin, Walter. *Charles Baudelaire: A Lyric Poet in the Era of High Capitalism.* London: NLB, 1973.

——. *Illuminations.* Edited by Hannah Arendt. New York: Schocken Books, 1976.

——. *The Origins of German Tragic Drama.* London: NLB, 1977.

——. *Understanding Brecht.* London: NLB, 1977.

Bernardet, Jean-Claude. *Brasil em tempo de cinema.* Rio de Janeiro: Civilização Brasileira, 1967.

——. *O Vôo dos anjos.* São Paulo: Brasiliense, 1991.

Bhabha, Homi K., ed. *Nation and Narration.* London: Routledge, 1990.

Brecht, Bertolt. *Brecht on Theater.* New York: Hill and Wang, 1976.

Buarque de Hollanda, Heloísa. *Macunaíma: Da literatura ao cinema.* Rio de Janeiro: José Olympio Ed./Embrafilme, 1978.

Burton, Julianne. *Cinema and Social Change in Latin America: Conversations with Filmmakers.* Austin: University of Texas Press, 1986.

——. "The Intellectual in Anguish: Modernist Form and Ideology in *Land in Anguish* and *Memories of Underdevelopment*." Working papers of the Latin American program of the Wilson Center, no. 132, 1983.

————. ed. *The Social Documentary in Latin America*. Pittsburgh, Pa.: University of Pittsburgh Press, 1990.

Callinicos, Alex. *Theories and Narratives: Reflections on the Philosophy of History*. Durham, N.C.: Duke University Press, 1995.

Candido, Antonio. *On Literature and Society*. Edited and translated by Howard Becker. Princeton: Princeton University Press, 1995.

Cohn, Norman. *The Pursuit of the Millennium*. New York: Oxford University Press, 1974.

da Cunha, Euclides. *Rebellion in the Backlands*. Chicago: University of Chicago Press, 1944.

Dahbour, Omar, and Micheline R. Ishay. *The Nationalism Reader*. Atlantic Highlands, N.J.: Humanities Press, 1995.

Dantas, Vinicius, and Iumna Maria Simon. "Bad Poetry, Worse Society." In *On Edge: The Crisis of Contemporary Latin American Culture*, edited by George Yúdice, Jean Franco, and Juan Flores. Minneapolis: University of Minnesota Press, 1992.

de Man, Paul. "The Rhetoric of Temporality." In *Interpretation: Theory and Practice*, edited by C. S. Singleton. Baltimore, Md.: Johns Hopkins University Press, 1969.

Derrida, Jacques. *L'Ecriture et la différence*. Paris: Seuil, 1967.

Eagleton, Terry. *Walter Benjamin; or, Towards a Revolutionary Criticism*. London: Verso, 1981.

Eisenstein, S. M. *Film Form*. Edited and translated by Jay Leyda. New York: Harcourt, Brace & World, 1949.

Eliade, Mircea. *Cosmos and History: The Myth of the Eternal Return*. New York: Harper, 1959.

Espinosa, Julo Garcia. "For an Imperfect Cinema." *Jump/Cut* 20, Special Section on Twenty Years of Revolutionary Cuban Cinema (May 1979): 24–26.

Fanon, Frantz. *The Wretched of the Earth*. New York: Grove Press, 1968.

Favaretto, Celso. *Tropicália: Alegoria, alegria*. São Paulo: Kairós, 1979.

Fletcher, Angus. *Allegory: The Theory of a Symbolic Mode*. Ithaca, N.Y.: Cornell University Press, 1970.

Foucault, Michel. *The Order of Things: An Archaeology of Human Sciences*. New York: Vintage Books, 1973.

Freyre, Gilberto. *The Masters and the Slaves (Casa Grande e Sezala): A Study in the Development of Brazilian Civilization*. Translated by Samuel Putnam. New York: Knopf, 1946.

Gabriel, Teshome. *Third Cinema in the Third World: The Aesthetics of Liberation*. Ann Arbor, Mich.: UMI, 1982.

Gellner, Ernest. *Nations and Nationalism*. Ithaca, N.Y.: Cornell University Press, 1983.

Genette, Gérard. *Figures III*. Paris: Seuil, 1972.

Gerber, Raquel. *O mito da civilização atlântica: Glauber Rocha, cinema, política e a estética do inconsciente*. Rio de Janeiro: Vozes, 1982.

Greenblatt, Stephen, ed. *Allegory and Representation*. Baltimore, Md.: Johns Hopkins University Press, 1981.

Hobsbawm, E. J. *Bandits*. New York: Laurel Editions, 1969.

———. *Nations and Nationalism since 1780: Programme, Myth, Reality*. Cambridge, Eng.: Cambridge University Press, 1990.

James, David. *Allegories of Cinema: American Film in the Sixties*. Princeton: Princeton University Press, 1989.

Jameson, Fredric. *The Political Unconscious: Narrative as a Socially Symbolic Act*. Ithaca, N.Y.: Cornell University Press, 1981.

———. "Third World Literature in the Era of Multinational Capitalism." *Social Text* 15 (Fall 1986): 65–88.

Johnson, Randal. *Cinema Novo × 5: Masters of Contemporary Brazilian Cinema*. Austin: University of Texas Press, 1984.

———. *Literatura e cinema: Macunaíma. Do modernismo ao Cinema Novo*. São Paulo: T. A. Queiroz, 1982.

Johnson, Randal and Robert Stam, eds. *Brazilian Cinema*, 3rd ed. New York: Columbia University Press, 1995.

Kadir, Djelal. *Questing Fictions: Latin America's Family Romance*. Minneapolis: University of Minnesota Press, 1986.

King, John, Ana López, and Manuel Alvarado. *Mediating Two Worlds: Cinematic Encounters in the Americas*. London: BFI, 1993.

López, Ana. "Toward a 'Third' and 'Imperfect' Cinema: A Theoretical and Historical Study of Filmmaking in Latin America." Ph.D. diss., University of Iowa, 1986.

Mesquita, Fernando. "A solidão lunar." *Cine-Olho* 5/6 (1979): 71–75.

Michelson, Annette. "Film and the Radical Aspiration." In *The Film Culture Reader*. Edited by P. Adams Sitney. New York: Praeger, 1970.

———. "Toward Snow." *Artforum* 10 (June 1971): 30–37.

Moreira Leite, Dante. *O caráter nacional brasileiro*. São Paulo: Pioneira, 1976.

Navarro de Toledo, Caio. *ISEB: Fábrica de ideologias*. São Paulo: Editora Atica, 1977.

Nichols, Bill, ed. *Movies and Methods*. Berkeley: University of California Press, 1976.

Paranaguá, Paulo, ed. *Le Cinéma brésilien*. Paris: Centre Georges Pompidou, 1987.

Pasolini, Pier Paolo. *Heretical Empiricism*. Bloomington: Indiana University Press, 1988.

Pécaut, Daniel. *Os intelectuais e a política no Brasil: Entre o povo e a nação*. São Paulo: Editora Atica, 1990.

Pépin, Jean. *Mithe et allégorie: Les Origines grecques et les contestations judéo-chrétiennes*. Paris: Etudes Augustiniennes, 1976.

Pereira de Queiroz, Maria Isaura. *O Messianismo no Brasil e no mundo*. São Paulo: Dominus, 1965.

———. *Os Cangaceiros*. São Paulo: Livraria Duas Cidades Editora, 1977.

Pick, Zuzana. *Latin American Cinema: A Continental Project*. Austin: University of Texas Press, 1993.

Quilligan, Maureen. *The Language of Allegory: Defining the Genre*. Ithaca, N.Y.: Cornell University Press, 1979.

Ramos, Fernão. *Cinema Marginal: A representação em seus limites*. São Paulo: Brasiliense, 1986.

Rocha, Glauber. *A revolução do Cinema Novo*. Rio de Janeiro: Alhambra/ Embrafilme, 1981.

Ropars, Marie-Claire. "Le Film comme text." *Le Français aujourd'hui* 32 (January 1976): 27–46.

Rosen, Phillip. "History, Textuality, Nation: Kracauer, Burch, and Some Problems in the Study of National Cinema." *Iris* 2, no. 2 (1984): 69–84.

Schwarz, Roberto. *Misplaced Ideas: Essays on Brazilian Culture*. London: Verso, 1992.

Sommer, Doris. *Foundational Fictions: The National Romances of Latin America*. Berkeley: University of California Press, 1993.

Stam, Robert. *Reflexivity in Film and Literature: From Don Quixote to Jean-Luc Godard*. New York: Columbia University Press, 1992.

———. *Subversive Pleasures: Bakhtin, Cultural Criticism, and Film*. Baltimore, Md.: Johns Hopkins University Press, 1989.

Stam, Robert, and Ella Shohat. *Unthinking Eurocentrism: Multiculturalism and the Media*. London: Routledge, 1994.

Weffort, Francisco. *O populismo na política brasileira*. Rio de Janeiro: Paz e Terra, 1978.

White, Hayden. *The Content of the Form: Narrative Discourse and Historical Representation*. Baltimore, Md.: Johns Hopkins University Press, 1987.

Willeman, Paul, and Jim Pines. *Questions of Third Cinema*. London: BFI, 1989.

Index

Ismail Xavier earned his Ph.D. in cinema studies from New York University. He teaches film theory and film history at the University of São Paulo, Brazil. He has published, in Brazil, books on film theory (*O discurso cinematográfico* and *A experiêcia do cinema*), on Brazilian cinema (*Sertão mar: Glauber Rocha e a estética da fome* and *Alegorias do subdesenvolvimento*), and on D. W. Griffith (*D. W. Griffith: O nascimento de um cinema*). In English, he has written chapters for *Brazilian Cinema* (edited by Randal Johnson and Robert Stam), *Resisting Images: Essays on Cinema and History* (edited by Robert Sklar and Charles Musser), *The Social Documentary in Latin America* (edited by Julianne Burton), and *Mediating Two Worlds: Cinematic Encounters in the Americas* (edited by John King, Ana López, and Manuel Alvarado) and has published in the journals *Cineaste* and *Film Quarterly*, among others. In France, he has written chapters for *Le Cinéma brésilien* (edited by Paulo Paranaguá), and he has also published in Spanish and Italian. He has lectured on Brazilian cinema in the United States, Japan, and France, and is one of the leading film theorists in Brazil.